THE
Formula

Also by Albert-László Barabási

Network Medicine: Complex Systems in Human Disease and Therapeutics
(editor, with Joseph Loscalzo and Edwin K. Silverman)

Network Science

Bursts: The Hidden Pattern Behind Everything We Do, from Your Email to Bloody Crusades

The Structure and Dynamics of Networks
(with Mark Newman and Duncan J. Watts)

Linked: How Everything Is Connected to Everything Else and What It Means for Business, Science, and Everyday Life

Fractal Concepts in Surface Growth
(with H. E. Stanley)

THE
Formula

THE UNIVERSAL
LAWS OF SUCCESS

Albert-László Barabási

Little, Brown and Company
New York Boston London

Little, Brown and Company
Hachette Book Group
1290 Avenue of the Americas, New York, NY 10104
littlebrown.com

First Edition: November 2018

Little, Brown and Company is a division of Hachette Book Group, Inc. The Little, Brown name and logo are trademarks of Hachette Book Group, Inc.

The publisher is not responsible for websites (or their content) that are not owned by the publisher.

The Hachette Speakers Bureau provides a wide range of authors for speaking events. To find out more, go to hachettespeakersbureau.com or call (866) 376-6591.

ISBN 978-0-316-50549-9 (hc) / 978-0-316-52647-0 (int'l)
LCCN 2018939520

10 9 8 7 6 5 4 3 2

LSC-C

Printed in the United States of America

Contents

THE
Formula

Success Isn't About You.
It's About Us.

My wife says she fell in love with me because I knew the temperature of the sun. I met her in a coffee shop while preparing to teach my students the basics of thermodynamics. "How could we possibly know such a thing?" she asked. The idea that I could pin a number — 5,778 kelvin, to be precise — on something so far away, something so untouchable, so violently, immeasurably incendiary — seemed like a magic trick. It's the kind of answer any parent would love to supply to the questions kids tend to ask. Instead, we admit, "I don't know," or speak in vague terms. "The sun is hot. Really hot." But we're talking about the glowing orb that illuminates our lives, the source of life as we know it. I found it baffling as a child that adults knew precious little about something so big.

My grandfather owned a fleet of trucks in his small Transylvanian village, but by the time I came along, all he had left of his business was his machine shop, a cavernous wooden shack where I spent every one of my vacation days. I loved that shop, which was in some ways my first laboratory, a place where I could safely break something down to its nuts and bolts, study its gears, and see exactly how it operated. Understanding what made something work—that was the fascination. It still is.

I come from a family of tinkerers. After Communism robbed my grandfather of his fleet of trucks, he fixed appliances for the whole neighborhood, examining the innards of an iron or a radio with patient confidence. My dad, a truck driver for the family business at a mere ten years old, could crawl underneath an ailing car, poke around for a few minutes, and emerge with blackened fingers and a pleased expression, the problem fixed. He spent his life always running something—a school, a museum, a company—approaching each job with the mind-set of a tinkerer, rolling up his sleeves and making it work no matter the circumstance.

Maybe it's a tinkerer's curiosity that turned me into a scientist. Early on, physics allowed me to explore the sprockets and gears of the universe and the very forces that control our lives. Looking for more challenges, I turned later to the complexities of networks and data. For a vigilant asker-of-questions, I've chosen the right corner of the scientific world to call home. As long as a line of inquiry is based on numbers—the more the merrier—I can pursue it doggedly, following its scent through the maze of data now available to researchers in our hyperconnected, technological world. Hunting down an answer inevitably leads to more questions, new possibilities that hover like gnats on the periphery of any research I conduct. I try to swat them away and stay focused on the task at hand, but I'm not that different from the kid I once was, stubbornly asking "Why?" in response to... well, pretty much anything. It is the quest for answers that gets me up in the morning and keeps me up at night.

These days I run the Center for Complex Network Research, in Boston, where my job is exploring the "why" behind topics as varied as how people or molecules interact, where and how links form, and what our interconnectedness can tell us about society or our biological origins. We've examined the topology of the World Wide Web. We're looking at how tiny hiccups in our genetic networks lead to disease. We're exploring how our brains control their billions of neurons and how molecules in food attach to our proteins, ensuring our long-term health.

I love this kind of stuff—the math behind our social fabric, the way numbers provide a framework for understanding the essence of our connectedness. When I use models and tools to delve into unlikely topics for scientific analyses, these frameworks inevitably deepen our knowledge.

That's precisely what we did with success. It took a few years, but after harvesting mountains of data on human accomplishment, we figured out a way to break the concept down to its constituents and study its gears. Our goal was to formulate success as a mathematical problem that computer scientists and physicists, using the unforgiving tools of quantitative science, could address in a definite fashion. It wasn't that different from pulling apart a bike, or using thermodynamics to fathom solar heat. Once we started seeing the mechanisms that create success, we began to answer the kinds of impossible questions I tortured my parents with as a child.

Exactly how, for instance, did we decide that *this*—the

5

blurry, unremarkable photo hanging in the Museum of Modern Art—is a masterpiece?

Why is *Carousel*, not *Cats*, the best musical ever?

Are expensive schools worth it?

Why are there a mere handful of superstars in any field?

Add these to the hundreds of other questions about success, achievement, and reputation that seem, like the sun's temperature, impossible to pin down. Is it our performance that pushes us up the corporate ladder? Do we get less or more creative over our lifetimes? Should we collaborate or compete with superstars? How do networks—social and professional—affect our access to success?

Believe it or not, quantitative answers can be found for all these seemingly unquantifiable questions. By examining the patterns in the data and identifying the mechanisms that produce success, we determined that we could address each of the questions head-on. Once we began to comprehend the universal forces at work behind our individual successes and failures, fascinating findings started to emerge.

•

We started with disaster, backhandedly landing on success. At the time, my lab was analyzing cell phone data to understand how people react to major catastrophes. Recognizing that this was a good opportunity for one to learn by doing, I assigned Dashun Wang, a gregarious, Chinese-born Ph.D. student, to help with the ongoing project. The endeavor resulted in a truly fascinating paper, one that I was certain would have a major impact on disaster relief efforts worldwide.

Except…no one else thought so. Try as we might, we couldn't get it published. The highest-tier and then some of the lowest-tier journals rejected it. We joked that we should have removed the word "disaster" from the title, since that likely destined it for failure.

A lifelong basketball player, Dashun shrugged off our disastrous paper as if it were a setback on the court. The ironies amused him. But when he and I met one night to discuss his next project, he was eager to move on.

"I'll do pretty much anything but work on another disaster," he said with a chuckle.

"Then let's make your next project a success," I said. "How about the Science of Success?"

I'd meant the question to be tongue-in-cheek. Except as soon as I said it, we both knew that we'd stumbled onto something interesting. Why *not* apply our methods to the study of success? It seemed that studying success would not be all that different from studying catastrophe. We can accurately predict the trajectory of a hurricane by examining a big pile of data points and using them as input for weather models. These predictions are hugely valuable in developing a response plan. Communities that lie in a hurricane's projected path prepare to batten down the hatches; the rest get ready for sprinkles and buy umbrellas. We don't question the validity of the forecast, though a century ago prophesying a monumental storm would have seemed like witchcraft. Why, then, couldn't we do something similar with success? Data collected in unexpected realms and filtered through sophisticated mathematical models, after all, can seem like a kind of magic.

• • •

We started out small and focused on a specific area: success in science. We realized that in the digitized era we now live in, we had troves of detailed records about our own discipline—catalogues of research papers going back over a century. Why not put science itself under our data microscope? The project sought to answer some of my most puzzling, fundamental questions: How does success emerge? How can it be measured? Why are some of my biggest heroes—remarkable scientists whose discoveries have enriched my life—so doomed to invisibility that they hardly appear in a Google search? And why are others whose work is not any more remarkable or novel propelled to stardom?

In no time, we started seeing patterns in the data, which turned into formulae we could use to *predict future outcomes* for ourselves, our colleagues, and even our professional rivals. As I'll discuss later in the book, we could actually fast-forward a scientist's career to determine her future academic impact, gauging her chances of making it big or having her contribution appreciated by only a few kindred souls within an already esoteric discipline. We also developed an algorithm to predict precisely who, among hundreds of contributors to a discovery, would get most of the credit, and—spoiler!—it was rarely the person doing the lion's share of the work.

The most unexpected outcome? Finding a courtesy-van driver at a Toyota dealership in Alabama who had inexplicably been overlooked for a Nobel Prize. And he's just one in the collection of characters we met on our journey toward understanding success. Among them were also the guy who crowdfunded $10,000 in eight minutes, a Harley-riding success researcher with a passion for Broadway musicals, and a former oceanographer turned winemaker whose discovery of ugly truths has changed the way I buy wine.

Our first Science of Success project took two years to complete, and its findings opened up a new realm of inquiry ripe for further exploration. The resulting paper, Dashun's first as lead author, was published in *Science*, the most prestigious journal out there. He and I were both a bit stunned. In running from disaster, we stumbled across success.

•

What I was learning about my own field of science captivated me, and it quickly became clear that we could use the same approach to examine success in other realms. Did the same patterns apply to accomplishment in sports, to rewards in art, to high achievement in sales? Could we foresee which TV show or book would become a sensation just as we could forecast the success of new scientific discoveries? Could we predict a career in business in the same way we could now anticipate an unfolding academic one? What if the patterns and regularity that we saw in the way scientists succeed and fail reflected some deeper truths that apply to all of us? What if our mathematical tool kit showed that success in all realms obeys the same universal laws?

To be honest, it was a risky proposition. A glance at the existing success-related literature, which lines an entire wall at my favorite bookstore, told me that most writing about the topic relied on inspirational messages and anecdotal evidence, a far cry from the hard theorems and flinty empirical data to be found on the science shelves.

But what those books also tell me is that people have a deep hunger to understand what contributes to success. It's a topic that obsesses many of us. And well it should. Success is not only a fundamental aspect of human experience, both practical and existential, but is also often a fundamental marker by which we measure the life we are leading. Whether we'll fail or thrive in our chosen careers or even hobbies matters deeply. When we make a discovery, produce a piece of art, or design a new gadget, we want to make sure it will have an impact on the world. We puzzle over the fine line between success and failure daily as we envision our own future trajectory or as we steer our children into adulthood. If only we could find patterns of success in a whole range of fields, perhaps we might be able to make sense of what we far too often attribute to chance.

Propelled by this possibility, I challenged my lab members to discover the quantitative laws that govern success. Each success story is bound to leave a trail of data points behind. I hoped not only to capture these trails but also to identify the patterns that success obeys and the drivers behind them. And we did just that, meticulously gathering data from multiple fields—the arts, academia, sports, and business—and analyzing it on a large scale. We purchased massive databases containing all the research papers ever written, allowing us to rebuild the careers of every published scientist going back a century or more. We bought access to the weekly sales patterns of all books sold in the United States, data that helped us examine the commercial success of each author independent of the genre they worked in. We were given access to information about global gallery and museum exhibits, which allowed us to rebuild the careers of all contemporary artists, identifying the invisible networks that guaranteed success for some of them. We scoured massive data sets pertaining to success in sports, business, and innovation. Then we put all of it under the quantitative microscope that our lab and others have developed over the past two decades. We took these tools—hardened by decades of work by computer scientists, physicists, and mathematicians interested in unveiling the secrets of the universe, curing genetic diseases, or finding valuable information in milliseconds among billions of Web pages—and the mathematical rigor behind them and applied them to the massive data sets that capture how we encounter and experience success. And to better survey the potential behind this new field, we also organized a symposium on the Science of Success, held at Harvard University in May 2013. Over a hundred researchers, everyone from sociologists to business professors, came to share their findings. As we put our heads together, we were suddenly seeing a *series of recurring patterns that drive success in most areas of human performance.*

Because the patterns that began to emerge were so universal, we started to call them the Laws of Success. Given that scientific laws are immutable, doing so probably seemed brash to outside researchers. But the more we explored and tested them, the more solid and general they appeared. Crucially, like the laws of gravitation or of motion, the Laws of Success can't be rewritten to fit our needs or beliefs, no matter how righteous or strongly held. And outright resisting them is about as futile as trying to fly by flapping our arms up and down. But—just as engineers use their understanding of fluid mechanics and plenty of tinkering to improve airplane technology—we can take advantage of the Laws of Success to invent our futures.

In the upcoming chapters, I will delve into the far-reaching scientific inquiries that support each law. My goal with *The Formula* is to outline our discoveries so that readers, aware of the complex but consistently reproducible mechanisms that generate success, can use this knowledge in their own lives. But this is not a self-help book. I like to think of it, instead, as "science help," a framework that uses science to understand and orchestrate outcomes. Scientific analysis can illuminate seemingly deeply irrational puzzles, turning our assumptions on their heads. In other words, science can help us make sense of the randomness of the human world—unveiling the mechanisms at work when we're passed over for a job, the underlying pattern that explains why some artists thrive while others fail, the lingering hunch that success is about more than just talent or how well we perform.

As I'll discuss in the conclusion, despite his evident genius, even Einstein's success was no foregone conclusion. In fact, much of his rampant recognition hinges on events completely divorced from his contributions to science. Across the board, the research indicates that we can't rely on sheer instinct, strong performance, or all the old inspirational clichés if we want our work to be appreciated, our accomplishments to be noticed, and our legacies to endure.

In fact, for the purposes of this book, we'll be defining success along these lines: it is the rewards we earn from the communities we belong to. In the case of Einstein—the "Man of the Century," according to *Time*—that reward is fame. But it can be recognition if you're a collaborator, visibility if you're a brand, renown if you're an artist, album or ticket sales if you're a musician, revenue if you're in business or sales, earnings if you're a banker, audience if you're a playwright, citations if you're a scientist, endorsements if you're an athlete, and impact if you hope to make a difference in virtually any field. These success measures all have one thing in common: they are external, not internal; collective, not individual.

This is not to say that we can't experience success as something deeply individual. Personal growth, satisfaction, and depth of experience are powerful and significant. Our framework for success doesn't preclude such measurements, nor should they be regarded as mutually exclusive from success as I'm defining it. They often go hand in hand, our satisfaction growing with the impact we've made. But as a scientist, I can't measure individual fulfillment any more than I can assign a number to happiness. Private definitions of success are unique to each of us, so they're invisible to our approach to big data. A perfectionist may perceive even a much-praised performance as a failure and argue that true success comes only when she feels genuinely satisfied with her labors. She wouldn't be wrong. Nor would the guy who finishes his unpublishable novel but considers it a success because he met a personal goal by completing it. These are triumphs essential to who we are and why we get out of bed in the morning. My life, too, is full of personal goals—to be a good father, an insightful mentor, and an astute speaker paramount among them. I'd love to find a way to explore success through this far more personal lens. Sadly, I haven't found a way to do so, since individual aims remain stubbornly inaccessible to our methods of research. They've proven to be unmeasurable so far.

Let's say you're a talented skater recovering from knee surgery. You work with your physical therapist; you toil through repetitive exercises. You set goals and make painful but incremental progress. Then the day comes when you don't need crutches. You take three steps. Ten. You eventually lace up your skates and get back in the rink, a moment of victory. This is when the triumphant music sounds, should Hollywood tell your story. Call it the biggest success of your life, and I'd fully agree with you.

Yet in this book we'll refrain from calling this "success." It's not that we'll ignore this kind of achievement. Rather, we'll call it performance. You reached an important goal through hard work. But the rewards were internal, centered on personal satisfaction and fulfillment. They matter, of course. They matter a great deal. They matter to you and to your physical therapist; they matter to your coach and to your family, just as achieving a milestone at work is significant to you and your boss. They may even enhance your future performance. But when I talk about success being collective and not individual, requiring a *community's* response, I mean that we need to be able to observe the ripple of impact your performance has on the people and environments you move within. We need to see how your performance matters to us.

Remember the old philosophical chestnut: If a tree falls in the woods and no one is around to hear it, does it make a sound? According to our new understanding of success, the answer is a resounding no. Audiences won't applaud your earth-shattering, disruptive achievement unless they can witness its impact. In an era when we can track human behavior with almost topographic accuracy, big data allows us to map success by measuring collective response to your performance. In the highly technological, plugged-in present, not only can we examine the circumstances through which success emerges, we can see how it spreads through the networks that connect us, touching faraway communities.

So while I recognize the importance of personal fulfillment, it's not a factor I can consider in my work as a researcher. Respecting that boundary has been oddly freeing. The popular definition of success reinforces the perception that "success" is as loose a concept as "love." The topic's vagueness kept scientists away—they assumed that it couldn't be studied. Realizing that success is a collective phenomenon throws that perception out the window. Once we defined success along external lines, a whole new set of possibilities opened up. We could measure and quantify it, using tools of scientific inquiry. And once we did that, we could unveil the laws that govern our success.

These laws are what separate the best seller from the bargain bin and the billionaires from the bankrupt. They illuminate how flawed competition protocols are, many of which effectively determine a winner by lottery. They show how "experts"—professionals who assess wine, classical music performances, figure skaters, or even other judges—are often no better at ascertaining quality than you or me. They explain why that guy who dominates staff meetings but shows up late and unprepared on all other occasions somehow becomes your boss. They show us that taking a risk on an underdog can have enormous impact, or that a single, initial donation can make or break a fundraising campaign. They even elucidate how a thoroughly terrible song—insert your nomination here—mystifyingly becomes a hit. The Laws of Success have governed our lives and careers as immutably as gravity through the centuries, and yet, until recently, we did not know they existed.

Before big data and the Science of Success, we assumed luck or hard work or talent, mixed together in some magic, unknowable proportion, were all that mattered—myself included. As an immigrant from Transylvania, first a political refugee within Europe and then a hopeful student, I believed that hard work alone was my best strategy. I was doubly committed to showing that I could succeed in America. But my only game plan for making it in science was to perform exceptionally, to make a discovery with lasting impact, to conduct research so groundbreaking that it couldn't be ignored. Years ago, my lab members taped a picture of the Energizer Bunny on my office door, with my face superimposed over its furry pink jowls. And even now I can't stop. I continue to work with a single-mindedness that can be infuriating to the people I'm closest to. These are things I can't really change about myself, though I've certainly tried. I believed in hard work as a child, and I believe in hard work now. But as the Laws of Success started to unfold before my eyes—as I saw patterns on a large scale that in individual cases seemed random—I was shocked by my own ignorance.

While I now know that performance remains crucial, I also know that it's only *one variable* in the formula for success. Other variables that we will unveil in the coming chapters are just as indispensable. When we break down and demystify the ingredients of success, we grasp what we can control in our lives—and what we can't. Because just like the laws of nature, the Laws of Success don't necessarily apply to all of us all the time. But they do come into play when we engage in specific activities. Aerodynamics are crucial if you're flying, friction if you're driving, and fluid dynamics if you take a boat. Different laws and formulas apply depending on what means of transportation you choose. The Laws of Success are similar—our insights into team success aren't going to illuminate the triumphs of an artist who works exclusively alone.

But we can use the laws to understand how invisible forces shape our successes and failures, knowledge I've found truly revelatory. As a kid, I was more of an artist than a scientist. Then, a few weeks into my first high school physics class, I earned an eight out of ten on a pop quiz that everyone else failed. I beamed in astonished pride when the teacher praised me. I don't think I was particularly gifted at physics, and I certainly wasn't passionate about it yet. The only reason I'd earned a decent 80 percent score was because a friend of my parents', an engineer, happened to be staying with us, and the night before the quiz he'd coached me through my homework.

Oblivious to the forces that had boosted my performance, I left the classroom that day with newfound confidence. It was the first success I experienced in science, and it stayed with me long after I'd graduated. It's fair to say that the rest of my life hinged on that moment. Because, without fully realizing it, I'd encountered the first of the many complex mechanisms at work that shaped my career. What underlies that experience—and all my later moments of personal triumph—are captured by the Laws of Success.

1

The Red Baron and the Forgotten Ace

In 1915, commanders in the German military received a complaint from a young cavalryman named Manfred von Richthofen, who wrote, "I have not gone to war to collect cheese and eggs, but for another purpose." The son of a prominent Prussian family, he was a military school graduate and passionate hunter, and he didn't want to spend the war in the army's supply branch. He wanted to see combat. Whether because of his enthusiasm or noble birth, he was granted his wish, a transfer to the air force.

It's true, von Richthofen's talents would have been wasted as an egg collector. He needed only twenty-four hours of training to take his first solo flight, in a brand-new Albatross biplane. With an open cockpit and skeletal frame balanced on two thin wheels, it was impossibly rickety by modern standards. Yet only a month later, von Richthofen had already scored six kills against Allied planes. He was fearless, sometimes flying four missions a day over the battle-gutted farmland of occupied France and descending on Allied pilots in brutal aerial assaults. He made wreckage of twenty-two planes in April 1917 alone, a month that came to be known in aviation history as "Bloody April" because of the extreme losses the Allies suffered. During his three-year career, von Richt-hofen gunned down eighty planes. That's more, by official standards, than any other ace pilot in World War I.

Von Richthofen also did something that now seems highly incongruous in our era of spending billions to make airplanes invisible to enemies. He painted his wasplike plane a taunt-ing, brazen red. The color of the aircraft, moving across the sky like blood smearing a butcher's apron, became the vivid source of his famous nickname: the Red Baron. It embodies the spirit of a brash nobleman who ordered a custom-engraved trophy from a high-end jeweler in Berlin for each of his kills. He accumulated sixty before Germany, squeezed by the hard-ships of war, ran out of silver. He continued to fight but quit collecting the cups—trophies made from base metal simply wouldn't do.

The Red Baron's story survives a century later, and not just in Germany. He is the subject of more than thirty books, including his own 1917 autobiography, which he wrote from a field hospital while recovering from a head wound. He's fea-tured in Hollywood movies, graphic novels, and comic books. Scores of documentaries have reenacted his aerial feats, ana-lyzing his achievements with breathy reverence. His fame extends from the bookshelves of war history buffs to the freezer aisle in the grocery store. If you really want to get your fill of von Richthofen, you can snack on a Red Baron frozen pizza while training on a Red Baron 3-D flight simula-tor. And of course he's immortalized in the playacting of the world's most beloved cartoon dog, whose animated battle with the Red Baron is embedded in the American childhood imagination and in the Royal Guardsmen's hit song "Snoopy vs. the Red Baron."

The product of a Snoopy-deprived Eastern European childhood, though, I'd never heard of the Red Baron until I came across a research paper, published in 2003, in a fairly obscure journal. The paper explored the performance of German World War I aces—pilots who had downed five or more aircraft over the course of the war. The performance of the fighter pilots was relatively cut-and-dried, determined by a single number, their total documented victories. With his eighty victories, von Richthofen was at the top of the list. Pilots such as Hans-Helmut von Boddien, with five, were near the bottom.

Compiling an accurate record of the pilots' performance served a purpose—the authors were curious how recognition related to it. Recognition, however, is generally much harder to measure. They couldn't use the rank or medals these pilots were awarded as a result of their achievements, because most of them didn't live to see the end of the war.

So they proposed a simple but clever solution. They used Google hits, measuring how many times people searched for these pilots by name on the Internet. The Google hits helped the researchers to gauge the degree to which the world remembered each pilot nearly a century later. This would be difficult to do if the German aces had common names like Robert Hall, one of the Allied pilots, given that there are many Robert Halls out there who have never downed a plane in their lives. The authors chose to focus on the German pilots precisely because they had singular names—such as Otto von Breiten-Landenburg or Gerold Tschentschel—circumventing a frequent problem we bump

21

up against when the subjects of our research point us toward numerous unrelated targets.

Altogether, the 392 German aces claimed a total of 5,050 victories. The eighty Allied planes that von Richthofen personally sent careening out of the sky is a stunning individual record. But it's a mere 1.6 percent of the total. Pocket change in the larger scheme. Yet he generated 27 *percent* of the German aces' Google hits. He takes up far more room in our collective consciousness than any of his compatriots.

At first glance, the Red Baron's legacy confirms the popular assumption that strong performance leads to success. It's as simple as that: if you fly flawless missions, pull off dramatic aerial stunts, and hit your targets with ruthless accuracy—if, in essence, you're the best at what you do—you'll be remembered for it, revered over centuries and across oceans. We're taught from grade school onward that perfecting performance is our best strategy for distinguishing ourselves from the crowd. The examples held up to us, the athletes, artists, writers, scientists, and entrepreneurs we idolize, all tend to perpetuate the same paradigm. The self-help gurus and football coaches, the educators and eager parents and pull-yourself-up-by-the-bootstraps politicians, even researchers studying the German aces: we all equate performance with success.

Except then there's René Fonck.

René who? you'll probably ask, echoing the befuddlement I felt when I came across a little-read article about him. His obscurity is downright bizarre. Fighting for the Allies in the same theater as the Red Baron, Fonck, a skilled French pilot, claimed to have gunned down 127 German planes. Seventy-five of these victories have been independently confirmed, making him, at the very least, the *second* most accomplished pilot of the war. If we add to his tally the most probable of his unproven claims, we arrive at a total of one hundred or more. That means that for all intents and purposes, Fonck was the Red Baron's equal in aerial warfare, and most likely his superior.

He was certainly a more technically proficient sharp-shooter than the Red Baron, rarely requiring more than five bullets to down a plane. Plus, he was a master of graceful maneuvering. One pilot compared Fonck's flying under fire to the quick up and down of a butterfly evading a predator. Whereas von Richthofen actually lost three battles — the last ending his life at the ripe young age of twenty-five — Fonck and his plane were never even scratched by enemy fire. He frequently came back from missions the sole survivor of his squadron, and doing so meant downing planes defensively, using calculation to ensure his escape. His tactics were far superior to von Richthofen's shoot-from-above hailstorm assaults. Yet all we know about René Fonck is contained in a hard-to-find autobiography and a few mentions of him here and there. He's largely been forgotten by time. It's as if the Red Baron, with every plane he downed, created lasting craters of impact, permanently carving his success into the landscape below. Fonck destroyed planes with equal or greater frequency, but they all crashed with a barely audible thud.

Why? That's a question that fascinates me. Take other examples: Claudette Colvin, an African-American teenager in Montgomery, Alabama, who refused to give up her bus seat to a white passenger in 1955. Her gesture presaged Rosa

Parks's by nine months. Same action, same city, same time frame. Yet no one mentions Colvin when students are taught about the heroes of the U.S. civil rights movement. Edison gets credit for X-ray photography, moving pictures, recorded audio, and the light bulb, when in fact *all* were discovered by other scientists or inventors. And then there are the Wright brothers, the inventors of the airplane according to the schoolbooks. Never mind that the first powered flight was executed nine months prior to theirs, by a New Zealander named Richard Pearse. Seemingly, it's the *last* person who makes a discovery that really matters, not the first.

Countless stories are right in front of our noses about deserving people who can't seem to jump-start their dreams. Our favorite restaurant fails, closing in the middle of a busy summer season. A brilliant uncle's gadgets remain little more than patched-together prototypes in his suburban basement. Our kids bang out chords for a piano instructor who's a true talent but never got a big break. We often chalk up such obscurity to bad luck, a crappy hand of cards. But if you're anything like me, you'll find such an answer unsatisfying. It simply doesn't make sense.

Until you begin to look at the data. The Red Baron's and René Fonck's vast difference in lasting renown, despite their indistinguishable performances, speaks to the most fundamental principle of the Science of Success, and our definition of the term "success" moving forward.

> *Your success isn't about you and your performance.*
> *It's about us and how we perceive your performance.*

> Or, to put it simply, your success is not about *you*, it's about *us*.

This definition of success is the axiom, or starting point, the foundational premise behind the research on success described in this book. Performance—or what you *do*, whether it's your bike-racing record or the number of cars you've sold or your score on a multiple-choice exam—is certainly a variable where you have some control. You can perfect your performance by honing your skills, practicing, preparing, and strategizing. You can even compare your performance against that of others and determine where you stand.

Success, however, is a whole different category. It's a collective measure, capturing how people respond to our performance. In other words, if we want to measure our success or figure out how we'll ultimately be rewarded, we can't look at our performances or accomplishments in isolation. Instead, we need to study our community and examine its response to our contributions. It's this clear distinction between success and performance that helped us in the lab to identify the universal patterns represented by each of the laws shared in this book.

The collective nature of success helps us explain why the René Foncks of the world go largely unrecognized despite their astounding or rare feats. Sure, recognition depends on the quality of your work; the Red Baron wouldn't be remembered if he were mediocre. But that's not the only factor, not by a long shot, as it were. You can perform well and not be acknowledged for it, an unfortunate truth that most of us know from experience. How often have we watched peers, with comparably meager or even lesser performances, get hailed for their work? Humankind is full of original artists and thinkers whose contributions are largely lost to history because their contemporaries failed to see their genius. You

25

may be writing the best code out there, or saving your company piles of money, or stashing a blockbuster away in a drawer, but if we're not aware of your achievements, then how can we recognize you for them? If we don't see, accept, and reward you for your performance, if we—and by "we" I mean more than just a few isolated voices—don't find your project worthy, it will likely falter, or stagnate, or barely make it off the ground.

•

Our new definition of success is foundational to the rest of the book. It tells us that success is *a collective phenomenon rather than an individual one.*

If our community is responsible for our success, we have to inspect the social and professional networks that generate collective responses to individual performances. Few of us start our journeys on a stage where thousands hail our accomplishments. Our initial impact is inevitably local, witnessed by our family members, colleagues, friends, neighbors, collaborators, and clients. Yet occasionally we set in motion ripples that reach beyond our immediate circles, radiating outward and activating a broad communal response. The most successful among us have mastered our networks, using them to achieve a place in the collective consciousness, snapping up valuable real estate in the brains of unlikely people.

The brain isn't a bad way to start thinking about such an enabling network, and collective consciousness isn't a bad way to evaluate our definition of success. We consider our brains as single entities capable of memory, sensation, and thought. But of course brains are composed of a very intricate and densely linked network of neurons. Every thought, feeling, and sensation we experience is caused by a train of excitations flashing through this neural web, with no single neuron solely responsible.

The networks that characterize our success are equally complex. Social platforms like Facebook barely permeate the dense social webs we're embedded in, and handing out business cards at a mixer—the emblematic act of networking—is only the most rudimentary way to use the professional webs enabling us.

In the language of networks, we are all nodes within an interconnected web that links us to billions of other nodes. In order to see the impact that you have on your collective environment, you must look to the other nodes in your network and check how they react in response to your performance. Our collective definition of success reminds us that we need to examine the networks we belong to, strategizing how we can use them to our future advantage. The landscape of a network, its highways and cow paths, its wildernesses and canyons, can reveal the routes to realizing our goals.

Here's a personal example of what I mean. As a scientist, my performance hinges on a single thing: discovery. Right? *Except that performance needs to be empowered by opportunity.* I grew up in Transylvania, a Hungarian kid in hermetically closed Communist Romania, where travel abroad was permitted only to other Communist countries. International conferences were off-limits. I had very limited access to scientific journals. I didn't even have much of a reason to learn English, since the odds I'd leave Romania were basically nil. So no matter how promising I may have been as a budding scientist, my access to the professional networks that are the lifeline for science were severely curtailed.

But then, in the summer of 1989, a phone call dragged me out of my dorm room in Bucharest and sent me packing to my hometown in Transylvania, my exams half done. My father, a museum director of some prominence, was among the last ethnic Hungarians to hold a leadership position in the Romanian political system. The victim of a nationalist purge of ethnic minorities from governance, he was suddenly stripped of his post and livelihood. One day he was running a network of museums; the next day he was checking tickets on local buses. The change was too visible, reflecting poorly on those who plotted his fall. So they plotted again, removing him from the picture entirely. Just like that, my dad and I found ourselves in Hungary, political refugees. It wasn't what I would have chosen for myself by any means—separated from my mom and sister, I can't remember a time I've ever felt so alone. But once I recovered from the shock of starting a life in a country where I had no friends or even acquaintances, I realized that those narrow-minded officials had done me a favor: by sending us away, they offered me access to a professional network that would have been off-limits in Communist Romania.

Indeed, just three months after, I was studying with a world-class scientist, Tamás Vicsek, who had returned from years of working as a researcher in the United States. He invited Gene Stanley, the most prominent name in my field, to a conference in Hungary, and at the reception Tamás held at his Budapest home, I had the chance to practice my shaky English on the guest of honor. Gene invited me to Boston for my doctorate studies, activating his own professional network to make sure that I was admitted. There were strings to pull, after all. I'd flunked the English-language qualifying exam, a minimal requirement for admission. Still, I somehow found myself in Boston, the Alexandria of modern science, a place teeming with opportunities.

I'm tempted to say that all this happened because I was a promising scientist, that my later success was thanks to my performance alone. But then I think of my peers at the university in Bucharest. Some of them took home the gold in physics competitions I didn't even *qualify* for. There was Dan, who'd already won the International Physics Olympiad as a ninth grader, beating the whole world in topics I wouldn't learn about for three more years. There was Cristian, a gentle giant, who could explain the solution to virtually any problem in his soft, pleasant voice. Both were measurably more accomplished than I was. Yet, lacking a path forward, neither made it in our chosen profession. So no matter how promising I was as a scientist, the same performance that helped me succeed in Budapest and Boston would have fallen on deaf ears in Bucharest. We'll discuss in a later chapter how networks both isolate and embrace us, shaping our prospects in invisible ways. Life in Communist Romania offered me a personal case study, a glimpse of the powerful role networks and the collective played in my own success, long before I understood the science behind them.

•

The Red Baron and René Fonck each achieved success according to a clear and countable military standard: the number of enemy planes brought down. Compared to their peers on either side of the battle, they were the best at this task. But the discrepancy between how the Red Baron and René Fonck are remembered has little to do with performance. The differences, instead, are due to the collective nature of success. And it's about the networks that detect, acknowledge, and disseminate our achievements to the larger world.

The Red Baron is often described as heartless and exceedingly vain, with cold, emotionless eyes. His autobiography is little more than an account of various acts of violence relayed in an off-putting, self-congratulatory tone. Yet, confronting the terrors of war, his peers were inspired by his bravado. When he flamboyantly painted his plane red, he became the quintessential symbol for the German propaganda machine, bolstering the morale of the German public. His proud face, shadowed by a jaunty peaked cap, appeared on trading cards. Newspapers claimed that the British military had created special squadrons whose only goal was his demise. For all these reasons, the Red Baron became a singular hero. Even his untimely death in combat—the circumstances of which were shrouded in conspiracy—was helpful in maintaining a mythology that might otherwise have been confined to the context of war. A baron by birth and a warrior in death, he was enshrined as an enduring symbol of patriotism and heroism.

The same factors on the other side of the front line should have also pushed Fonck to prominence. And in many ways they did, at least at first. During the war, he received all the honors an ace pilot could hope for. His notoriety even got him elected to the French Parliament. But then the public turned on him. His first mistake was that he wasn't killed. Surviving World War I, he landed in politically murky waters during the

Nazi occupation of France during World War II. He also failed as a demonstration pilot, crash-landing on takeoff while attempting the first flight from Paris to New York.

But details aside, the key distinction between the two men is that one was useful to his network and the other was not. The Red Baron's success was about what was happening politically and socially during the war, not only about how many planes he shot down, or how vain he was, or how he felt about his accomplishments. We remember him today because he was once vital to the German propaganda machine. His reputation was left in the hands of those desperate for a hero to galvanize their spirit. The broad public, responding to the Red Baron's performance, created a myth about him that served its purposes. In other words, *the network found him useful and chose to amplify his success.*

The Laws of Success will help us understand how to jumpstart this kind of community interest, so that our performance resonates widely. If our goal is that our work matters to others— and who doesn't want that?— then we need to understand how collective interest in our contributions is generated through the intricate webs we are embedded within.

In the Red Baron's case, his network created a legend so prodigious that it quickly transcended battle lines. Remember those *Peanuts* cartoons where Snoopy salutes the Red Baron from the sinking plane that is his doghouse, as smoke billows around him? It's this sportsmanlike gesture of respect in the face of certain defeat that I find particularly telling. His foe's reputation for aerial combat is so great that even Snoopy, a cartoon dog fighting in the limitless realm of the imagination, doesn't presume he stands a chance.

But as I invoke Snoopy as an arbiter of success, it is important to clarify that the Red Baron was not only successful. He was also *famous*. His unlikely appearance in an American cartoon decades after his death is proof positive. Which raises an important question. Can we separate success from fame? Do we have to?

•

The largest round table I have ever seen is in the Nobel Forum in Stockholm, where the Nobel Committee confers each year to decide on its laureates in physiology or medicine. Leading to that room is a corridor with a portrait of each winner. I once visited the forum and lingered in the hallway full of portraits, absorbing the serenity of the space. It felt like visiting a chapel, a shrine to the secular saints who move medicine forward. Each portrait is of a scientist of outstanding performance. And each had experienced exceptional success—their peers had recognized the importance of their work and acknowledged its impact by awarding them the highest honor a scientist can aspire to. Although we don't usually associate celebrity with science, if there's fame in science, they've achieved it.

But as I took in name after name, portrait after portrait— more than a century of hardworking, passionate people whose discoveries had literally saved millions of lives—it occurred to me, stunningly, that I didn't recognize a single face. Not one.

It gave me tremendous pause. I felt chastened, humbled by an obvious truth that had somehow eluded me.

Success and fame are very different animals.

For example, as a writer Vladimir Nabokov is undoubtedly a success. He's known for a lush, complex body of work in addition to *Lolita*—thousands and thousands of pages. But if you ask anyone other than an English major who Vladimir Nabokov is, you're likely to be met with a blank stare or, at best, "The guy who wrote that book about the pedophile?"

It goes without saying that Einstein is a successful physicist. His renown extends beyond the small and insular world of science, a rare feat. Show a picture of him to anyone on the street, and he'll declare, "Einstein, of course!" But if you ask what he's famous for, you'll hear a hesitant answer framed as a question. "He was a genius, right?"

There are multitudes of Nabokovs and Einsteins out there. They accumulate success through their performance, and then their success brings them recognition, radiating far beyond their professional networks. And once people become recognizable names outside of their professional networks, to the point that their future performances are secondary to our appreciation of them, we bestow the mantle of *fame*. Fame is the rare side effect of exceptional success. It's not the purpose of this book to put fame under the microscope, but neither can we shy away from it.

Still, it's fascinating to think about the people who share the strange domain of "famousness." If you want to know who's more famous than Jesus (hint: it's not the Beatles), you can search the Pantheon Project, an online tool created by César Hidalgo, my brilliant former student, now a professor at MIT's Media Lab. According to César, the truly famous are those known beyond their local spheres. Instead of measuring fame using Google hits, as in the ace pilots study, he uses Wikipedia pages—or to be precise, the number of languages a person's Wikipedia page is published in. To be included in the pantheon, a person's renown has to have crossed national and linguistic barriers, and must be represented on Wikipedia in at least twenty-five languages. This single requirement narrows the famous down from practically any minor celebrity or vaguely notable person to 11,341 individuals, members of a fascinating and motley crew.

On the website, you can explore these legendary figures using a vast array of search criteria. Who was the most famous person born in 1644? Bashō, the master of Japanese haiku. The most famous person born in Barcelona? Seventeen people make the list, but Joan Miró, the painter, tops it. The most famous musician of all time? Jimi Hendrix. What about the world's most famous criminal? Charles Manson ranks third, behind Jack the Ripper and my fellow Transylvanian Elizabeth Báthory, the alleged serial murderer. The most famous American of all time? Not George Washington or Bill Gates. It's Martin Luther King Jr.

We shouldn't be surprised that our Red Baron makes the pantheon, as the forty-fourth most famous military figure, the fifth most famous person born in 1892, and the fourth most famous person born in Poland. His Wikipedia page appears in forty-three languages and has attracted over 8 million views. It's as if his crimson biplane has defied physics, propelling itself through space and time. He leaves René Fonck—who isn't even in the pantheon—in the Wiki-dust, a heroic achiever fogged in by obscurity.

The most famous person ever? According to the Pantheon Project, it's Aristotle. Though far less flashy than the Red Baron, he has remained important in many locales, languages, and eras. Perhaps it's not a coincidence that the giant of both philosophy and lasting fame had insight into success that is relevant several thousand years later. "This [honor], however, appears to be too superficial to be what we are seeking, for it seems to depend more on those who honor than on the one honored." In other words, being honored is an unreliable means to happiness, since it relies on the giver rather than the recipient. Not a bad way to rephrase our definition of success.

Aristotle is a shining example of the majority of people in the Pantheon Project's rankings who have made meaningful and far-reaching contributions, reinforcing the idea that performance is crucial to enduring success. But there are also twenty-one members of the project's "celebrity" category, and they're an interesting bunch. The top ranking belongs to Lina Medina, the youngest person ever to give birth. (She was only five years old at the time, a horrifying thought.) A few beauty pageant winners, socialites, and heiresses figure in the mix, reminding us that fame can be utterly divorced from anything we'd recognize as achievement or even content.

Kim Kardashian is the fourteenth most famous celebrity of all time, appearing in forty-four language editions of Wikipedia. If René Fonck is an example of outstanding performance without success, then Kardashian is his opposite: an unmistakable instance of success without obvious performance. We know from experience how difficult it is to generate reward even with superior achievements. How is it possible to do so without them?

That's a question that has always bothered me, chafing against the hard-work ethos we're all raised to believe in.

With that in mind, we'll now get into the heart of this book, starting with an important question. How do *success* and *performance* relate to each other? While there clearly is some relationship between the two, the case of Kim Kardashian reminds us that the concepts aren't equivalent.

THE FIRST LAW

Performance drives success, but when performance can't be measured, networks drive success.

As we journey from tennis courts to art galleries, we'll see why it's not the reputable schools we attend that makes us succeed, but our success that makes a school reputable. Most important, we'll learn to see the largely invisible networks that shape our success.

2

Grand Slams and College Diplomas
Why Hard Work (Sometimes) Works

My former wife and I considered ourselves fortunate. Our son, Dániel—a likable, smart kid—was doing all the right things. He was taking four college-level classes in the eleventh grade. He had helped launch a school newspaper and put late nights and weekends into editing it. He was on the swim team. He was curious and had multiple interests, and his grades were excellent. His teachers and peers liked him. He seemed happy. And we were happy that everyone was happy.

It wasn't until Dániel started applying to colleges that we realized he had a boulder-sized obstacle in his path—his naive, foreign-born parents. You see, we were both educated in Europe—his mom in Sweden and I in Romania—and we believed in a sole metric when it came to success: performance. Do well in school and you'll succeed. The elite high school I attended in Romania had based its admissions on one exam taken by thirteen-year-olds, with odds of admittance a slim three to one. After tenth grade, I took another cutthroat test, which whittled the number of my classmates in half. Finally, my application to the university hinged on a similar factor—my score on an exam in physics and math. Nothing else mattered, not my extracurricular activities, not the many days I'd spent in the art studio, dreaming of becoming a sculptor, and not even my grades or my research paper that had been accepted by a prominent physics journal in Romania. It seemed as if my performance alone, reflected in exam scores, determined my fate. It never occurred to me that college admissions in the States would be different.

A faculty son, Dániel considered the University of Notre Dame his second home, and for many years his hope had been to return there. But after we moved to Boston, his world opened up. He spent a summer working at MIT and another at Harvard. Then there was Stanford, which he'd fallen in love with when he and I visited the Bay Area. Because his numbers were good—his GPA spoke to his academic abilities—we believed that any of these schools were well within his reach.

It wasn't until I started looking at his application materials that it dawned on me what those colleges were asking for. Essays about unique life experiences. Recommendations from teachers. Interviews with college administrators. A wide range of extracurricular activities. A track record of excellence in one specialized area. Plus, top grades and SAT scores, and constant reminders that these measurable factors were secondary to the rest. My heart sank. Despite spending two decades on the faculties of several major American universities, I'd been clueless about what it took for my students to get into my classroom. Why was such an important process as school admissions so opaque and subjective and, in the end, so unpredictable?

It was the first time in my life that I was faced with the

question, what does it take for our kids to succeed in a world where we lack a clear metric of performance? To find an answer, we need to discuss, first, an area where performance is uniquely accessible—sports. So let's start with the Woman with the Ising Tattoo.

•

The Girl with the Dragon Tattoo was an international hit when Burcu Yucesoy applied for a job in my lab. I had begun noticing the tattoos people had wherever I went, but the striking one on Burcu's left arm really hit home. It was a black-inked rendering of the Ising Hamiltonian function, the formula that underpinned much of her doctoral work. Having spent years focusing on an obscure realm of physics that she affectionately called "finicky, capricious, and frustrating," she was ready for something different. Moreover, she was articulate and her scientific abilities were impressive. Yet I kept returning to that tattoo, thinking, *What a nerd!* I loved it. She was hired.

A few months after the interview, she finally joined my lab, where we were already exploring how success emerged in science. Before we could begin in earnest, though, we encountered a major problem: the data that would allow us to measure performance, which seemed like a key prerequisite to success, was hard to find.

But then my neighbor in Budapest, Tamás Hámori, a former professional tennis player, told me about a rich trove of data gathered by the Association of Tennis Professionals. It tracks performance in painstaking detail, he explained, keeping an accurate record of each pro match and assigning points to players based on the outcomes. For instance, a winner of a Grand Slam championship earns two thousand points, whereas a player eliminated during the second game in this tournament only earns about ten. These points, updated weekly, determine each player's relative ranking. As with kills for World War I ace pilots, these points allowed us to compare the tennis players with high accuracy. This was precisely what we needed—an area where performance was definitely measurable. So Burcu's task looked straightforward: use tennis to unveil the relationship between performance and success.

Clearly, tennis was not what Burcu had in mind when she applied to my lab. In fact, sports were almost *never* what Burcu had in mind. She'd played tennis one summer as a middle schooler at a camp in Istanbul. There was even a photo of her, bespectacled and dwarfed by her enormous racquet, in the local newspaper.

"I was so bad I thought my racquet had a hole in it," she told me, laughing, recalling the misery of lobbing balls back and forth across a net, her sneakers and eventually her face streaked red from the clay court. The article about her tennis camp had been stashed long ago in a box in her mother's house, replaced by scientific awards and certificates.

Perhaps eager to tackle the sport from an angle more advantageous to her skill set, Burcu took the assignment and ran with it. Soon, however, a complication began to emerge: while there was a near-perfect tool to gauge a player's performance, there wasn't yet a measure to quantify "success." According to our new foundational premise, success is not about *you* and your performance; it's about *us* and how we perceive it. So if winning in tennis is a clear-cut case of *performance*, then *success* must mean something else—for example, recognition and income.

It's no secret that top athletes are richly rewarded for excellence on the court, but the vast majority of an elite athlete's income comes from endorsements. The tennis star Roger Federer earned an astonishing $58 million in one year alone from endorsing various brands. Advertisers want access to his huge fan base. His exceptional rewards are not linked to his day-to-day performances; they reflect the cumulative *visibility* generated by his wins and losses.

Burcu hoped to find data on the behind-the-scenes decisions in corporate offices that led to these massive sponsorships. Yet she could only collect information on the top stars; not much registered for smaller deals or middle-ranked players. So she decided to focus on what drives the endorsements in the first place—a player's fan base, since that's the catalyst for the size of the deals. She could have turned to Google to figure out how many of us really care about a player, as we'd done for the German pilots. Yet because the tennis players do not have names as distinctive as Hans-Helmut von Boddien or Otto von Breiten-Landenburg, the results Google offered were hard to interpret. She therefore turned to Wikipedia—with its feasts of personal and professional details—since Googling any tennis player would immediately guide us to his or her Wiki page anyway.

Burcu simply ignored the layers of trivia that Wiki editors lovingly uploaded about the marriages, breakups, and off-the-court antics of their favorite players. She peeked instead under the hood of the site, examining layers of data that gave clues about Wikipedia readers' visitation patterns. This allowed her to reconstruct how many people clicked on, for instance, Roger Federer's Wikipedia page over a given period of time.

Using Wikipedia hits as a proxy for popularity, Burcu then moved to our real purpose: to determine how skills and victories translated into "success" as we're defining it. She began by compiling a detailed timeline of each player's performances between 2008 and 2015, recording all his wins and losses, together with the points earned in every match. She then invented a formula that combined these performance measures with the aim of predicting the visibility each tennis player *should* earn based on wins and losses. The process was time-consuming; it took almost two years to complete.

But it paid off.

As Burcu crunched the numbers, a pattern emerged. No matter if a player was top-ranked—Roger Federer, Novak Djokovic, Andy Murray, Rafael Nadal—or an up-and-coming novice on the circuit, there was a remarkable synchronicity between her predictions and the athlete's true visibility. Performance was so married to success that Burcu could *accurately anticipate the number of people likely to flock to a player's Wiki page on any given day following his performance on court.* She could foresee periods of low Wiki traffic for poorer-performing players, along with the valleys created by injuries. But she could also predict the huge peaks of attention for an unexpected win against a prominent player. And once she had the performance data, Burcu could *predict* success.

There was only one way to interpret her results: Success in tennis is determined by a single factor—strong athleticism. At least on the court, the dogma of the classic, hard-work-yields-reward strategy holds true. *Performance drives success.*

This is the starting point. If you're a tennis player, keep your eye on the ball and perfect your game. (Pick any sports cliché and insert it here, then call your childhood coach and thank him for his wisdom.) But this isn't the case only in sports. You can't be a successful lawyer without a solid command of knowledge that attracts clients. You can't be a renowned architect without a strong background in structural engineering and a keen eye for design. Your sensational tech product can't have too many glitches.

Burcu's formula was as elegantly designed as the tattoo on her arm. Still, our findings were a little disappointing. We'd been hoping for insights beyond the obvious. Instead, what we discovered reinforced the most basic premise of all: performance is the key to success. Sure, we found a dramatic, quantitative correlation between performance and success. But how dramatic is that?

•

If there was a silver lining in Burcu's findings, it was the hope it gave me that Dániel, my son, would land in the college of his dreams. Tennis came as close as I could imagine to the Romanian school system, where test scores alone are expected to determine measurable outcomes. This belief, however, lasted only until the college responses started pouring in, and then reality took over. Stanford, Dániel's top choice, said no. Harvard also turned him down. These rejections, added to a pile including letters from Brown, the University of Chicago, and the University of Pennsylvania, were emphatic proof that we weren't in Romania any longer. Putting my faith in performance alone was a flawed, heartbreaking tactic. It got to the point where I was afraid to ask what was in the latest envelope.

Luckily, there was also good news. Dániel got accepted at Notre Dame, his original dream school for years. Having taught for a decade there, I knew it would offer him an excellent education. So every time another no landed in our mailbox, we reminded each other that he still had an outstanding place to go.

Then we got more encouraging news, though it ended up creating something of a dilemma. An acceptance arrived from Northeastern, my current employer.

Dániel now had a choice, but it wasn't an easy one. Notre Dame came with a substantial price tag. Northeastern wouldn't cost a dime because of its generous benefits package, which allows the children of faculty and staff a tuition-free education if they qualify academically. What does Notre Dame offer that Northeastern doesn't that justifies the difference?

Well, there was data for that. Let's start here: graduates of elite colleges have a leg up on peers who attend lower-ranked colleges. An Ivy League grad will average over $70,000 as a median annual salary a decade down the road, while graduates of other schools can expect less than half that—$34,000. The disparity is particularly high at the higher ends of the income spectrum. The top 10 percent of Ivy League grads earn an average of $200,000 or more within ten years of leaving school, whereas the highest earners in the other schools make a hair under $70,000.

When Dániel was applying to colleges in 2012, hoping that his hard work would pay off, Notre Dame was ranked nineteenth in the country. Northeastern was only sixty-ninth at the time.

Notre Dame was in a prestigious, almost Ivy League–level category. Northeastern was free.

Many parents and students face a tough choice when the offers finally roll in: Should we mortgage our future to guarantee the best education for our children? It's a deeply emotional decision. Yet, after learning there was data available to help us shape our decisions, my thinking changed entirely. It turned out that despite the clear-cut statistics, choosing Notre Dame over Northeastern would have *absolutely no bearing* on his future earnings. Not even going to Stanford or Harvard would make a difference. Rather, performance and ambition, working in tandem, would determine his future success.

•

Boston Latin, the first high school in the United States, is still the crown jewel of the Boston school system. Ranked in the top twenty high schools in the country, it's public but highly selective. Just as I had to do in Romania, kids must do well in an exam to get in. If your kid doesn't make the cut, she will be automatically enrolled, based on her exam scores, in Boston Latin Academy, a similarly named but second-ranked school. If she doesn't get admitted there either, she can attend the O'Bryant High School of Math and Science. After that, she has to enroll in a "non-exam" public school.

There's a reason kids (and their parents) clamor to enroll in Boston Latin: the graduates collectively boast the fourth-highest average SAT score in Massachusetts, fast-tracking them into elite colleges. Latin Academy is also impressive, in the eightieth percentile for the state. O'Bryant's average scores might be only in the fortieth percentile, but they're substantially better than the city's non-exam-based schools' dismal averages. So if you're a parent living in Boston, you'll do everything possible to ensure your kid lands at one of these exam schools. And if your kid misses the cutoff, it would seem, on the face of it, that you're setting her up for failure.

But are you? A few years ago, a trio of economists asked that very question, carefully comparing the students who just made it into Boston Latin with those who barely missed the necessary score. Often just tiny percentage points on a test determined the outcome. That means students on either side of the admissions line were virtually indistinguishable when it came to their initial academic achievement and intellectual promise. There was a key difference: some were lucky enough to spend the next years in a fabulous school, while others, every bit as intelligent, were forced to go elsewhere.

Naturally we'd assume that the students who attend a superior school, taught by stellar teachers and motivated by brilliant peers, will perform measurably better on achievement tests by the time they graduate. Except…they don't. Not even by a little bit. It doesn't matter what we look at— PSAT, SAT, or advanced placement test results. *There are no differences* between Boston Latin graduates who just made it into the school and those who barely missed their chance and ended up at Latin Academy. And the same is true for those who missed out on Latin Academy and ended up at O'Bryant, a much-lower-ranked school. They still did exactly as well as those who crossed the admissions line, gaining entry into

Latin Academy. For those who took the exam and missed the final option of O'Bryant, ending up at a non-exam school? They, too, did as well at graduation as the students who'd barely made it into O'Bryant.

Take a moment to grasp the implication. I know I had to. We've established that, as a group, the Boston Latin kids do perform better when compared to their counterparts at Latin Academy. Their SAT scores are higher. No one disputes that. What the data tells us, though, is that the difference—despite what parents think, teachers suggest, and principals claim—is not because the school enhances their performance. It's because *high achievers continue to excel no matter what education a school offers.* The Boston Latin students have that superior collective SAT score at graduation because the entrance exam selected the top performers to begin with. And they simply carried those abilities through high school. In other words, Boston Latin doesn't make your daughter a better student. It's your daughter who makes Boston Latin into the elite school it is.

The message is clear. The school doesn't ultimately matter; the student does. And this is not a critique of the Boston school system—the conclusion held for all high school systems where there was data to address these same questions. Researchers found identical results from New York City to Romania to Hungary, where my younger kids went to school for five years. These outcomes hinted that it didn't matter if we sent Dániel to Northeastern University or the University of Notre Dame. It was his ability that would determine his success once he graduated, not the school he attended.

But could I really use high school data to guide my son's college choice?

I didn't have to, because two Princeton economists took great pains to sort out which factors determine the long-term success of college graduates. They started by comparing students who applied to elite universities but ended up, for various reasons, at less prestigious ones. Remember that the data is pretty clear on this score: the median annual income of Ivy League graduates is about $70,000 ten years later, twice the pay of non-Ivy grads. Yet to the surprise of the researchers, the graduates of humbler schools that snubbed the Ivy League were earning just as much as Ivy League alums. In other words, a student who won entry to Princeton but decided on Northeastern still possessed the earning power of a Princeton grad. It's the Latin schools all over again: the school doesn't make you great; you are great to begin with!

Burcu's tennis findings make a cameo here: performance drives success. A college student's measurable performance, captured by her SAT scores and class ranking at application time, determines her future income.

But the most unforeseen conclusion of the Princeton study came when the researchers looked at those who weren't accepted into Ivy League colleges. After accounting for all performance measures for students, such as SAT scores and rankings in their high school class, the key factor determining income a decade after graduation was not the college they attended. The single determinant of long-term success was derived from the best college a kid *merely applied to*, even if she didn't get in. Meaning that if she applied to Harvard, got rejected, and went to Northeastern, her success was on a par with that of Harvard graduates who matched her SATs and high school grades. In other words, it's performance and ambition—*where she thinks she belongs*—that determine your daughter's success.

A few things I hasten to add, with a bit of a caution. Forcing your child to apply to Harvard as some future guarantee of big earnings obviously defeats the purpose. Ambition, after all, is innate. While the results are unequivocal that confidence and self-belief play a huge role in success, they have to match strong performance.

Nor am I suggesting that elite colleges don't impart tremendous benefits. The data shows that African-American, Latino, and other underrepresented social and cultural groups, along with first-generation college students, benefit greatly from access to these schools.

But if you miss out on an elite spot—if you're like Dániel, the high-achieving child of educated middle-class, though naive, parents—there's plenty of hope. You might not have been tapped by the establishment powers that be, but you have the crucial ambition and ability to compete.

•

In the end, Dániel attended Notre Dame.

You might sense a contradiction. Why did I, the numbers guy, decide to throw all that tuition money out the window? Well, back in 2012, I was not yet aware of the data that would have helped me decide. Nor did I know that in the years to follow Northeastern would halve its number in the national ranking, coming closer to Notre Dame's. But as the data we've covered in this chapter indisputably shows, strong college ranking has less impact on a student's future than what the student brings to the college. It's a convincing argument that ambition and achievement can defy our assumptions and even the playing field. And while Burcu's findings about success on the tennis court unequivocally confirmed the inspirational messaging of tennis coaches everywhere—that success depends solely on performance—my son's experience with getting into college was deeply puzzling to me. Here were two rare realms—tennis and school achievement—where performance was measurable, leaving little room for disagreement about what constituted excellence. In both those realms, long-term success coincided with performance-based rank to an undeniable degree.

It's tempting to make the sweeping generalization that exceptional performance always wins. Yet for that to be true, we must be able to measure performance. SAT scores and tennis rank provide this metric, but such accurate performance metrics are nearly impossible to obtain in most fields. You don't need to look far to see this—take a team sport like soccer, and you'll see how difficult our task is. Sure we know how many goals and assists a player makes, but we can't really parse his performance from his teammates' in a way that passes scientific muster. In fact, we saw this in action recently, when we analyzed the postgame grades judges assigned to each player in an Italian soccer league. These experts had been hired by three different Italian newspapers to examine individual performance on the field. A full 20 percent of the time, one judge gave a high grade to a player while the others saw a deplorable performance. A deeper analysis showed that the judges had no idea how most of the players performed. Defenders, for example, were assessed based on how the team did, the goals scored and the overall goal differences. The hundreds of little moves and choices defenders executed during the ninety minutes of game time — tackles, successfully foiled passes, assists, and aerial duels — left no mark in the memories of the judges as they rated each player. These judges, and the rest of us, seem to forget that a strong soccer player on a weak team may score plenty of goals but not actually win games. Or he might score fewer goals because his teammates fail to "set him up for success." Even if he's a star on an excellent team, it's difficult to determine whether his team's win is solely due to his own performance or the collective effort of the group. Move him from a great squad to a weak one, and our player's performance weakens. Assembling a team for success is a complex challenge. And measuring and rewarding individual performance in a team setting is, of course, even trickier than it is with one-on-one sports, as we'll see later.

The bottom line is this: gauging individual performance is a challenge even in sports, where the winners and losers are clearly defined. But what happens when we don't have a precise way of delineating high and low scorers? Who decides the winner and the loser then?

To find an answer, we'll next turn to an area where performance is impossible to measure.

And we'll see networks take center stage.

3

The $2 Million Urinal

Why Hard Work Doesn't Work

"SAMO saves idiots and Gonzoids," someone wrote in block letters across a door in a Manhattan alley. A strange graffito, sure, but not that different from other tongue-in-cheek poetic statements that were suddenly popping up all over the city in 1977.

"SAMO is an escape clause," declared one.

"SAMO is an end to playing art," announced another.

"SAMO does not cause cancer in laboratory animals," insisted a third.

Then, in 1979, came a final, succinct decree: "SAMO is dead."

And SAMO did die, but only in the way that artistic collaborations often end, when two people working together go their separate ways. The better known of the two artists behind SAMO was Al Diaz, who despite his youth had a long track record in graffiti art. Three years earlier, his work had been featured in a book about graffiti by Norman Mailer, which was about as much notoriety as an underground graffiti artist could hope for. Diaz did solo work, but he also created in tandem with a friend under their single moniker, the genesis of which is unabashedly adolescent. The duo smoked pot, which they dubbed "the same old shit," a phrase shortened to "same old" that morphed into SAMO. Under their assumed persona, they hit the streets with paint cans in hand, scribbling messages across the city. Then they had a falling-out.

In science we like controls, which, for example, might help us gauge how two individuals with similar starting points diverge over time. Many of our deepest understandings of topics like nature versus nurture or genes versus environment come from such twin studies, which follow the lives of siblings with exactly the same genetic makeup. In fact, the previous chapter's academic "twins"—students who barely land in elite schools and their less fortunate counterparts—helped us parse out the role of schools in our success. SAMO offers a kind of "twin study" in art. Two students who are the same age, from the same environment, make art that's impossible to tell apart. Suddenly they become untwinned, breaking abruptly out on their own. What happens then?

Al Diaz is still a player in the New York art scene, but if you've never heard of him, you're not alone. His biggest claim to fame remains SAMO, a project that's been dead since his partner took to the streets solo nearly forty years ago.

Diaz's partner in crime is also long dead—succumbing to an overdose at twenty-seven. But his art is immortal. Just two years after "SAMO is dead" was scrawled across SoHo, Diaz's partner created a large untitled painting of a skull made with spray paint and an oil stick. It recently sold for a record-breaking *$110.5 million*. His name was Jean-Michel Basquiat.

When it comes to success, Basquiat and Diaz are a striking example of how people with a common beginning experience wildly divergent outcomes. Their careers began at the same time and place. Their work was initially indistinguishable. But Diaz has made art in relative obscurity ever since. Basquiat, on the other hand, was a sensation as a living artist and a rampant success as a dead one.

So how do we explain Diaz's and Basquiat's divergent trajectories?

They differed in one essential aspect: Diaz was a loner. Basquiat, on the other hand, was an unapologetic networker. This was evident even during their adolescent SAMO phase, when Diaz insisted that they keep their shared identity a secret. Basquiat? He outed the partnership to the *Village Voice* for one hundred dollars.

That difference was part of a pattern. Indeed, Basquiat assembled his relationships in the art world like a carefully curated gallery show. As a brash near-teenager, he approached Andy Warhol, then the reigning patriarch of the New York art world, sweet-talking him into buying one of the postcards he hand-painted and sold on the street. Basquiat capitalized on this transaction, using it to build a relationship with Warhol that would last the rest of his life. And though he was not enrolled there, Basquiat hung around the School of Visual Arts, eventually meeting and then dating Keith Haring, who was just then becoming one of art's most glittering names. Basquiat also befriended the producer of the cable program *TV Party* and began appearing on the show, a role that gave him some local celebrity.

Perhaps most important, he sought out Diego Cortez, a

well-connected East Village artist. It was Cortez who included Basquiat in a group show that featured no fewer than twenty of his drawings and paintings, which hung side by side with works by Robert Mapplethorpe, Haring, and Warhol. A handful of New York's prestigious dealers took notice. As the sun rose the morning after the show's opening, Basquiat hustled back to his father's Brooklyn apartment and shouted, "Papa, I made it!" And indeed he had. Some of the works he'd exhibited that night sold for $25,000, an enormous sum in the early 1980s. By carefully and aggressively building a series of meaningful connections, Basquiat went from homeless teenager to A-list artist in under two years. Diaz, on the other hand, continued to make underground street art.

It helped that Basquiat was passionate, driven, and died of a heroin overdose at a young age. But what's surprising is how little his success has to do with the excellence of his art. He had, after all, the same artistic DNA as Diaz, to the point that their work was often deliberately indistinguishable. Nor was it the inherent quality of *Untitled*—that 1982 painting of a black spray-painted skull on a deep, colorful background— that made it the priciest piece by an American artist ever sold at auction.

The fact is, no one can assign value to masterpieces or assess their worth by simply looking at the art itself. Instead, we have to look at the invisible network of curators, art historians, gallery owners, dealers, agents, auction houses, and collectors that determines what gets into museums and the price we're willing to pay for them. These networks not only determine which works hang on museum walls; they even command which works we line up to see.

Which means we've arrived at a topic that a book about success can't avoid. Since success is a collective phenomenon, measured by how our community reacts to a performance, it's impossible to understand the phenomenon of success without also observing the network it takes place within. But networks are singularly important in areas like art, where performance and quality are hard to measure. In fact, an interconnected web of relationships determines success in art to a degree that even I, a network scientist, find stunning. How do networks perform this predictive magic? How do we create value when there is none?

•

In 1917, Marcel Duchamp walked into a plumbing supply store in New York City and selected what's known as a Bedfordshire-style urinal from the array of bathroom fixtures on offer. When he returned to his studio with his gleaming porcelain find, he laid it on its back, signed it "R. Mutt," named it *Fountain*, and called it art. Displayed at an angle and out of its normal context, it *was* oddly beautiful, but aesthetics weren't really the point. Duchamp submitted the signed urinal to the Society of Independent Artists—which he served as the founder and director of—for exhibition. The society was so forward-thinking that its stated purpose, in fact, was to avoid the highbrow selectivity of stuffy museums. Instead, curators vowed to accept works by anyone who wished to be included, as long as they paid a small membership fee. The exhibition was the largest of its kind, and it nonjudgmentally featured art by big names and complete unknowns in the same space.

But *Fountain* was too much even for the society's open-minded curators. Not only did Duchamp anonymously submit a functional, premade object to an art exhibit, which was unheard of at the time, but he chose a deeply impolite *urinal.* The society balked, refusing to display the piece. And so *Fountain* met an unceremonious end. Only a single photograph of it, by Alfred Stieglitz, survives. The urinal itself was presumably discarded in an early-twentieth-century trash heap, buried among the flotsam and jetsam of a bygone era.

The point Duchamp was making, though, lives on. The piece was an in-your-face provocation, one that shook the very foundation of the art world. Today, many art historians consider *Fountain* to be the single most important work of modern art. To give you a sense of its importance, Dimitri Daskalopoulos, a Greek collector, forked over almost $2 million in 1997, and not even for the discarded original. He paid that sum for one of *seventeen* replicas released fifty years later by Duchamp's dealer. "For me," Daskalopoulos said, "it represents the origins of contemporary art."

I agree with him. You could argue that *Fountain* is a deeply serious practical joke or an irreverent work of serious art. It's probably both. It's also, of course, just an ordinary, factory-made urinal, nothing more, nothing less. The object becomes art not because it's handmade or aesthetically pleasing but because it embodies an idea. Dare I mention the old cliché "One person's trash is another person's treasure"? Or "Beauty is in the eye of the beholder"? Duchamp was the first artist to act overtly on this. And he was keenly aware of something else: despite its grandiose museums and galleries, the art world is small and insular, with an evolving set of values all its own. A urinal might be just a fixture in a bathroom, but displayed in a gallery with a placard and an artist's signature, on equal footing with acclaimed masterpieces, an ordinary object is suddenly imbued with extraordinary meaning. Context matters when we assess value.

Fountain illustrates how difficult it is to understand success in areas where quality and performance are inherently absent. As an art collector myself, I'm choosing my words carefully. But I *do* mean to say that there is no quality in art. I'm not being disparaging. I make time to visit contemporary art museums and stop by galleries in every city I travel to. Still, I'm also taken aback by the extraordinary value of some of these pieces, especially considering these price tags do not reflect inherent quality. The simple truth is we have no way of objectively determining the value of any work of art or the performance of its maker. And so all forms of art—poetry, sculpture, novels, even a badly executed interpretive dance— are, essentially, priceless. So how, then, do we explain Basquiat's *Untitled* and the myriad other masterpieces that have fetched more than a hundred million dollars in recent decades?

To answer that question, consider Rembrandt's *Man with the Golden Helmet*, which, up until the mid-eighties, attracted droves of art appreciators to the Bode Museum in Berlin. Vendors outside the museum hocked postcard reproductions of the painting, which depicts a contemplative-looking man wearing a glittering, feather-adorned helmet. His gaze is fixed downward, as if he's lost in thought. The painting was the most popular work of art in the entire museum, and was undoubtedly beautiful. But when scholars announced that

60

The Man with the Golden Helmet had been misattributed to Rembrandt—its true maker now downgraded to an unknown Dutch artist in Rembrandt's circle—the crowds vanished. Nothing about the painting differed. The man with the golden helmet was still captured vividly on canvas, his eyes eternally cast down. But virtually overnight interest waned, its value plummeted, and few could remember what the fuss was about.

Or the opposite happens. There's the painting of Christ by Leonardo da Vinci, one of only twenty or so paintings attributed to him, which in 2017 sold for a record-shattering $450 million. The last time it had changed ownership was in 2005, when a consortium of art dealers purchased it...for less than $10,000. What explains the Everest-sized leap in its value? Back in 2005 it was thought to have been painted by one of da Vinci's disciples, not by the master himself. It's the same painting, just as remarkable or unremarkable as it ever was. Nothing changed but its context.

Even the wildly famous *Mona Lisa*, perhaps the best-known single artwork in history, spent some of its life on humble office walls, coyly smiling down at the keeper of royal buildings during Louis XV's reign. Open up any art history book, and you're bound to find pages justifying its reign over the art world: the subject's enigmatic smile, the unique techniques da Vinci employed, the painting's robust composition. The truth is, though, that up until a century ago, the *Mona Lisa* was just one of many valuable paintings at the Louvre. It became a household name only after it was stolen in broad daylight in 1911, creating an international hunt for the thief. It turned into a worldwide mystery playing out in major cities, like New York, Paris, and Rome, trailed by stranger-than-fiction anecdotes—at one time Picasso was wrongfully arrested as an accomplice in the crime. The drama that surrounded the *Mona Lisa*'s two-year disappearance is what made the painting such a quintessential treasure. If it were ever to sell, it's estimated that it would fetch an unheard-of $1.5 billion. If art has no inherent value, then where does that $1.5 billion price tag come from? Networks. The art world is a wonderful illustration of the *First Law of Success:*

> *Performance drives success, but when performance can't be measured, networks drive success.*

As we saw in the previous chapter, if we have metrics to use—on the tennis court, say, or in your business's quarterly reports—it is performance that drives success. It's easy to spot the difference between a professional athlete and an amateur when they play the links side by side. We respond by rewarding excellent performers financially and socially, often in disproportionate measure. But if you hang a piece of modern art next to a child's finger painting, grumpy uncles are wont to say that they look exactly the same. I don't agree, but they do have a point: determining which work is "better" is sometimes a tricky proposition. We can take cues from context and make an educated guess. One hangs on a kitchen refrigerator, the other on a gallery wall. One hangs in a small-town gallery, the other in New York's MoMA. One sells for $50, the other for $5 million. The Duchampian reality is that these cues shape our perception, frame our understanding, and set the market price. As we'll see next, they are also shaped by networks.

·

I have spent the past two decades documenting how networks work in numerous realms from genetics to business, but until recently, anyway, art was not one of them. That's because the art world is as secretive as the Swiss banking system. So much so that even art world insiders—the very people whose job is to help particular artists on their path to success—often have a limited understanding of why a particular work lands in a major museum or sells for dazzling sums at auction.

Luckily, data is a genie that's hard to keep stuffed in a bottle. When I dropped in on a meeting with Chris Riedl, a young faculty member at the Network Science Institute at Northeastern University, and his postdoc, Sam Fraiberger, I expected to learn more about Chris's research into T-shirt sales. But my ears perked up at the end of the meeting, when Sam mentioned that he had access to a massive trove of data pertaining to the art world.

I've been passionate about art since high school, when I had my sights set on being a sculptor. At fourteen, I spent a month working as an artist's assistant in the Lázár Castle, a mesmerizing Renaissance relic in Transylvania's Carpathian Mountains. So I've long wanted to explore art through the lens of networks and big data. And according to Sam, here it was: really big data, capturing the careers of roughly half a million artists working worldwide from 1980 to 2016. It contained details on hundreds of thousands of exhibitions at more than 14,000 galleries and close to 8,000 museums over the thirty-five-year time frame. It also included information about the nearly 3 million artworks sold at auction during that same period. The data was provided to us by Magnus Resch, a German art historian living in New York, who built Magnus, an app designed to help art lovers recognize and price artwork in galleries and museums.

The Magnus data allowed us to pull up an artist at random and examine his or her full artistic career. For example, I was curious about Mark Grotjahn, an abstract painter featured recently in the *New York Times* for doing something unusual in the art world: he took an active role in managing his own career, sidestepping dealers and setting his own prices. That's taboo—but, at least in his case, highly effective. Using Magnus's data set, I could look at Grotjahn in isolation, observing the rapid increase in prices that his tactics induced. Grotjahn sold only one painting at his second solo show—for a lowly $1,750—and none at his first. In the mid-2000s, he started exhibiting very aggressively, which boosted his sales. His best sale to date, in 2017, was for almost $17 million for a piece on auction at Christie's in New York. This is helpful information if you're interested in Mark Grotjahn and curious about the worth of his art. But if we want to capture how Grotjahn got where he is, we need to look past his specific individual career and examine the unseen network responsible for his success. Because that network isn't specific to Grotjahn. In fact, all artists' success relies on it.

Multiple dependencies govern how the art world places value on an individual work. Artists derive prestige from their affiliations with specific galleries and museums; in turn, the prestige of these institutions stems from the perceived importance of the artists they represent and exhibit. In other words, there's a symbiotic relationship between artists and institutions, and it's based on little more than mutual belief in one another. Artists want nothing more than to have their work exhibited at esteemed galleries, and galleries succeed or fail by attracting well-regarded artists. That means that prestige in the art world is as subjective as it is valuable. And value is created by invisible and visible influences; numerous, often conflicting interests; and lots and lots of money.

The Magnus data set offered us a way to observe and analyze the millions of tacit transactions that determine the emergence of influence in art. By reconstructing the exhibition histories of half a million artists, we could unveil the network that offered access to coveted institutions. We did so by mapping the unseen links that shape how artists move among galleries and museums. Two institutions—say, Museum A and Gallery B—are linked if an artist who exhibited at Museum A moves next to Gallery B.

Why is this a meaningful way to link institutions? Because curators look to one another to validate their decisions. If a gallery sees that an artist is exhibited by other institutions whose instincts it trusts, it's far more likely to take that artist on. So moving your artwork from A to B is not merely a transaction. It's preceded by a lot of research, consideration, and valuation on the part of gallerists and curators.

The outcome of our effort was a map that captured how art moves around the world. There were a few major hubs, which represented the few institutions that were linked to an exceptional number of other institutions. The network's hubs were, without exception, the art world's most influential galleries and museums—New York's MoMA, Guggenheim, and Gagosian Gallery, trailed closely by the Pace Gallery, Metropolitan Museum of Art, Art Institute of Chicago, and National Gallery of Art in Washington, D.C.—all American exhibition spaces. These were densely linked to European institutions like the Tate, Centre Pompidou, and Reina Sofia.

If your work is exhibited at one of these hubs, it's as if you hop onto a merry-go-round of success, looping around and around to other major institutions with ease. Your sales and the skyrocketing price tags on your work also become a foregone conclusion. These hubs are the conduits of artistic success. By showing at major galleries or museums, you're *guaranteed* to be a superstar in the art world.

But as we looked more carefully at artists' routes to success, we found that there are only a select number of galleries that will catapult your career to superstardom. Instead, most galleries and museums are part of tightly knit communities that are so busy networking among themselves that they hardly connect to the main cluster. If you're an artist working with one of these "island" galleries, and another one of its institutions opens its gates to you, you can easily access all other galleries on that island. But you'll be trapped there—none of them can teleport you to the mainland, where the action is.

It was devastating to unfold this map and see so few routes to success on it. As I inspected the results, I thought of many talented friends who exhibit in numerous isolated Eastern European galleries. I suddenly understood how trapped they are in a cliquish and unforgiving industry.

Seeing where the network hubs are located, it's tempting to conclude that if you want to succeed, all you need to do is move to New York, or London, or Paris. But, interestingly, our network map showed that success didn't boil down to mere geography. The big-name hubs networked mainly among themselves, no matter the distance that entailed. Smaller galleries situated within walking distance of MoMA, or the Gagosian Gallery, were strangely not part of the same network. And if you start somewhere outside of the major gallery network, you end up finding yourself back at the same small-scale galleries where you started out. Even if you show your work in a gallery next door to the Guggenheim, the road that will take you to that glittery hub might be inexplicably impossible to find.

Warhol, for a while the highest-grossing artist in the world, was one of the first to understand this. "To be successful as an artist," he said, "you have to have your work shown by a good gallery for the same reason, say, that Dior never sold his originals from a counter in Woolworth's." There's symbiosis to success in art. As we've seen, success is essentially a feedback loop, where galleries make names for themselves by taking on big-name artists, and big-name artists earn their fame by showing at reputable galleries. Tricky, right?

The dirty but open secret in the art world is that once you've made it, it's in everyone's interest to keep you "made." If a collector pays a million dollars for a piece of art, it's in her interest and the artist's interest and the gallery's interest that the work in question be worth at least that much moving forward. Galleries don't survive without collectors. Nor do museums. Collectors sit on museum boards. They donate major works to these institutions, providing exposure to artists from their personal collections. And they influence fellow collectors. If you're an artist whose work comes up at auction and it looks like it might not sell, your gallerist or collector will be there to buy it back, even bidding against each other, so that the final price captures the valuation they wish to see. And if no one's interested in buying your art? In a normal economy, galleries would drop the prices on your work, hoping to recoup some costs.

Not in art. You never see a "30 Percent Off Sale" sign hanging in the window of a gallery, or "EVERYTHING MUST GO" painted across a display window. Galleries will dig their heels in and simply hang on to pieces they can't sell. It's a pyramid scheme that pushes prices in only one direction. It works because there's no meter to gauge the quality of any given piece, no objective way to measure an object's inherent worth. The emperor is never without some article of clothing. Forget talent, creativity, or aesthetics. Insiders shrug those attributes off as quickly as they forgot the *The Man with the Golden Helmet* and his beautifully downcast eyes. Value in art is in the network. Any work, from the *Mona Lisa* to Basquiat's *Untitled*, is garage sale material without it.

While the art world may lack performance metrics, it doesn't lack order. In fact, the patterns that characterize the art market allowed us to do something that even I didn't think would be possible at the start of the project. Like fortune-tellers, we could predict the fate of almost any artist whether she was starting out at the periphery of the network or at its heart. If we used her first five exhibits as input, the patterns of where she would show next were so predictive that we could map out her trajectory decades into the future. In our simulations, just as in the real data, elite artists continued to exhibit at high-prestige institutions. For artists starting at the periphery, success was largely local and painfully incremental.

Why did our predictions work so well? Precisely *because* performance in art can't be measured. Since there is no way of establishing that any work of art is truly better than another, the network takes over, establishing value. In a way, that aptly reflects our premise in chapter 1: Success depends not on you or your performance but on us. The network is what carries the collective response to your performance.

Taking all this in and thinking about the young artists I admired, I had every reason to be concerned, especially for my friend Botond Részegh, a Transylvanian artist whom I've known for over a decade. His fantastic illustrations helped tie together the science and history narratives in my previous book, *Bursts*, and I've long admired his paintings, a few of which hang on my walls. Plugging his career into our map should have created a sense of dread about his prospects. Many of his exhibits were in galleries very much on the network's periphery.

By choice, it turned out. Years ago, he was offered the opportunity of teaching at the most important art school in Romania. He made, however, the seemingly unwise choice to move back to Csikszereda, the Transylvanian village he and I are from, devoting his life to his own art instead. That's a choice that put him about as far as he could get from the glittery center of the art world.

Could anyone like him make it? We went back and scoured the data, looking for people like Botond, artists who started on the network periphery and made it nonetheless.

There they were. A small fraction of artists, 227 out of half a million, who'd begun their careers at third-tier institutions but ended them on the high-prestige merry-go-round. They'd started at the bottom but managed to break through, finishing at the top. And since we were curious about what factors contributed to their success, we spent weeks scrutinizing them, trying to understand how their careers differed from the art world's norms.

While each of them had a unique journey, as a group, these 227 artists shared several unusual patterns. They broke through quickly, within the first decade of their careers, mirroring the rapid rise in the ranking of elite tennis players. Indeed, players who reach the best ranks typically distinguish themselves in their first twenty tournaments. Excellence in tennis is not achieved by slow improvement in skill—instead, young players who hope to reach the top echelons of the sport arrive with a remarkable skill set, winning match after match.

Since we can't measure skill in art, the question was, what would predict the rise of these 227 artists? There was one factor: a relentless and restless early search. The data showed that these artists avoided the comfortable and common route of exhibiting repeatedly at the same galleries. Instead, they cast a wide net, as the saying goes, reaching outward and showing at institutions of widely varying location and reputation. And whether by accident or intention, they touched some galleries that are stations on the path to the center of the art world. In other words, the secret to their artistic success hinged on their ambition and eagerness to shop around. Rather than remaining stubbornly loyal to a few exhibition spaces, they surveyed their options and took advantage of a wide range of opportunities.

Which suddenly put Botond's career in a more hopeful light. You know, in addition to his talents putting brush to canvas, he's also the kind of person whom you meet over a beer and implicitly like and trust. Not only are you immediate friends, you're suddenly handing him the keys to your house. Which made him a born networker. And he doubled down on this skill—he runs a local nonprofit gallery, where he exhibits prominent artists, building connections to them and their curators and gallerists. More important, he travels as much as his limited budget allows, sleeping on friends' couches in far-off cities where he can rub elbows with gatekeepers to the elite club.

These qualities helped him achieve the impossible, at least according to our map—the work he makes in an isolated Transylvanian village is now shown in prestigious New York galleries. How did he do it? By fully recognizing that the canvases he painstakingly applies paint to—large, blurry images rendered in subdued tones—are just the entry ticket to the party. It's up to him to navigate the network by mingling widely, connecting to as many partygoers as possible.

So, while it's easy to feel hopeless if you're working off the beaten path, it's worth remembering that social and professional networks—not mere geography—are what determine *anyone's* success. Networks brim with opportunity, partially because they're held together by powerful hubs, people who are, well...really good at networking. These connectors are eager to utilize their relationships to support people and causes they find value in. They're especially good at seeing opportunities in the social fabric that other people miss. Connect with them.

Remember, performance needs to be empowered by opportunity. We need to reframe the all-too-frequent assumption that aiming for the top means scraping our way up from the bottom. If performance in all professional realms were as cut-and-dried as in tennis, that might work. But climbing the corporate ladder isn't realistic if we can't prove we're the best at what we do. Instead, we need to bring the corner office or that prestigious gallery or that hoped-for interview closer to us.

How? Replace the corporate ladder with a social bridge. We never work in isolation—even when we think we do. Our collective definition of success requires us to think about the ways that our work impacts others. If we want to bring the world-up-there nearer to our doorsteps, we need to find the hubs that can accelerate our trajectories and reach out to them. We need the ambition to aim for the top right away. That's what Ivy League applicants and skillful young tennis players do. That's what the big names in the art world do. And that's what good networkers do. No matter the field, discipline, or industry, if we want to succeed, we must master the networks. Because as the First Law of Success reminds us, the harder it is to measure performance, the less performance matters.

So…how hard *is* it to measure performance?

In exploring the First Law, I've deliberately focused on two extremes of the success game—individual sports, where performance is meticulously and accurately measured, and visual art, where performance is impossible to gauge. Most professions fall somewhere in between these two extremes, so success for the vast majority of us can't be pinned to a single variable. If you're a lawyer, a salesperson, a teacher, or an investment banker, *both* performance and networks matter, to varying degrees.

The next part of the book will focus on this in-between territory. Lacking a single metric to identify and reward superior performers, we unconsciously use several, evaluating one another both qualitatively *and* quantitatively. In other words, we use our best judgment.

The problem is, our best judgment always fails.

THE SECOND LAW

**Performance is bounded,
but success is unbounded.**

The Second Law explains the hidden factors that shape our choices. It tells us why experts are doomed to failure when they try to select the best wines or the most accomplished violinists. The law explains why Tiger Woods's competitors play measurably worse when he's on the green and why the last interviewee almost always gets the job.

4

How Much Is a Bottle of Wine Worth?
How Do We Decide When We Can't Decide?

In the tasting room, pristine glasses shimmer under the fluorescent lights. Flights of wine are arranged on tables that clusters of judges hover over. The bodies of the numbered bottles are cloaked in black plastic, disguising the often beautifully designed labels. Poured anonymously into glasses, though, the wines are beautiful. Rose-gold or deep burgundy or pale amber, they brighten the clinical surroundings. The judges lift and swirl the wine to study its body before sniffing the scent and sipping for taste. Their brows furrow as their mouths search for the subtleties that make particular varietals sing. They tick boxes and make notes on their clipboards. They sometimes taste twice. Regardless, it's a job they approach with scientific seriousness.

This is a world Bob Hodgson knows well. He's a soft-spoken winemaker in his late sixties, with a short-trimmed white beard and thin-rimmed glasses. He looks more like a college professor, which he once was, than a devoted servant of Dionysus. The owner of a California vineyard who retired from a career in oceanography, Hodgson was surprised by the often confusing results his wines earned in competition. His '93 Zinfandel was a gold medalist in one competition and outright dismissed in another. Some panels shrugged off his reds while others adored them. Puzzled, he decided to become a judge himself. But that experience didn't bring much insight either. He often found that his favorite Chardonnay barely registered in the final reckoning or that an underwhelming Merlot somehow took home a top prize.

Hodgson eventually resigned from judging because such discrepancies led him to believe that he just wasn't very good at it. Yet the success of his vineyard rested on his peers' critical assessments, and he couldn't escape the uneasy feeling that the process was flawed. A great deal was at stake; cases and cases of wine, stockpiled in his warehouse, hung in the balance. But no matter how he looked at it, the outcomes of competitions were far from consistent. If anything, they seemed consistently random. Eventually, the scientist he was raised a skeptical eyebrow.

The California State Fair Wine Competition is North America's oldest, and perhaps for this reason one of its most prestigious. Winning a gold medal here allows wineries to increase the price point of their wines, significantly improving their chances of survival in a competitive market. Hodgson was curious: Just how accurate and consistent were judges at detecting superior bottles? Since he served on the competition's advisory board, he asked his fellow board members to let him conduct an experiment.

When the 2005 panel convened for that year's round of judging, on the surface everyone followed the same, time-honored protocols: evaluating each wine's sweetness, acidity, tannins, fruit, and body; taking thorough notes; sniffing, sipping, swishing, spitting. But there was something different about the day's deliberations. For the purpose of Hodgson's experiment, *the judges were tasting the same wines repeatedly.* Meaning that over the course of a tasting, they encountered the same wines served back to them three times in random order. Suddenly, the flaws in the system—inconsistencies that Hodgson had previously only suspected—became glaringly apparent. One judge gave an 80, the lowest grade, to a wine in the first sipping. A moment later, tasting it again, he assigned it a decent 90. When presented with the same wine a third time, it didn't ring a bell, so he awarded it a 96, a rating worthy of a gold award. "They scored the identical wines as if they were different," Hodgson recalled. He concluded that chance has a great deal to do with the awards that wines win.

•

Usain Bolt, the fastest man on earth, beats Yohan Blake and Tyson Gay by only 0.11 second. That's a 1 percent difference, detectable only by the sophisticated chronometers and video recordings used at top-level competitions. In a contest between Bolt and me, of course my performance would be laughable. But the difference between our speeds is actually not that great: Bolt runs less than twice as fast as I do, not a hundred or even ten times faster. That's because, physically, even his speed has a limit. We call it "bounded" in science, and many excellent runners come close to that upper bound— some so close that it's impossible to tell who's the fastest without using accurate tools. It's easy to tell tall from short, or fast from slow, or swill from grand cru, but far harder to tell tall from tall and fast from fast and grand cru from grand cru.

The problem Hodgson detected stems from a simple issue. The wines that judges encounter in competition are, generally speaking, exceptional performers. And that's precisely the case in *most* competitions. Usain Bolt and Hodgson's wine competitions both provide evidence that *performance is bounded*.

That may sound abstract, but it has precise meaning in the quantitative world I work in. It means that our performance follows something like a bell curve. Often used for height or IQ, a bell curve is a graph with a large rounded peak tapering away at each end. It shows the distribution of probability, capturing the differences among us. Most people are of average height, located near the peak of the bell curve, for example, with a few tapering off in the very short or the very tall range. But there's a reason that giants are the stuff of fairy tales. Bell curves decay exponentially as you depart from the average, meaning that it is exponentially rare to find outliers, individuals of exceptional height. And because the bell curve applies to our speed as well, we'll never find runners competing with Ferraris. Even the best, the Usain Bolts and Tyson Gays and Yohan Blakes, are forced to sprint along in the bell's upper taper, practically stubbing their toes against the farthest bounds of performance.

It might be hard to believe, but the single fact that performance is bounded allows us to forecast future outcomes in many sports. A few years back, Filippo Radicchi, a fellow Science of Success researcher at Indiana University, looked at the history of Olympic records going back to 1896 and discovered that each improvement in performance lines up along a bell curve. That alone allowed him to predict *future* Olympic records. Prior to the 2012 Olympics, for example, Radicchi predicted that the best time in the men's one-hundred-meter dash would be 9.63 seconds, give or take 0.13. Sure enough, Usain Bolt clocked in at 9.63 seconds precisely, breaking the previous record. Ditto the women's champion, who Radicchi predicted would cross the finish line in 10.73 seconds, give or take two-tenths of a second. Shelly-Ann Fraser-Price, whose final time was 10.75, fell within Radicchi's margin of error.

And because performance is so bounded, it allows us to predict, with impressive accuracy, what our own ultimate limits are. Radicchi tells us that the most humanity can ever hope to achieve in the hundred-meter dash is 8.28 seconds. That's the upper bound for human performance in sprinting. The current world record falls a mere second and a half short. Unless we develop superhuman technology or genetically engineer new athletes or pump our competitors full of dope, no one will ever run faster than that.

If performance weren't bounded, athletes could come along and blow previous record holders away. But they won't. And so we know that, after a certain point, convincingly out-performing our competitors isn't possible. That's a humbling realization, a reminder that you might be a fantastic surgeon or a brilliant engineer or a deft pianist, but there will always be plenty of other surgeons or engineers or pianists who are just as skilled. You might have spent hundreds of thousands of dollars on tuition to elite programs and toiled for thousands of hours to rise to the upper echelons of your chosen field, but you're not going to find yourself surveying a vast empty expanse when you get there. You'll find yourself in the company of at least a few other individuals who have similar talents and experiences and education, people equally motivated and hardworking. Your performance will be measured against theirs, and that measurement will, over time, tell us something about the limits on achievement in your field. All of us at the top will find ourselves repeatedly bumping up against the same bounds in performance.

Which raises an important question. If we're surrounded by excellent competitors, how do we distinguish the best from the best? How do we decide when we can't measure?

•

Wine competition judges don't fail because they lack expertise, preparation, or thoroughness. They fail mainly because the wines they're judging are all excellent. Even I could probably detect the blatant inferiority of a cooking wine poured from a gallon jug were I to sip it side by side with a two-hundred-dollar bottle of Pinot Noir from an artisanal vineyard. But determining which bottle of good champagne to buy for a New Year's Eve party, I hate to say, is a choice I'll likely make based on the price tag alone. I lack the palate to gauge what differentiates excellent from extraordinary. But, according to Hodgson, so do *experts*.

Even though performance does drive success, the problem is that the differences among top contenders are so tiny that they're often nearly immeasurable. This complicates the message on that trite-but-true "Practice Makes Perfect" poster we all remember hanging in the junior high gym. Practice is certainly important, and many people get pretty close to perfection. Yet most of them do not get the rewards of it by becoming successful. So as we near the upper bound, performance is simply not the deciding factor.

Outwardly, the judges at wine events have the easiest job in the world. After all, they sometimes get to taste 150 excellent wines a day. But in reality, their task is enormously difficult. Vineyards submit only their best bottles for a competition, so judges confront wines that are nearly indistinguishable. And they have no "stopwatch," no simple tool, to determine which anonymous glass of Malbec, raised to the nose and swished in the mouth, is, definitively, a winner. We lack appropriate stopwatches in most areas of human performance: in violin contests, in pop music competitions, in awarding literary prizes, in choosing the doctor of the year, or, as we saw in the last chapter, deciding which artwork in a gallery is the "best."

Does the bounded nature of performance mean that all wine competitions are flawed? Hodgson's data certainly suggests so. After repeating his experiment for four consecutive years, he came to the startling conclusion that any given judge was consistent in scoring the same wine *only 18 percent of the time.* In the rare cases where Hodgson saw consistency in a particular wine's scores, it was almost always low-scoring across the board—that is, if a judge didn't like that particular bottle of Chardonnay to begin with, then she didn't like it on the second or the third try. We're good at calling out the crap. For better wines, though, the judges flip-flopped a whopping 82 percent of the time. The same wine often ranged from gold medal to no mention on the same judge's scorecard.

These results troubled and fascinated Hodgson. He wasn't

out to undermine the community that gave a home to his passion. He wanted, instead, to understand and improve the system. So he started to examine his data from a different perspective, hoping to discern good judges from bad ones. Were there "gold-medal judges" who could reliably detect gold-medal wines where their peers struggled? Hodgson returned to his data, scouring it for accurate, high-performing judges. And he did find some: about 10 percent of the judges each year were pretty consistent. If they ranked a wine gold-medal-worthy on the first try, they ranked it gold-medal-worthy on the second and third tries also. When they didn't like a wine, they rejected it again and again. That was encouraging! If he could identify and reengage these dependable judges year by year, he could turn wine judging into a reliable science. But then he did a final test, comparing these gold-medal judges' performances to their performances in other years. And once again, the news was unsettling. He could find no correlation between judges' past track records and their current reliability. The super-consistent judge one year was unreliable the next. There was, apparently, no particular skill set that could be taught or honed, not a single dependably superior palate on panel after panel of experts.

"I'm not going to bite the bullet and say it's completely random; I don't think that's true," Hodgson concluded. "But that's what the results indicate." As a judge once himself, Hodgson might not want to admit it, but I will: The data is clear. The gold medals attached to bottles in wine stores are based on junk science. I'm not implying that prizewinning wines are bad. To the contrary—they're all *excellent*. And that's precisely why winning a wine competition comes down largely to chance.

•

Several years ago, I had the opportunity to see Lang Lang perform at a symphony hall. Known for his dazzling flair, he's arguably one of the best pianists in the world. I'd never seen him play before, but as the performance began, I found it increasingly difficult to follow the music. Instead, my attention was totally absorbed by Lang Lang's gestures. The exaggerated tilt of the body as he hit notes in the higher octaves, the fluttering of his fingers as he lifted them dramatically over the keyboard. Sure, I was amazed by his talents but also bemused by all his gesturing.

As it turns out, there's a purpose to his showmanship. Chia-Jung Tsay, a researcher at University College London, asked both professional musicians and novices to predict which of three finalists would win a classical music competition. One group listened only to the audio of each performance. Another was given both audio and video. Finally, some were shown *only the video* without the sound, a ridiculous proposition if you're asking them to select the best musician.

Prior to the experiment, both experts and novices felt strongly that the audio alone would offer the best chance at predicting the winner. This was, after all, a *music* competition. But Tsay found that the groups that relied on the sound only could select the winner from among the musicians just about 25 percent of the time. Given that there were only three choices, that's worse than if you were guessing on a multiple-choice test! Both the experts and novices relying on the sound disagreed with the jury, picking someone else for the top spot.

Surprisingly, the group best able to pinpoint the winner consisted of those who watched the video with the sound off, making their choice among performers who were passionately executing music that couldn't be heard. In that group, novices and experts alike guessed correctly about 50 percent of the time. In other words, *those who couldn't actually hear the music did twice as well as those who did.* The experts did no better than the novices at identifying the most deserving performer, and in some cases they did *worse*.

Now, stop for a second and absorb what that means: *The original, expert jurists must have also selected a winner based on what they saw and not what they heard.* If we follow the data, we arrive at the astounding conclusion that the Lang Langs of the music world are revered, but it's not because they produce markedly better music than their competitors, the performers who don't draw a sold-out crowd. They're revered because they're excellent musicians who also *look the part*.

Someone once told me how she hired a guy because he was wearing pink socks. All the candidates were equally qualified, and after a long day of interviews only the bright-colored socks stood out. These pink socks aren't that different from Burcu's tattoo, which, I must admit, made as much of an impression on me as her outstanding CV. In fact, if I run down the lists of selling points of each person I've hired, it's often these gestures or cues that stick with me. A joke someone made on the way out. An intriguing skill listed on a résumé. A striking pair of glasses or a funny laugh. As the hiring manager, I want to get a sense of a potential employee's values or personality during an interview. Since only qualified candidates make the cut, I'm inevitably reading *them* more than their résumés.

Applied to our own lives, this suggests we should bring our genuine self to an interview. An unlikely answer or an interesting personal anecdote might just give you a leg up. Given how bounded performance is, if you can find small ways to stand out, it makes enormous sense to do so.

To be clear, I'm not encouraging you to place all your faith in a gimmick. There's a fine line between distinguishing yourself from the crowd and sending that crowd scurrying. Remember, when we lack hard data to go on, the factors that sway us are subtle or even unconscious; you don't need a whole song-and-dance routine. Burcu didn't get her tattoo to impress me; it was already inked onto her skin. But it reflected a facet of her personality that made her unique, and when performance is bounded, these little things can make a huge difference.

If the music research tells us anything, it's how important the unspoken aspects of our self-presentation are. Lacking the ability to distinguish based solely on the music, judges make decisions grounded in other aspects of the performance. A musician's clothes, perhaps. The style with which he plays. His showmanship and facial expressions. *These* become the factors that float to the surface in murky, hard-to-quantify musical waters.

•

No competition, regardless of its prestige, is immune to these biases. Take, for example, the Queen Elisabeth International

Music Competition, which is to classical music what *American Idol* is to pop music. The contest has been making stars since 1937, first in violin, then in piano, voice, cello, and composition. The violin prize consists not only of a large check but also a four-year loan of a coveted Stradivarius. Most important, it brings prestige, opening doors to elite concert halls and lucrative recording contracts around the world.

The competition has a long reputation for fairness, observing a number of protocols to prevent bias. Each year, eighty-five hopeful performers are invited to compete from all over the world. Once they arrive in Brussels, they're whittled down to twelve finalists who are then given the same concerto, composed specifically for the competition. Asking everyone to play the same new score ensures that no one can win on the strength of her personal selection honed over time. Additionally, a random draw determines when finalists perform, and distribution of the concerto is staggered, ensuring that musicians have exactly a week to practice prior to their final performance. Nightly throughout the week of the finals, two candidates play for the judges during assigned slots and are evaluated on the spot. Judges can't change their scores after they submit them, and they don't confer during the evaluation process. In its attention to detail, the competition is the best attempt by classical music to select and reward the most talented performers.

Yet the process *still* fails. Let's look at the piano competition. Eleven contests were run under identical rules between 1952 and 1991. Since performance slots are randomly assigned, the most talented performer could land anywhere. But we see some pretty peculiar things if we inspect the forty-year record. First, no one performing on the first day ever won the competition. There were only two performers on the second day and there was one who performed on the last day among the grand prizewinners. *Half of the remaining eight winners all happened to perform on day five of the competition.* Strange, isn't it?

Of course, this could happen by chance. When we repeatedly throw a die, we tend to think that a 3, 5, 6, 3, 1, 2 sequence is far more likely than a 6, 6, 6, 6, 6, 6. If we do roll all 6s on the first try, we intuit it as divine intervention. The truth is that both sequences appear with exactly the same probability. So we *could* chalk the music competition results up to an uncanny coincidence. But two economists put the competition under their statistical microscope and came to the resounding conclusion that chance couldn't explain *this* outcome. Instead, those who were asked to perform during the first day of finals indeed had a much lower probability of winning, *systematically ranking almost three positions below those who performed on the fifth day.* The order during a given night also mattered. Those who performed second tended to be ranked one position higher than the opening act. Gender also played a role. All things being, as it were, equal, men were routinely ranked about two positions above women. A female performer who opens the finals will be ranked about *six* positions lower than a male performer with identical talent who performs second on the fifth day.

Clearly, gender bias plays an enormous role in who wins the competition. But it isn't the only determining factor.

Experts point to two other effects, both rooted in the way the competition is organized. First, it is unique in its requirement that all participants play the same concerto, a policy put in place to create an even playing field. But the concerto is new to the violinists and the judges alike. Very few jury members can fully hear music by simply reading the score—the subtlest parts of the piece emerge only after repeated listening. When the judges first hear the concerto from the initial finalists, their unfamiliarity with it is acute. They grow increasingly familiar with the piece as the competition unfolds. On the first day, overtaken with the freshness of the music, the jury members are likely less mindful of a musician's interpretation, nuanced approach, or the particular color or tone elicited.

Second, even if the judges *were* able to appreciate the first performer on his or her own merits, this musician is also doomed by another policy aimed at fairness: the hard-and-fast rule that jurors cannot change their evaluation in retrospect. Imagine you're a judge and the first musician knocks your socks off. Would you risk giving him the maximum grade? Probably not. Doing so would back you into a corner if you happened to hear an even more impressive performance later. As the competition draws on, the members of the panel not only listen better, they also evaluate better. They're also increasingly eager to generously reward what they like, relaxing their grades over time.

Wine and classical music share an aura of refinement that may bias us toward "expert" opinion. We're intimidated by all we don't know when it comes to such "sophisticated" topics, so we tend to lean hard on the evaluation of those who can take a strong whiff from a stem glass and proffer the strange and specific descriptor of "slightly melted tarmac" or "a wheelbarrow full of Ugli fruit." Or those who seem to be able to easily discern the subtle emphasis a particular violinist places on a passage in the middle of a concerto. In these esoteric realms we don't question the decades-old protocols.

But no matter where we look, the same flaw in protocol—researchers call it an "immediacy bias"—effectively determines competition outcomes. We saw it in the Queen Elisabeth competition. The later performers, those with the highest immediacy in our brains, come out ahead. This is also true of Europe's famous, long-standing pop song competition, the Eurovision Song Contest. The later a singer performs in the evening, the higher the chances that he or she will take home the trophy. And it's true in figure skating, where the skaters perform in random order during the first round, sliding out onto the ice hopefully and, one by one, executing dances that include maneuvers or figures similar to those of competitors. Laden with bouquets and waving regally from the sidelines, they are judged immediately after their performances. We watch them on TV as they wait in suspense. When they hear each judge's verdict booming from the intercom, their faces relax into relieved laughter or grimace in pain. The camera briefly showcases the drama. Then it pans to the next skater in a spangled leotard who poses in the center of the ice.

It seems transparent and fair, but it isn't. Scores systematically increase according to a skater's position in the roster. Those who compete later appear—miraculously, consistently—to skate much better. Once again, fates are determined by the order of performances.

•

If such clear bias exists in how we evaluate figure skaters, wines, classical music, and bubblegum rock, why wouldn't we expect to see similar problematic biases in how we evaluate other realms of performance? Performance is bounded, no matter your profession, which makes distinguishing among top performers inevitably difficult.

Another example I find particularly startling is the manner in which aspiring courtroom judges in Spain are evaluated. Many hopeful, well-prepared applicants appear before a panel of experienced justices, to be quizzed in three categories: "general culture," "languages," and "history, law, culture, and economy." It's not hard to imagine the anxiety that taking an oral exam before an array of revered experts might induce, especially when your career hinges on the results. It's the stuff of cold-sweat nightmares: authority figures peering down, asking probing questions on a wide range of topics. All you can do is cross your fingers and rack your brain.

But in this case the moment of truth doesn't come in the hot seat. Rather, your chance of success is predetermined several weeks prior to the exam. That's because if you happen to draw a Monday slot—and you could draw a slot on any day of the week—the deck is already stacked against you. As a brave, early-week pioneer, you have about a 50 percent chance of passing your law exam. Whereas if you draw a Friday slot? Lucky you! You now have a roughly 75 percent chance of becoming a judge. The vast discrepancy in outcomes has little to do with your relative performance, which we assume would vary based on your knowledge, preparation, and expertise regardless of the day of the week. Isn't that why we conduct the exams to begin with? And yet the judge deciding the verdict in Spain's next major case may have benefited from the same immediacy bias witnessed in a slew of other contexts.

Perhaps it doesn't matter. Any of these would-be judges presumably fall within the upper bounds of performance in the field. The outcome may not be flawless, exactly, but interviews and contests are a decent means of choosing candidates in a crowded field. Right?

I almost buy it. But then another example sneaks up on me: the way the FDA approves new medical devices. At approval meetings, a chairperson seats people around a conference table according to her discretion. After initial presentations by the device manufacturer and two formal reviewers, the chairperson asks the committee member seated nearest to the reviewers to comment. The chairperson then guides the discussion, going clockwise or counterclockwise in the room, allowing each member to raise issues. In theory, this gives everyone a fair shot at voicing potential concerns.

But it doesn't. *The device's approval is typically determined by those who are asked to speak first.* They're the ones who get to frame the key questions. The later speakers are unable to raise new issues effectively; the concerns of the first speakers have been posed and set the tone. In other words, *where people sit in a meeting, and the order in which they speak, can impact whether a medical device is approved for public use.*

Think about that the next time you're in the OR. A doctor might have been able to offer you an innovative new therapy had the key argument for it been voiced early! While that's an alarming finding, think about how it fits with your work experience. As a university professor, I serve on a number of committees. After grabbing a coffee and a pastry from the back of the room, I try my best to engage in the discussion. I might even bring a few notes bulleting issues to address. But as the conversation heads toward a consensus, disagreeing is like swimming against a riptide. Sure, I can try to reverse course, but positions have emerged and people are suddenly on either the defensive or offensive. Who wants to raise nit-picky questions when most have started looking at their watches or checking their texts? If I don't feel passionately, I put my doubts aside and move on with my day.

But it's not always that simple. Not if someone's job is on the line or we are ending a student's career with our vote. And not, as in the case of the FDA's committees, if the outcome affects our health. The idea that such decisions largely come down to where people are seated in an unassuming conference room? I find that deeply troubling.

The problem is, people need to sit somewhere. Performers can't all compete at the same time. By definition, judges almost always have to, as the phrase goes, use their judgment. But then we see—with FDA approval processes, judging proto-cols for figure-skating contests, qualifying exams, violin com-petitions, and wine tasting—that the mechanisms designed to ensure evenhanded competition in a range of fields often have the opposite effect.

In many ways, the boundedness of performance sets most competitions up for failure, forcing judges to decide not between good and bad, slow and fast, or experienced and novice. Rather, they're asked to choose among people who all nudge the upper limit of performance in their fields. If not for the chronometers in a race, often even a keen-eyed, veteran judge can't know for certain who leaned first over the finish line. Candidates of top caliber competing for a prize or job can be even more perplexingly impossible to tell apart.

I'm not suggesting that decision makers flip a coin. It might be fairer, though, to select the ten best competitors, acknowledge that we can't really tell them apart, and give them all the prize. Otherwise we're asking judges to do the impossible. We risk decisions based on variables that have little to do with performance; we risk men getting routinely ranked higher than women. We witness awards going to a performer who sticks in the minds of judges merely because exaggerated gestures ingrained a vivid mental picture in the audience.

•

If you hope to succeed in any realm, you must remember that your competitors are just like you — prepared, accomplished, and ready for the job. When I interviewed for my first faculty position at the University of Notre Dame, I was the least experienced of the candidates. I'd finished my Ph.D. only six months earlier, and the ink on my diploma was barely dry. At twenty-seven, I was the youngest in the pool. Sure enough, as I later learned, the committee members had already informally decided to give the position to a well-deserving candidate before I set foot on the campus. Yet I somehow walked away with the job. My advantage over the other hopefuls? I was the last to interview.

When a student now asks for advice before job interviews, I think about my own experience in the job market and the Science of Success that has since put it in context. "When is it?" I ask, but not as a casual question.

Excellence has qualified him for the job. But, given that performance is inherently bounded, I can also say with near surety that many of the other candidates will be just as qualified, setting up a tough challenge for the hiring committee. That means the "what" and the "who" of the interview—its content and its participants—are less important than the "when."

"Put it off! Put it off for as long as you can!" I implore my student, who, eager to get the job, is bewildered. That is, until I explain that one should inquire politely as to when the hiring committee plans to make its final decision, and then one should try to get an interview as close to that deadline as possible. As the committee nears the end of its process, the decision makers get smarter. The final candidate walking through the door very likely won't answer questions better than the guy before him. *The questions he's asked are better,* informed by the interviews that came before, just as a judge hones her ear with each iteration of a concerto performed for her.

While it's disheartening to realize how arbitrary most evaluation processes are, that awareness can also liberate us. Because if we perform well, any of us could be that final "best candidate." Our exceptional but bounded performance is what puts us in contention, gets us in the room, or lands us on the stage. The choice wouldn't be difficult if we weren't good at what we do. So when the inevitable self-criticism and self-doubt creep in after a defeat, we can tell ourselves, with relative surety, that the setback isn't about our failings, our flaws, or our shortcomings. Far more likely, it has to do with something as haphazard as timing.

Understanding the inherent randomness in every selection, we can better appreciate how success is often a numbers game. If you want to win competitions, you need to enter a slew of them. If you want to get a job, you must send out plenty of résumés. If you want a starring role, you need to step up for audition after audition. You can't always control whether you're the first or last to take the stage, but just as you need to buy multiple tickets to widen your odds of winning the lottery, you're far more likely to score a preferred spot on the roster if you keep showing up.

The good news is that once you get that first win, the data shows you'll win again and again. *There's a secret, mindlessly metastasizing aspect to reward.* Success can self-generate, growing in proportion to its size. If you win once, you'll win again. And again. And again.

We've created such a mystique out of the idea of success that it can often seem like some sort of hallowed realm populated only by superhumans. I can imagine the ever skeptical Hodgson uncorking a bottle of Pinot Noir and insisting that I let him in on the secret of why some achievers keep on winning no matter what. What's the secret of that kind of power?

Turns out there's data to help understand that, too.

5

Superstars and Power Laws
The Rewards Are Limitless

Tiger Woods was a mere nine months old when he first knocked a ball off a tee. These early attempts were left-handed, literal mirror images of his father's swings. When he corrected himself a few weeks later, abruptly switching to a right-handed stance, Earl Woods realized his son, still toddling in diapers, had exceptional talent. "I knew he was gonna be the best in the world," the elder Woods said later. "I just knew it."

At two, Tiger Woods won a pitch-and-putt competition for kids ten and under. At four, he began to work with professional coach Rudy Duran, who was amazed to witness the knobby-kneed kid mechanically hit numerous perfect shots during their first session. Grainy video footage shows Woods, wearing an outsized red trucker hat and tiny white golf gloves, hitting balls across the driving range with adult seriousness. A mustachioed Duran kneels nearby, as if bowing before a child king.

At six, Woods placed eighth in a ten-and-under Junior World competition. At eight, he won. By fifteen, he was the youngest player to win the U.S. Junior Amateur Championship. He then took his first U.S. Amateur Championship when he was eighteen. And on and on. His later achievements as a professional golfer—he pretty much laid waste to the competition from the minute he joined the PGA ranks—are legendary.

Given his résumé, it's tempting to conclude that Woods is a rare exception whose performance isn't bounded. He has the lowest scoring average in PGA history, after all. A list of his records, assembled for his forty-first birthday, contains forty-one entries. I was surprised, then, when I looked more carefully at the numbers. The PGA maintains detailed statistics of each player's performance, including driving distance, percentage of fairways hit, percentage of greens reached in the regulation number of strokes, and average number of putts per round. It's nearly impossible to find a more perfect bell curve in the real world than when you look at how these four performance criteria are distributed among the players. They truly reinforce just how universally bounded performance is: most players are average, and the few who stand out do so by a tiny margin. Tiger Woods, of course, practically kisses the upper bound in all four areas.

But he's not the best in all of them. For example, in 2013 when he was PGA Player of the Year, his average "strokes gained" from the tee to the green was 1.600; Henrik Stenson's was 1.612, and Justin Rose's was 1.914. In this area, both Stenson and Rose performed better than Woods. Or take his 2013 drive distance, a gauge of how far he typically hit—an impressive 293 yards. That put him in thirty-fifth position in that category. The top player that year, Lake List, had a drive distance of 305 yards. Despite his talent, Woods, like the rest of the competition, has bounded performance. If he wins, he does so by a fraction of a swing, eked out by masterfully combining different skills. No matter what criteria we look at, he's not that much better than his competitors.

But while Woods's performance is clearly bounded, his *success* is limitless. In 2009, Woods became the first athlete to net more than *a billion dollars* over the course of his career. That same year, he became the second-richest African-American, trailing only Oprah Winfrey. Even in 2015, when he no longer dominated golf, he was ranked ninth on the *Forbes* list of highest-paid athletes. An enormous amount of his wealth comes from endorsement deals, which run the gamut from golf paraphernalia to sports drinks to razors to cars. The five-year deal Woods negotiated with Nike in 2000 for $105 million was, at the time, the largest contract an athlete had ever signed. As part of the agreement, he received a percentage of the sales of Nike's golf apparel and equipment. He was so central to the brand that for years he collected royalties on it, pocketing a profit with every swoosh-emblazoned fleece vest sold at a pro shop.

Woods is what economists call a *superstar,* someone exceptionally rewarded for exceptional performance. Superstars exist because *success is unbounded.* By performing even a fraction better than your competitors, your reward can easily be hundreds, sometimes *thousands* of times greater. Economist Sherwin Rosen described superstars as "relatively small numbers of people who earn enormous amounts of money and dominate the activities in which they engage." The obvious examples include movie stars, pop singers, high-profile CEOs, and investors. Think George Clooney, Jennifer Lawrence, Will Smith. Katy Perry, Lorde, Bruno Mars. Bill Gates, Richard Branson, Warren Buffet, George Soros.

There is a disproportionate relationship between the quality of superstars' work and their success, meaning that slightly better performance can lead to an outsized amount of success. "Lesser talent is a poor substitute for greater talent," Rosen wrote, reminding us that, given the choice between an exceptional singer and one who's just pretty good, we'll choose the former. This no-brainer choice prompts all of us to listen to the same songs, read the same books, and watch the same tennis players. It therefore skews the market toward those individuals deemed particularly talented.

It's hard to fathom how massive the rewards can be for those who reap them. Here's an example that helped me understand the unbounded nature of success: When my book *Bursts* came out in October 2009, I couldn't help but check who else was competing for the valuable attention of my potential readers. *The Lost Symbol*, by Dan Brown, was topping the *New York Times* Best Seller list. In second place was *The Last Song*, by Nicholas Sparks. I wasn't surprised to see a *Da Vinci Code* sequel taking top billing, but I was curious about the runner-up. *The Last Song* is a romance and Brown writes thrillers, but they loosely belong to similar categories of commercial fiction, books for escape and relaxation, to be read on beaches and in airports. *The Last Song*'s number two ranking is, of course, as close as you can get to number one. It'd be easy to conclude that if Sparks worked a little harder or his publicist performed a little better, he could unseat Brown. What, I wondered, could Sparks have done differently?

The answer is . . . *nothing*. Sure, number two is almost number one. But when I looked at the sales data, I discovered that *The Last Song* sold 120,000 copies that week, an astonishing number. Keep in mind that most best sellers sell in the range of 3,000 to 5,000 copies a week. The other 99 percent of books sell far fewer. By all standards, Sparks had achieved dramatic success. But *The Lost Symbol,* only a single position higher than *The Last Song,* sold *1.2 million*. Brown didn't just edge out Sparks. He sold an incredible ten times the number of copies. Is *The Lost Symbol* ten times better than *The Last Song?* Unlikely. The difference in their sales has nothing to do with performance, which is inherently bounded. Instead, it shows how limitless success can be.

•

This key distinction between performance and success is captured by our *Second Law of Success:*

Performance is bounded, but success is unbounded.

Just as our understanding of the bounded nature of performance is based on a precise formula, a bell curve, the unbounded nature of success is based on a different mathematical relationship called a *power law*. Bell curves decay exceptionally fast at high values, a scenario that simply doesn't allow for outliers. That's why the best score in strokes in golf is 1.919, and not 10 or 100. By contrast, power law distributions have slowly decaying tails, meaning that they allow for a few exceptionally large outcomes, extremes that would be impossible in a bell curve.

Remember the bell curve mentioned in the previous

chapter that described height? In a world where height followed a power law and not a bell curve, most of us would be fairies, no more than a few inches tall. But it would not be unheard of to run into the occasional towering giant, someone who looks down on the world from a height of a hundred feet or more. And if you consider a world population of 7 billion or so, you'd even find one or two rare and monstrous beings at least *eight thousand feet tall.*

Power laws describe the distribution of the most accepted success measure: wealth. They are the reason why the combined wealth of the top eight richest people in the world is more than the combined wealth of the world's bottom 50 percent. A power law's ramifications are inscribed on the placards and Internet memes of the Occupy Wall Street movement. We, the 99 percent, are anonymous and plentiful, like stars in the Milky Way, lacking the luster and distinction of more visible counterparts but nonetheless composing the majority of the known galaxy. Superstars are the few exceptionally shiny, bright, visible 1 percent—those who have unlocked the key to a rich-get-richer effect and who reap the rewards of seemingly limitless wealth.

When economists like Rosen—who measure success in a single dimension, dollar bills—talk about superstars, they really mean the superrich. Any economist will tell you that the odds aren't high that you or I will fall into that category, but Tiger Woods is an outlier in a field where most of his peers make $100,000 a year. Whether we aspire to being businesspeople, pop singers, pro athletes, artists, or social activists, it's easy to conclude that regardless of our performance, superstardom is beyond our grasp.

Except…maybe it's *not*. Success isn't only about money—there are multiple dimensions to it. So while wealth may come with superstardom, superstardom doesn't require wealth. Because if we look at how the people around you respond to your performance, then superstars start to pop out at us like constellations shining through the lens of a new, more powerful telescope. Here's what I mean. You may be the most respected book agent, or architect, or engineer, yet the odds aren't high that you're a billionaire.

We might be tempted to define superstardom solely in financial terms, but power laws facilitate a broadening of our definitions of success. This is probably one of the most fascinating outcomes of any foray into the Science of Success: the realization that regardless of the success measure we're talking about—impact, visibility, audience, or adoration—its distribution follows the same power law as wealth. And thanks to the power laws, there are always a few individuals whose successes are many orders of magnitude higher than everyone else's. We call them outliers. They tend to be people with outstanding performance. But as we saw in the previous chapter, they are, at best, only slightly better than their peers. What distinguishes them from everyone else isn't their performance; it's their success. So as we explored success in multiple arenas, we realized we had to expand the until now strictly economic definition of superstardom.

•

Steven Weinberg is the best-paid physics professor in history. As a physicist who developed a theory that unified electromagnetism and the weak forces affecting subatomic particles—the same concept that Einstein pursued unsuccessfully for much of his professional life—Weinberg's contributions to science are stunning. His theory led to groundbreaking work by other researchers, including the discovery of the "God particle," or the Higgs boson. As you might imagine, he was exceptionally rewarded for his exceptional performance. He earned a Harvard professorship and received the Nobel Prize in 1979.

It turns out that Weinberg's not just a whip-smart scientist; he's also a skilled negotiator. The University of Texas at Austin attempted to woo him from Harvard in 1982, offering a salary that matched their president's. Weinberg turned it down. Instead, he asked for pay on a par with the university's football coach. This was *Texas*, remember, and Weinberg knew where the priorities lay. When he left the Ivy League and moved west, his salary *did* match the coach's. In 1991, he made around a quarter of a million dollars. That was an unheard-of sum for an ivory-tower academic, especially at the time.

As stunning as Weinberg's salary was, though, it was only five times the average physics professor's. Contrast that with today's business world, where a typical CEO rakes in roughly 271 times the salary of his average employee. If Weinberg were a superstar by an economist's definition, his income should have exceeded $200 million. Weinberg's inability to rake in money at that egregious level helps us understand a key feature of superstardom. Exceptional reward only comes from talents that are easily and cheaply disseminated. As Rosen put it, "A performer or author must put out roughly the same effort whether ten or a thousand people show up in the audience or buy the book." To be a superstar economically, in other words, your performance must scale.

Think of the university's football coach, a position that pulled in a quarter of a million dollars in 1991. His talents, which helped secure wins for the Longhorns, do scale: broadcasts of the games reach millions of fans. So when the popularity of college football exploded over the past two decades, the income of the coach also exploded, without any additional effort on his part. He became a superstar. Today, the head coach at the University of Texas earns over $5 million yearly, more than any other university employee, around twenty times what he made in 1991. Weinberg, who according to public records now earns in the neighborhood of $575,000, on the other hand, has merely doubled his income in the decades since his hire.

More than half a million dollars is nothing to thumb your nose at. It's an exceptional salary. But there's a reason why Weinberg's pay doesn't mimic the football coach's. He's there to teach, and his salary is derived from tuition dollars. His classes aren't taken by vast multitudes. In 2011, he began teaching an undergraduate course on the history of physics, from the Greeks to string theory, so an audience of maybe several hundred students, tops, benefits from his talent. He has no enthusiastic fans decked out in bright jerseys swarming his lectures, no one tailgating his presentations, no one cheerleading from the sidelines during his classes. If we're measuring Weinberg's success in economic terms, his impact just doesn't scale.

Yet Weinberg's case perfectly illustrates how limited the economic definition of superstardom can be. The truth is, Weinberg *is* a superstar if the metric we use is scientific impact. That's a currency, like dollars, that can actually be measured. Take his paper that introduced electroweak interaction and, decades later, earned him the Nobel Prize. It inspired thousands of other papers, spawning related groundbreaking work and pushing the discipline forward. We know this because it was cited 14,000 times by other scientists, implying that 14,000 research papers were influenced by Weinberg's work.

Because citations in science also conform to power laws, measuring success in science isn't much different from doing so in business. Success is unbounded in academia as well. But our success metric isn't money; it's scientific impact, measured in citations. Just as most wage earners don't rake in astounding sums, most papers—however laboriously and passionately researched—get few or no citations. That means that the majority of research projects fly almost completely under the radar. Papers like Weinberg's are the rare exceptions, earning outsized scientific attention and superstar status. Such outliers remind us that academic success is like success in any other realm. It sees no boundaries.

Citations, then, serve as currency in the scientific world. I don't mean that as a figure of speech. Rather, it's possible to put actual monetary value on each citation a paper receives. We can, in other words, calculate exactly how much a single citation is worth.

Any guesses?

Shockingly, in the United States each citation is worth a whopping $100,000. We know this by looking at the amount of money the nation spends on research in hopes of furthering a variety of scientific causes, from medical breakthroughs to innovative products, or new insights on the origins of our universe. If we then divide that figure by the total number of citations collectively generated by the papers these funds paid for, we can estimate the cost of a single citation. With that we can translate Weinberg's superstardom into numbers even an economist can understand. His seminal paper, which has received 14,000 citations over the years, has had a scientific impact worth an extraordinary $1.4 billion! That is the approximate total cost of all the research inspired by Weinberg's 1967 discovery.

How can Weinberg have such an outsized impact? The answer is the same if we ask how the Dalai Lama can attract billions of admirers, or how Beyoncé can boast millions of downloads. The unbounded nature of success isn't about Weinberg, the Dalai Lama, or Beyoncé. Success, remember, is about *us* and how we reward performance. We cite Weinberg's paper in a manuscript we've labored for years to write. We show up in droves to hear the Dalai Lama speak. Millions of us download and enjoy Beyoncé's songs. The currency of success can vary—and the Dalai Lama is a good example of how superstardom can coexist with an unflinching anti-capitalistic stance—but what is universal is that there is no upper limit on how much of it a superstar can earn. It's unbounded.

•

In Weinberg's case, or, for that matter, in Tiger Woods's, superstar status seems a deserved result of exceptional talent. These are people who, despite their necessarily bounded performance, have distinguished themselves from their particular packs and been rewarded accordingly. But it's worth remembering that both Woods and Weinberg have made names for themselves in fields—golf and science—where performance is somewhat measurable.

But it's also true in art, where, as we saw in chapter 3, quality and performance are impossible to measure. A quick glance at the art data showed success in art is very uneven. While most artists are exhibited fewer than ten times in their careers, a handful are shown thousands of times—or in Andy Warhol's case, over *10,000 times*.

And let's also consider the superstars who are, well…considered stars—pop singers, for example, whose talent is really in the ear of the beholder. We have no good way of determining if Justin Timberlake is measurably better than a guy singing on a subway platform, but Timberlake is surely rewarded as if he is. He ranks number nineteen on *Forbes*'s list of the world's highest-paid celebrities, and his music reaches fans all over the world, a reach that is crucial to superstardom. That's because scalability is necessary for power law distributions. To reap enormous reward, the product you provide must be easily reproduced. Sherwin Rosen, as he was developing his economic theory of superstardom in 1981, predicted that advances in technology would further exaggerate the superstar phenomenon by allowing a few performers to access an even larger audience. These looming figures would, at the same time, reduce the reach of their less visible peers. The already wide gap between the band playing in the local bar and the band playing on TV would widen further.

Rosen was right. In 1982, when Timberlake was just another infant mewling in a crib somewhere, the top 1 percent of pop stars took home roughly a quarter of concert ticket revenue. Now Timberlake and his fellow top twenty hit makers rake in more than half of that purse. Not only do people spend more on entertainment than in previous decades, the rise of MTV,

DVD players, MP3s, and Internet streaming during Timber-lake's lifetime has expanded his audience and rewards. And as he and his cohort of outsized names and personalities—Taylor Swift, Justin Bieber, Lady Gaga among them—take up more room in our collective eardrums, the would-be up-and-comers share less and less.

Disproportionate reward is a dynamic we all recognize in the post–Occupy Wall Street era. Wealth distribution fol-lows a power law, encoding hard truths. A few individuals are grossly enriched while a considerable portion of the world is literally starving. The math behind the unbounded nature of success is cemented in inequality. In the collective conscious-ness, superstars belong to a separate society peopled by the rare and lucky. They tower over us, untouchable. And when we do find ourselves in their presence, we handle them with kid gloves. If we happen to see them in a coffee shop or bump into them on the street, we make note of the occurrence as if we'd witnessed a miracle. We name-drop our association to them. And as we angle for their attention, we change our own behavior in subtle ways, which affects our ability to succeed.

•

Tiger Woods squints into the distance, somehow spanning the space between his small white ball and the hole he aims to drop it in. On the green, he casts a long, sharp shadow. His competitors hover on the periphery, observing the legend at work. We wait to be stunned. Part of what's incredible about Woods is his consistency. In the first decade of his profes-sional career, he won 54 out of 279 PGA competitions, placed in the top three in 93 events and in the top ten in 132 events, meaning he was highly ranked in well over half the competitions he entered. Despite his bounded performance, he set the high bar that other players aspired to reach. His excellence forced everyone to try harder.

Or that's how the thinking goes. Competition is good for us, we're told. It makes us sharper, more disciplined. We all do better if we're challenged by strong, competitive peers.

But what happens when that rival is a superstar? Does some of their shininess rub off on us, too?

Not really. It turns out that competing against a superstar has the opposite effect: it *measurably lowers our performance.* We know this thanks to Jennifer Brown, an economist who explored the sway superstars have on the rest of us. Using data from over a decade of PGA tournaments, she pieced together a dramatic pattern of psychological intimidation. How, for example, did Vijay Singh do when playing in a tournament with Tiger Woods, and how did he do when Tiger Woods was absent?

It turns out that lower-ranked players who never expected to stand a chance against Woods were rarely affected by his presence. But he seemed to have deeply intimidated his close competitors, those who rubbed elbows with him in the upper bounds of golf's bell curve. The halo of his superstardom radiated into the consciousness of fellow top-ranked players more than any other factor, negatively affecting their performances.

Let's look at the data Brown collected. In order to qualify for tournaments, golfers have to make the cut in the first round. Highly ranked players' first-round scores were, on average, 0.6 stroke higher (meaning weaker playing) when Woods was present than they were when he was absent.

Given that first-round scores often vary only slightly among top golfers, this alone was a striking finding.

But the effect *only got stronger* in regular and major tournaments. Golfers competing against Woods tallied final scores between 0.7 and 1.3 strokes higher. Since fewer than two strokes often separate first- and second-place golfers, the effect essentially determined the winner. The outcome was so striking it even has a name—the Tiger Woods effect—a phrase that captures how our performance suffers in the presence of superstars.

•

In April of 2008, Tiger Woods underwent knee surgery. He returned to the sport after a short break in June, handily winning the U.S. Open, but his pained expression indicated that something was still amiss with his knee. A second surgery took him out of play for eight straight tournaments. Woods took another extended break when his unraveling marriage became household knowledge in November of 2009 and he read an emotional apology letter to fans and the press. By the time he returned to competitive play in April of 2010, he'd missed a World Golf Championship event and the Arnold Palmer Invitational tournament, both of which he'd attended in previous years.

Brown compared the scores of the tournament participants during Woods's extended absences to their prior scores on the same courses. Her findings are striking. When Woods was recovering from surgery, his top-ranked competitors were playing not just subtly but *remarkably* better: *4.6 strokes better* on average. This time, even lower-ranked and unranked players improved. And when Woods took a break to get his personal life back on track, his fellow golfers' tournament scores were roughly 3.5 strokes better. These are astoundingly large changes in player performance. Their significance is perhaps best illustrated individually. For example, when competing in the same field as Woods, Vijay Singh shot fifteen strokes over par in 2007. But the year Woods was out nursing his knee, Singh came in ten *under* par. No matter how we look at the data, the conclusions are consistent. Woods's competitors are victims of a significant superstar effect.

So, presumably, are the rest of us. It's safe to assume that a Tiger Woods effect exists in a myriad of other fields: business, academia, politics, and the arts. Yes, healthy competition is good; it improves our performance. But competing against superstars is a whole different story. How often have we stumbled in the presence of a hero or mentor, our confidence imploding like a tire meeting a nail? How often do we defer to the judgment of superiors, convinced their wisdom and competence usurps ours? And how often do we let admiration interfere with objective assessment of our abilities? Our intimidation in the presence of luminaries is so deeply embedded that we probably don't notice how much it skews outcomes in favor of those whose success is already rampant. Vijay Singh must have been horrified to see how much Woods unnerved him and the degree to which it affected his performance.

It's important to remember, though, that if we're not neck-and-neck competitors, there are numerous benefits to working with superstars. There's a straightforward message in this chapter, one that's useful for everyone from individual team members to managers and hiring committees. *Superstars suppress you if you compete against them, but they may boost you if you cooperate with them.*

For example, research shows that when a university hires a scientific superstar of Weinberg's ilk, he improves the productivity of the entire department by an astonishing 54 percent. Strikingly, this is not just because of the outsized contributions of the superstar himself, which account for, on average, only about a quarter of the department's total productivity increase. The remaining upswing is by others — an indirect result of his or her presence. Superstars can be game-changers. They attract new hires, people hoping to bask in the brilliance they emit. The effect seems to last, too — productivity remains high even eight years after a superstar's hire.

More surprisingly, a superstar's impact is just as profound when he or she departs. In a separate study of absence-as-presence, Pierre Azoulay, an MIT professor, asked a morbid but important question: What happens to a research field when a superstar scientist suddenly dies? Azoulay's findings are a reminder of the deep influences that shape our professional successes and failures. After a superstar's death, the collaborators' productivity drops 5 to 8 percent. This isn't a temporary response, a blip reflecting the turmoil the sudden death produced. It's *permanent*, lasting the length of the collaborators' careers.

These are odd findings in light of the Tiger Woods effect.

We'd expect a superstar to cast a shadow on his or her community, impeding the growth of her lesser-known colleagues like a tree blocking the sun from a garden. We'd assume that a superstar's abrupt disappearance would even the playing field, allowing the less lofty to thrive. In fact, the opposite happens. Collaborators aren't able to capitalize on their newfound elbow room, and instead the loss diminishes the work of those remaining. That speaks to the crucial role superstars play in science. Collaborators rely on their esteemed colleagues' insights to advance their own research and careers. It's a good reminder of why superstars are highly rewarded.

•

Also worth remembering is that all superstars are bounded by the limits of performance in their field. True, they're excellent at what they do, but the Second Law tells us that their performance is really only fractionally better than their peers'. That means that we have a better chance of successfully competing with superstars if we see them as unthreatening as they see us. Even though we may imagine that Tiger Woods, squinting into the green expanses behind him, is surveying competitors who look as tiny and harmless as his own two-year-old self, they really only trail him by fractions of a swing.

That's good news for the rest of us. If we know that performance is bounded, we can remind ourselves that we're capable of besting superstars. The subtle psychological factors that diminish our performance in the presence of luminaries are less powerful if we're aware of them and if we remember that superstars are just as capable of failure as the rest of us. In moments of intimidation, we can bring our heroes down to our level.

One of the most fascinating aspects of Brown's research is how clearly it showed scores in professional golf fluctuating during Tiger Woods's "hot" and "cold" periods. When Woods was performing exceptionally well, his superstar effect loomed particularly large, influencing the scores of the top-ranked players by roughly two strokes. Conversely, when Woods experienced a cold period, his poor performance seemed to boost other players' confidence. During these slumps, the adverse effect his presence usually caused *disappeared*. Suddenly Woods was fallible. It was no longer a foregone conclusion that he'd win.

Hopelessness, not superstars, is what's so defeating. We're less likely to show up to the polls if we think our underdog candidate doesn't stand a chance and less likely to apply for a job if we think another applicant is a shoo-in. And we're less likely to speak up if we believe someone else in the room inherently knows far more about the subject. But if we come to competition assuming equal footing, we're far more likely to succeed.

Remember how Pierre Azoulay found that an academic superstar's death led to a decline in her collaborators' publication rates? This seems to suggest that our reverence for those who achieve superstar status is deserved. But his subsequent analysis is heartening for the underdogs and innovators out there. While examining the ripples caused by a superstar's death, Azoulay discovered that non-collaborating scientists in a superstar's discipline—those she never worked with while alive—saw, on average, an 8 percent *increase* in their publication rates when she died. These newly productive scientists were outsiders, usually younger researchers who'd been trying to find their way forward in a space dominated by the luminary. With the absence of the superstar, they were now able to question the existing dogma in their field, stepping out of Goliath's shadow.

In an era of Goliaths—when CEOs and pop stars and corporations reap disproportionate rewards—we need to believe that the Davids of the world can still compete. And we can, especially if we routinely remind ourselves that the Second Law plays out universally. If we keep in mind that, in terms of performance, superstars are not outliers, we may rid ourselves of the Tiger Woods effect, overcoming any sense of inferiority and increasing our odds of winning. We may be able to innovate with confidence, bringing creative ideas to the table without questioning our right to be there.

If the Second Law tells us anything, it's that superstars aren't infallible. Since the heights they tumble from are substantial, they crash-land with a bang. Scandal can overwhelm fame. We certainly see it in science. If a superstar is guilty of misconduct, falsifying results, or committing plagiarism, the penalty is bigger than it would be for a less prominent researcher. There is a 20 percent drop in citations for his or her *whole body of work*, not just for the work thrown into doubt. If superstars represent the gold standard for performance, then a single scandal can deeply deteriorate his or her credibility. In a world lacking objective performance measures, one verifiable misstep can easily force us to discover that the emperor has no clothes.

And it's true in golf. Tiger Woods's infamous transgressions off the course have overshadowed his performance on it, at tremendous personal cost. When his misdeeds came to light, he experienced what might be called public shaming, an intense and relentless airing of his personal failings. The media scrutiny he's endured in the years since speaks to how much we expect from superstars, and how much we penalize them when they disappoint.

"His entire identity and sense of self was taken away by the scandal. Shame is among the most powerful and destructive of human emotions, and Woods has been marinating in it ever since," Alan Shipnuck writes in *Golf.* "During his heyday, Woods could hit any shot and putted better than anybody ever has, but what separated him from everyone else was his heart and his head. His belief in himself was absolute, and unshakable....Success begat success. But all of that is gone now."

It's almost as if Tiger Woods was overshadowed by his former self.

•

The Second Law—Performance is bounded, but success is unbounded—perfectly illustrates the disproportional relationship between performance and success. But it tells us nothing about the roots of this disconnect. As I charted success in numerous fields, I repeatedly saw power law distributions. While this told me something important about the limitless nature of success, each chart seemed to reinforce the old adage: Life isn't fair. Luckily, the next law will help elucidate the mysterious mechanisms that create the dynamics we experience in our everyday lives. *Why* do superstars dominate in realm after realm? *How* do any of us become a runaway success in the first place?

Well, one way is to make a card game about kittens that defuse nuclear bombs.

THE THIRD LAW

Previous success × fitness

=

future success.

It's the law that shows us how a subtle phenomenon, *preferential attachment,* governs all success, from a petition's popularity to reading comprehension in children. When fitness and social influence work in tandem, success has no boundaries.

6

Exploding Kittens and Sock Puppets
How to Kick-Start Your Success

For Elan Lee, it began with a stream of e-mail messages arriving at such an unrelenting pace that his Gmail account stopped working. Strangers sent balloon animals, TacoCat plush toys, and legal threats. Fox News showed up on his doorstep unannounced. As the reporter plunked herself down at his desk, Lee felt disoriented even in his own apartment. So he hand-scrawled a list of talking points for the reporter, holding it up like a makeshift teleprompter as the camera started rolling.

Kickstarter campaign launched three days ago
Effort to fund "Exploding Kittens" card game
Reached campaign goal of $10,000 in first eight minutes
Has already raised more than $3 million

Exploding Kittens was a card game Lee had conceived with the help of two friends, Matthew Inman and Shane Small, and the premise was seemingly ridiculous. Cards depicted cats who could set off nuclear bombs by walking across keyboards—cats whose nefarious intentions could be defused only with laser pointers, goat wizards, and catnip sandwiches. The game was like a harmless, diverting round of Russian roulette, but with strategy and lots of gags.

Hoping to raise $10,000 to print the cards, Lee and his friends posted their concept on Kickstarter. They had a month to raise the funds. When they met their goal within *eight minutes*, they were gleeful. At the $100,000 mark, they became hysterical. When they hit $1 million, they were stunned. At the $2 million mark, they were...terrified. Lee stuck a Post-it note on his laptop screen to hide the box where Kickstarter clocked the campaign's total donations. "You ever have the feeling where you're up on a tall cliff...and you look out at the void and it sort of pulls you? And it's not cause you're suicidal or anything, you don't want anything bad to happen to you, but you think, like, 'What if, what if?'" Lee quipped. Referring to the campaign's website, he continued, "Well, in the bottom left-hand corner there's a box that says 'Cancel Funding.' I stare at that every day." This was early February, only twelve days in.

When the barrage finally abated—a quelling that occurred only because the month allotted for fundraising had elapsed—Lee and his friends had amassed $8.8 million from over 200,000 backers.

On the face of it, Exploding Kittens was like any of the other hopeful campaigns out there seeking seed money. And Elan Lee resembled any other entrepreneur, keeping fingers crossed that he'd reach his desired goal.

Except he wasn't.

Lee might not have anticipated that the dollars would rain down in such enormous numbers, but many signs were in fact pointing to the Category 5 hurricane of success headed his way. It *was* odd that so many people were throwing hard-earned money at an already funded card game, but when Lee launched his site to fund his project, he had a secret weapon—no, not a feline-defused nuclear bomb!—and it set him up for success. We'll discover what that was soon enough. Now, though, let's explore why so many projects fail to attract attention in the first place. In other words, what is the fuel that allows successful campaigns like Exploding Kittens to soar?

•

While the launch of Exploding Kittens evokes thoughts of almost effortless success, the truth is that as many as 70 percent of Kickstarter projects fail. They populate a sort of Kickstarter graveyard: the small-town heavy-metal band that can't record that hoped-for album, the struggling Web sitcom unable to raise the funds to shoot its next episode, the would-be chicken-and-waffle food truck that never was. At first glance, it'd be hard to pinpoint exactly what separates Lee from those hopefuls who, seeking seed money, repeatedly nudge their friends to "like" and "share" on social media, send out last-ditch pleas as their deadline draws near, and then disappear forever into the Internet ether. Faced with a sea of professional-looking videos put together by earnest entrepreneurs, what matters when we do or don't ultimately decide to click the fund button?

We find an answer in the work of Arnout van de Rijt, a

Dutch-born experimental sociologist. Growing up, he'd been a clarinetist, and a good one, taking home the top prize in the local classical music competition year after year. Despite his repeated wins, he thought some of his competitors—like his friend, a pianist—were more talented than he. Clarinet was a rare instrument and most of the truly talented kids played piano or violin. The budding scientist in him wondered whether his chosen instrument's rarity played a role in his repeated success. These kinds of questions are the reason he's dedicated his career to exploring how success emerges in numerous fields.

Take, for example, an experiment he conducted using Kickstarter, which offers some hints about the forces that catapulted Exploding Kittens into the stratosphere. Arnout randomly selected two hundred new Kickstarter projects whose donation tallies read, like a college kid's ATM receipt after a series of bad financial choices, a glaring $0.00. He contributed a small amount of money to half of them and snubbed the other half, designating it as his control group. Then he sat on the sidelines, watching their fates unfold. No project saw the lightning-quick uptick in donations that Elan Lee witnessed. But what Arnout found was striking in its own right. Those who received his initial donation *more than doubled* their chances of attracting further funds. Meaning that his pet projects, selected blindly, vastly outperformed the half he left for broke.

Arnout didn't personally know any of the people soliciting funds and didn't find their videos particularly compelling or their causes exceptionally worthy. His contributions were not substantial, equivalent to the few bills and loose coins one might drop into a street musician's guitar case. *Yet his random donations seemed to mark these projects for success.*

What Arnout observed was a phenomenon that we've seen over and over again in a range of fields. *Success breeds success.* In other words, those seen as successful attract more success, regardless of their performance. This is called *preferential attachment* in scientific literature, a term I coined in 1999 when I sought to explain how websites like Google acquire millions of links while billions of other sites with compelling content and services struggle to gain any visibility at all. Preferential attachment, a concept that emerged out of that research, tells us that the rich get richer, celebrity builds celebrity, and nothing succeeds like success.

This rich-get-richer phenomenon has been documented in scientific fields ranging from physics to economics over the past century. The sociologist Robert Merton called it the Matthew effect, after a passage from the Gospel according to Matthew that did a decent job of describing the concept, albeit with outdated diction: "For unto every one that hath shall be given, and he shall have abundance." This means that preferential attachment, in basic terms, was evident as far back as biblical times.

Let's look at preferential attachment within the context I first witnessed it: the World Wide Web, the hugely complex network composed of over a trillion websites. Each site on the Web is navigable by URLs that allow us to surf from one page to another with a single click. Because it's open to all, and wildly diverse in its array of offerings, the Web has been repeatedly touted as the ultimate platform for democracy, providing each website with an equal opportunity to flourish.

But that's not true and never has been, which we discovered in 1998 when we first mapped a portion of the Web using a homemade, primitive search engine not unlike the one that Larry Page and Sergey Brin, the founders of Google, were cobbling together around the same time.

Our map revealed something surprising about the rapidly growing World Wide Web. This was no egalitarian network where all voices could be heard. Instead, the vast majority of websites were virtually invisible in a mesh of other websites. A few sites act as hubs—Google, Amazon, or Facebook, for instance—attracting hundreds of millions of links and expanding because of preferential attachment. Search engine algorithms tend to rank sites by counting the number of times other sites link to them. The more incoming links a website has, the easier it is to find via browsing or search engine rankings. Consequently, the more links you have, the more likely that you will collect additional links and increase your visibility online. Substitute "website" for pretty much anything or anyone else belonging to a network: Hollywood actor, real estate agent, toy manufacturer, or even priest, and you'll see how deeply preferential attachment shapes the world around us.

Some basic examples to reinforce the point:

The more clients a real estate broker has, the more referrals she'll get. That's why it's so hard to get started in the business.

An actor will continue to land roles if he's in a film that wins applause. He might only have a cameo appearance to start, but the more his face pops up on our screens, the more a casting director or producer will want him in a new project.

Preferential attachment is responsible for the kind of snowballing success experienced by superstars like Tiger Woods or

Justin Timberlake, turning them into the hubs in their respective networks. If success were as bounded as performance, there'd be a limit to their fan base. But as Elan Lee's deluge of donations confirms, there isn't. The runaway popularity of Exploding Kittens reflected the unbounded nature of success captured in the Second Law. But the engine that makes these hubs or superstars is preferential attachment—success breeds success. In fact, the concept is necessary and inevitable in achieving exceptional impact, reward, and visibility. It's what propels superstars to the kind of dizzying heights that Lee was briefly tempted to jump from.

•

Recently, a friend of mine, Carrie, went to a routine doctor's appointment with her month-old son, a tiny little creature who blinked sleepily at her from what appeared to be the bakery scale he was perched upon. The appointment went well. As she stood to leave, wrapping the baby in an unnecessary number of layers to brave the elements on the walk to the car, the doctor handed Carrie, oddly, a black-and-white kids' book with a picture of a rabbit on the front. "Make sure you read to him every day," she said, as if explaining the dosage on a bottle of pills.

The idea seemed laughable. Was a doctor seriously prescribing books? Her story brought to mind the many "Oh, Americans!" moments I still experience after decades in the States. But it has since struck me as profound. The book doled out at the pediatrician's office is an important reminder of just how deeply a rich-get-richer phenomenon underpins our lives at the very outset.

Had my own son been born into a house with few books and parents who weren't readers, maybe the only reading material he'd have been exposed to in the first few years of his life would have been the small library he'd collect on doctor's visits. A child unaccustomed to books will likely not read much as he gets older. Exposed to fewer words, he'll develop fewer strategies for decoding them. As he advances through the grades, his literacy is on increasingly shaky footing.

That's a feedback loop with a dismal result: Research has shown that the least motivated readers in middle school read only 100,000 words a year. Compare that with the average middle schooler, who reads roughly a million words, or that rare reader like my daughter, Izabella, who—dragging impressive tomes in her oversized backpack—absorbs as many as *10 million* words annually. She pores over a library's worth of books on her summer vacations. She's had time to practice and build her skills. She can use a wide and vivid vocabulary to express herself, and teachers have praised her from first grade on. The recognition she experiences leads to further recognition. Knowledge breeds knowledge, skill breeds skill, expertise breeds expertise. And each of these leads to success, which builds on itself.

Preferential attachment, then, expands the divide between the educational haves and have-nots, a phenomenon that continues to snowball over a lifetime. It points to the chasm between children who are born, at least theoretically, with an equal chance at literacy and those who never catch up because they missed out from the start.

Given what I know about preferential attachment, I'm

convinced we also must parent our own success, wisely guiding our projects from the get-go. Without a playbook or a prescription, that's easier said than done. If accruing success in any field depends on...well, the success we've already accrued, then how does anyone become successful in the first place? How do we nurture preferential attachment? How does that Realtor get those initial sales?

It's a familiar Catch-22. When a college student applies for a summer job waiting tables in her hometown diner, she's asked, "Do you have any experience?" by the hurriedly summoned manager. Being honest, she confesses that, no, she doesn't. "Sorry, we need someone with experience," the manager shouts over his shoulder as he rushes off to make a fresh pot of coffee. On her way to the parking lot, disappointed and puzzled, she asks herself a chicken-or-egg question half out loud. "How the hell am I supposed to *get* any experience without any experience?"

•

By now there is overwhelming evidence that each time we see a runaway success—superstars, hubs, the extremely wealthy—preferential attachment has played a role. But underneath this soulless, mechanistic explanation, a central question lingers. What if preferential attachment is rooted in something even more fundamental: variations in talent or privilege, or the inherent social advantages a fortunate person is born with? That is, do those who repeatedly win do so because they are simply better or because they have consistently deeper resources?

These foundational questions prompted Arnout to conduct another experiment, this time turning to Wikipedia. Articles on Wikipedia are collaboratively written by pseudonymous "editors"—people like you and me who are willing to offer expertise on specific topics. Little known to those who do not regularly contribute to the site is that any user can offer virtual awards to editors whose contributions are deemed exceptional. The awards are meant to promote "Wikilove," a concept the site defines as "the spirit of collegiality and mutual understanding among Wiki users." Awards that Wikipedia calls "Barnstars" can be given to anyone by anyone who's logged in as an editor. There are no judges deciding who deserves a prize.

Because the Barnstars are meant to honor editors who are frequent and significant contributors, Arnout first identified the most active 1 percent of all editors, about twenty-four hundred altogether. Then he randomly selected two hundred of these dedicated Wiki nerds and split them, again randomly, into two groups of one hundred editors each. For all practical purposes, the two groups were indistinguishable, consisting of editors with equal commitment to Wikipedia. That is, until Arnout's experiment began.

Unknown to the editors, Arnout destined one group for success and let the other group flounder. He did so by arbitrarily awarding each person in one group a Barnstar. He withheld the awards from those in the second group. In essence, he created two parallel universes that differed in only one respect: one group was openly recognized for their contributions to the site, the other was not. Then Arnout sat on the sidelines and watched what happened.

• • •

The prizewinners got really busy. In fact, their productivity in editing sites jumped by 60 percent compared to the non-starred control group. They were also more motivated. But perhaps the most striking finding was this: Twelve of those whom Arnout rewarded with a Barnstar were subsequently granted one or several more Barnstars by other Wiki users over the three months he monitored the groups. Compare that with only two editors in the control group who received further awards. *The people who received a first, random Barnstar from Arnout became "awardable." They were far more likely to receive a second or third one from somebody else.*

It's tempting to reduce all of this to a simple reward dynamic. The Barnstar increases effort, which in turn brings success. Winning an award bestows confidence, teaches us how to win, enhances our recognition, and increases the resources that breed further success. But the beauty of Arnout's experiments is that he was able to rule out this possibility. True, as a group the Barnstar recipients showed increased effort, but the twelve doubly or triply awarded editors exhibited no greater productivity than their fellow group members. Most important, the results told Arnout that it's not talent, quality, or commitment that drives the accumulating pile of prizes to the already rewarded. By randomly selecting the groups, he avoided that possibility. The experiment took effort and talent out of the equation, demonstrating that regardless of performance, reward led to further reward. Success bred success. It was really as simple as that.

Wikipedia awards might seem trivial compared to grants or scholarships or promotions, more akin to the gold stars teachers distribute to committed readers in first grade. But I've witnessed this exact phenomenon play out in my own profession, when an Arnout-like figure bestows an award on a deserving colleague, launching him or her onto a path of expanding success. In every case I can think of, the honor seemed justified, and I was happy to see the scientist recognized.

But instead of spreading the love around, the opposite happened—our already recognized colleague started to receive more rewards. There's an easy case to be made for nominating an honored scientist for further accolades. His history of acclaim breeds confidence, not just in him but in us, too. It reduces any uncertainty about his merits and can be used to justify his further success.

When the Second Law's dictates about performance make one contender difficult to distinguish from another, remember, factors such as "awardability" can drive our success. I can't help but think that the judges of the Queen Elisabeth competition aren't really that different from Arnout. After selecting twelve finalists, they pick one performer virtually at random and give him a prize, launching his or her trajectory of success. I'm not just speculating here. The same team of researchers that discovered the competition's biases has proven how crucial winning is for a musician's career. They did so by analyzing the number of recordings each performer makes in the years after the competition. They also checked who was listed in the British Gramophone Classical Catalogue, or the Diapason, its French counterpart, which signals that someone has made it in classical music. And they examined the critics' perceptions of each musician's post-competition accomplishments. The researchers also asked music critics to rank each participant on a scale of 0 to 4, encapsulating expert opinion about every competitor's subsequent career.

Their findings show that a high ranking in the Queen Elisabeth competition, and the early visibility that came with it, kick-started musicians' success. Once that happened, preferential attachment started a chain reaction, pushing them to new heights. The musicians with high competition scores were more likely not only to get their work recorded but also to be listed in catalogues and earn the praise of critics. This of course makes sense if you believe that talent alone determined their competition ranking. But we know they all had talent; the performances of the finalists are virtually indistinguishable to the judges. It's chance and bias, plain and simple, that shape the final ranking. Yet those who are singled out and rewarded, *even arbitrarily*, experience major, long-lasting benefits as a result of the preferential attachment. An awarded musician becomes "awardable."

•

There's a "social proof" aspect to this phenomenon, one you can re-create in real time at a farmers' market with friends. Ask them to huddle enthusiastically in front of a vendor's wares, and see if a line begins to form on itself with almost magnetic power, inviting others to queue up. The carrots sold at that stand are probably no tastier than the carrots at the one across the way. It's the buzz of eager customers that makes the rest of us curious to discover what the fuss is about. We don't want to miss out on *those* carrots, which suddenly seem fresher and crunchier and sweeter, more vibrantly *orange* than the carrots we can get, far more easily, from the neighboring vendor.

Preferential attachment underlies most of our choices, everything from what products we buy to what causes we endorse. When prompted by a friend on social media to sign a petition, a similar phenomenon comes into play. We might or might not care, but we're more likely to engage if multiple people nudge us. When that same petition comes around a fourth or fifth time, having been shared and signed by numerous friends, we are, perhaps, ultimately convinced of its worth. It *must* be an important cause. *It matters to lots of my peers.*

To see this in action, consider Change.org, an online service that allows users to set up a campaign with a few clicks of a mouse. Over 30 million individual petitions have been created this way, on issues from local to global, from mundane to dire. With a signature, I can request further funding for my neighborhood youth center or request that the electoral college change an election result. I can ask to have profanity banned from a website or urge a governor to grant clemency to a death row prisoner. While some of these receive millions of signatures—especially those pertaining to world affairs or events in the national news—most only garner a few.

Curious how a campaign gains visibility, Arnout once again created an experiment. He selected two hundred early-stage campaigns and granted a dozen signatures to a hundred randomly selected ones. By now you can anticipate what he discovered: preferential attachment applies even to ideological scenarios. The causes Arnout randomly supported were far more likely to accrue further signatures than those he snubbed. That means that even when we're presented with an issue of potentially deep political or ethical importance, an issue about *justice*, say, an unjust mechanism comes into play. We may think of these petitions as a way to further democracy, but what Arnout discovered is that while all causes are created equal, it is previous success, not a cause's moral urgency, that drives its later success. A lot of petitions come through my Facebook feed, on a lot of varied topics. On rare occasions I sign them, usually when the issue at stake is one that I find particularly compelling: freeing an imprisoned scientist in an oppressive regime, or sparing a university from political interference. I click on sign because I care. That's a decision that feels personal and private. But only the popular causes reach my feed. It's not that I don't care about the rest. I probably do. But no one suggests that I look into them. These are the causes that lack that initial nudge; preferential attachment hasn't been activated enough to catch my attention.

•

"I don't need to really say anything about the plot of this book," Nicodemus Jones declared in his Amazon review of *A Quiet Belief in Angels*. Written by the British author R. J. Ellory, it was a new mystery novel only available by advance purchase. "All I will say is that there are paragraphs and chapters that just stopped me dead in my tracks. Some of it was chilling, some of it raced along, some of it was poetic and languorous and had to be read twice and three times to really appreciate the depth of the prose. . . . It really is a magnificent book."

As an author myself, that's feedback I'd happily accept.

Especially since it happened to be the book's first Amazon review. We know how crucial such a strong initial endorsement is for future success, and Jones kick-started *A Quiet Belief in Angels* by providing a credible critique early on, before anyone had a chance to appreciate the book's apparent magnificence. Like the Wiki-awards that Arnout doled out, Jones's generous feedback generated the positive momentum necessary for further accolades.

Not that Ellory needed extra praise. This was his fifth book, he already had a devoted fan base, and two of his previous books had been shortlisted for prestigious awards. Still, any new novel requires an enthusiastic readership to sell copies. Without strong praise at the start, *A Quiet Belief in Angels* might have languished in obscurity like so many other deserving efforts. What if, for example, Jones had deemed it "another in a seemingly endless parade of same-old-same-old police procedurals that seem to abound in the UK"—a direct quote from the critique he offered for *Dark Blood*, by Stuart MacBride? Such a scathing initial assessment could have left *A Quiet Belief in Angels* fighting for survival. Instead, the new novel went on to sell more than a million copies worldwide, becoming Ellory's biggest success.

Invisible early birds can play an alarmingly substantial role in the success or failure of a new project. I like imagining Arnout, as a scientific Tinker Bell, anonymously sprinkling fairy dust into not yet appreciated corners of the Internet. The unwitting participants in his experiments benefited more than they probably realize from his meddling. If they knew that their later successes were a direct result of his initial, purposeful nudge, I'd imagine they'd be startled. Likewise I can sense the heavy satisfaction of R. J. Ellory when he received such a glowing first review.

Except that Ellory was not startled at all. To the contrary: he and Nicodemus Jones, his avid endorser, were the same person. Jones was Ellory's pseudonym, a name he used in order to praise his own books and eviscerate his competitors'. Assuming a false identity, *he'd written his own laudatory review*. There's a name for this ethically questionable practice—it's called sockpuppeting—and it's more common than you might realize. In the decades since the Internet has made such an approach easy to pull off, numerous creators have used the tactic. For obvious reasons, it's sad that authors we admire stoop to deception when promoting their books. It's sadder still to realize how effective it can be. Because how, after all, do we select a book to dedicate precious evening hours to? We check if others found it worth their time. Arnout's experiments tell us how crucial a role early reviews play—they kick-start success.

But does sockpuppeting really work? Since we rely on ratings and reviews when making decisions about everything from vacuum cleaners to hotels, sockpuppeting raises valid questions about the accuracy, fairness, and trustworthiness of systems we take for granted. If we can so easily manipulate rating systems to our benefit and to the detriment of others, we should be alarmed. Can Jones's laudatory review enhance a book's success? Can his damning one kill a promising new novel?

Sinan Aral, one of the young stars in the new field of computational social science, designed another clever online experiment to answer these questions. He did so by manipulating the "up-votes" and "down-votes" responding to comments on a popular news aggregation site. The up-votes are endorsements by other users that are meant to recognize insightful or useful comments. Down-votes signal that a comment is redundant, irrelevant, or inappropriate. When Sinan offered an initial up-vote to a comment, he found, of course, that the comment was far more likely to get subsequent up-votes. The experiment showed, once again, that success breeds success.

But the question I was most curious about was this: What happened when he artificially down-voted a comment, whether or not it deserved it? Will an initial criticism lead to preferential "detachment," a quick plummet to irrelevance? Can the R. J. Ellorys truly kill their competition with well-timed criticism?

Sinan's findings were unexpectedly heartwarming. He saw no downward spiral when he arbitrarily down-voted a comment. There was no preferential "detachment." Instead, over time, other users of the site corrected the judgment by systematically up-voting it, eventually erasing Sinan's contrarian influence. Reason prevailed and the negative feedback got canceled out.

In an online world that can feel deeply unkind—read the comment sections on various websites to experience disgust at the inhumanity of people toward one another—Sinan's findings are reassuring. In the virtual universe, the Tinker Bells, scattering fairy dust Arnout-style, are more powerful than the sockpuppeteers. The R. J. Ellorys of the world may wreak some individual havoc, but they are perhaps less influential than they hope. A first good review is essential for success. But an initial scathing review won't necessarily attract further derision. Preferential attachment is a force of good. It refuses to serve those who would use it nefariously.

•

How do we use this powerful, positive force to nurture our success, then?

We start by thinking hard about how to generate the initial momentum that we now know is essential to success, first by encouraging those who've already praised our creative projects to do so publicly. Remember that one of Arnout's more fascinating findings is that it doesn't really matter who offers initial support, as long as *someone* does. But it's worth asking how much initial success is sufficient for further success. How many kicks does it take to kick-start something?

Kickstarter itself offers some answers. We already know that one small donation makes a significant and lasting impact on a campaign. But Arnout's next experiment tested how multiple random donations to a single source fared. In cases where he withheld funding altogether, 68 percent of projects failed, not attracting other donations. By contrast, only 26 percent floundered when they received one of his blind donations. But when he went as far as offering *four* blind donations, *only 13 percent of the projects failed.* In other words, more initial support *virtually guaranteed* success.

There was an interesting catch, however. Additional donations resulted in progressively smaller returns. A single initial donor attracted 4.3 additional donors. But the three following donors attracted only 1.7 more donors apiece. In monetary terms, Arnout's initial investment, which averaged $24.52, returned a remarkable $191.00 on average. But the return on his three subsequent investments only yielded half of that—$89.57 each. Simply put, the push provided at the get-go by the first donor made a much more significant impact than was caused by those who followed suit. Repeated interventions yield decreasing returns.

This shows, then, that a person clicking a project's fund button for the first time is doing more than daring to invest in that project's goals. *He's kick-starting preferential attachment, launching the project on a path to success.* The initial act of endorsement, therefore, is hugely important. It can make all the difference to a budding business, a struggling artist, a burgeoning reader, or a fundraising campaign. Anyone hoping to benefit from preferential attachment needs to keep this in mind. Arnout's meddling with crowdfunding also tells us that, yes, you need success to be successful, but even the biggest success starts out small and singular. You know that framed dollar bill hanging by the cash register in the home-town hardware store? It's not just symbolic. The first sale a business experiences *is* its most important. The initial customer dares to invest in the store's future. He's getting the ball rolling, launching it on a trajectory toward success.

Which brings me back to the graveyard of broken dreams, Kickstarter. Many of the failed projects on the site represent genuine effort and real worth. Yet instead of endorsing unknowns and underdogs, we too often choose the superstars in our networks. *That's* the mechanism behind wealth inequality and unbounded success. Preferential attachment explains why life isn't fair. To even the playing field, we need to find ways of recognizing, acknowledging, and championing talent early to set the snowball of achievement in motion. If we, for example, want our kids to succeed academically—who doesn't want that?—then it's vital to remember how ubiquitous preferential attachment is, and how, as we saw earlier, it's ingrained in our children's chances at success or failure.

Humans are inherently leery of risk. We are therefore always on the lookout for previous endorsement, some indicator that any promise we offer will have some ready-made company. We award the "awardable." We risk little when we nominate an Oscar winner for another acting prize or offer a coveted fellowship in music to a Queen Elisabeth competition winner, or—like one of Exploding Kittens' many enthusiasts—make a donation to an already fully funded crowdsourced campaign. As our definition of success dictates, success is a collective phenomenon. We are all, together, responsible for it. Particularly in areas where we lack a way of gauging talent, quality, and performance, we're more likely to rely on the perceived wisdom of the crowd. Yet doing so has far-reaching consequences, amplifying the already existing inequalities in how success is distributed.

•

Though I was not one of its original Kickstarter donors, I'm a big fan of Exploding Kittens. The game amuses and exhilarates not only my younger son, an eight-year-old adrenaline junkie, but also me, as I too find it funny and engaging. While playing, we've been known to have such a good time that someone else in the house has to come and quiet us down. As far as I'm concerned, the game's early backers had amazing instincts and the avalanche of endorsement that the card game received was well deserved. But Exploding Kittens could have just as easily been a tedious experience. How could any of the backers have anticipated how fun the game would be without trying it out first?

The answer is that Exploding Kittens had the initial kick-start built into it. Here's why: Its first donors, entering their credit card info within seconds of the game's launch, were fans of Matthew Inman, the artist who drew the goat wizards and the pig-a-corns and the weaponized back hair of cats featured on the cards. Inman was already a major force in the world of comics for his website, The Oatmeal, and for books like *Five Very Good Reasons to Punch a Dolphin in the Mouth.*

Unlike Exploding Kittens, The Oatmeal wasn't an overnight sensation. Its audience got built one comic at a time, triggering preferential attachment along the way. When Inman created a website in 2009 to share his dry, minimalistic, and character-driven drawings accompanied by witty commentary, he was still working as a Web designer. But his art created a stir on Digg and Reddit, giving him exposure he's quick to acknowledge he wouldn't have gotten in a pre-Internet era. It took another year for his comics to begin attracting 20 million visitors a month to his website. At that point, he could quit his job and self-publish a book that sold so well he had to hire a few family members to help fulfill orders. That book led to a book deal with a traditional publisher and an appearance on *Last Call with Carson Daly.*

Elan Lee, Inman's friend, offers us an example of how to use preferential attachment to the benefit of our creative projects without sockpuppeting or manipulating donors. Lee primed the game for success by collaborating with a "hub," a person with a substantial following already. Inman's fans, familiar with his work, were easily attracted to Exploding Kittens. By spreading the word among the right networks, Lee ensured that the game, as its name promised, would blow up. Though we'll see in the next chapter that quality plays an essential role, the storm of donations in this case could not be attributed to the game's merit, since none of the backers had a chance to test it before forking over money. Instead, it was Inman's fan base that catalyzed the funding process as soon as the Kickstarter page went live.

Just as I love playing Exploding Kittens with my younger son, Leó, I loved reading to my older son, Dániel. He allowed me to delve into the Harry Potter series, thick hardback tomes that were all the rage as he came of age. While one purpose of my efforts was to help him build his vocabulary, each word serving as a building block for another, far more gratifying was watching how riveted Dániel became by the stories. Bending toward the pages with that rare kind of imaginative attention, he was transported to an alternate universe.

Of course, Dániel loved Harry Potter. I read the first two volumes to him in Hungarian, but when the third came out he just couldn't wait the extra few months it took for the Hungarian translation to be released, so he read the books in English by himself. I remember the adventure we went on to secure a copy of the final book in the seven-volume series.

We traveled to Nagyszeben, a charming medieval city in the heart of Transylvania, and while our car was no Ford Anglia, flying Harry and Ron to Hogwarts, it seemed we, too, were on a magical journey.

We were willing to make that special trip because Harry Potter is not only mind-bogglingly popular, it's also pretty darn *good*. There's a catch to preferential attachment when it affixes to something extraordinary. Every now and again, like the cry of "Incendio!" when a Harry Potter character summons red and orange flames, something comes along that's so exceptional it's as if a charm has ignited it.

And the puzzle becomes, what exactly was the magic spell?

7

The Ear of the Beholder

How Quality Defies Social Influence

Kate Mills, publishing director at Orion Books in the UK, pulled *The Cuckoo's Calling* from a stack of manuscripts gathering dust on her desk. The crime novel, written by a former military police officer named Robert Galbraith, had some compelling qualities—beautiful language, an assured voice, and an intriguing main character with a prosthetic leg. She perused the book, deemed it "perfectly decent, but quiet," and promptly passed on it.

Galbraith, however, eventually found a publisher willing to take a chance. When the book was released in April 2013, Geoffrey Wansell praised *The Cuckoo's Calling* in the *Daily Mail* as an "auspicious debut." Despite Wansell's enthusiasm, though, the book didn't have much luck developing a readership and initially sold only a paltry five hundred copies, hardly an omen of good things to come.

But then a rumor started circulating that Galbraith had the same agent and editor as J. K. Rowling, of Harry Potter fame. Galbraith also had an uncanny ability for describing women's clothes, an idiosyncrasy that raised eyebrows. The rumor prompted London's *Sunday Times* to consult a computer scientist who did indeed detect puzzling linguistic similarities between Rowling's *Casual Vacancy* and Galbraith's debut. Backed into a corner, Rowling eventually admitted that the buzz was true. *She*—Britain's most famous living author—was Robert Galbraith, the unheard-of military police officer whose name graced the glossy front cover. The next day, *The Cuckoo's Calling* instantly became an international best seller.

In writing pseudonymously, Rowling was essentially conducting her own research into the Science of Success. She hoped to publish "without hype or expectation," allowing herself the "pure pleasure" of receiving unbiased feedback from readers and critics. She was testing the merits of her own writing as objectively as she knew how to do, by eliminating the shadow of influence cast by her gargantuan popularity.

Stephen King conducted a similar experiment more than thirty years earlier, when he used the pen name Richard Bachman to see if the success he'd garnered was due to luck or talent. King chose to publish his Bachman novels with as little marketing effort as possible, making life deliberately tough for his pseudonymous persona. It was a persona that King sketched out in detail. Bachman's novels included an author photo of a ruggedly handsome man gazing moodily from the book jacket, and an author bio that listed time spent as a merchant marine and as a chicken farmer in rural New Hampshire. According to the bio, Bachman spent his evenings writing, "always with a glass of whiskey beside his Olivetti typewriter."

Like Rowling, King was outed before he could unmask

himself—this time by a bookstore clerk who detected striking similarities between the two writers' styles. But, prior to being outed, King wrote four books as Bachman. His last one, *Thinner*, was reviewed as "what Stephen King would write if Stephen King could write," and it sold roughly 40,000 copies. Yet, once the book was attributed to King, it became a best seller, selling ten times as many books. Overshadowed by King, Bachman perished in obscurity. In later interviews, King summed it up this way: in 1985, Bachman died suddenly of "cancer of the pseudonym, a rare form of schizonomia."

"Cancer of the pseudonym" seems apt in Galbraith's case, too. Rowling surely hoped *The Cuckoo's Calling* would gain a wide readership on its own merits. Without Rowling's name gracing the cover, however, it failed to find an audience. This lack of initial interest was not unfamiliar to Rowling. Twenty years earlier, she'd been a single mother collecting welfare when twelve different publishers passed on the first Harry Potter novel. She was as destitute "as it was possible to be in modern Britain without being homeless," she confessed. Her story is a classic rags-to-riches reminder that talent and determination can pay off in superstar proportions. But, apparently, only occasionally: Why did *Harry Potter* become a success on its own merits, while *The Cuckoo's Calling* tanked until Rowling's fame resuscitated it? How can the same talent write a book that fires the imagination of 500 million readers, and then another one that attracts a mere five hundred?

Well, maybe *Harry Potter* is just a much better book than *The Cuckoo's Calling*. It could be as simple as that. We might have trouble articulating how we tell junk from gem, but we know the difference once we see it. When evaluating everything from personal trainers to hotels—or when deciding which products we'll add to our cart—we seek excellence. We lap up, without hesitation, the book, the movie, the car, or the service that appears to be better than the competition.

But even if a police procedural wasn't exactly Rowling's strong suit, *The Cuckoo's Calling* sprang from the same creative wellspring. Hence the initial question remains: Why did that book's sales spike only with her name attached? If you're Kate Mills leafing through manuscripts looking for the next best seller, a small error in judgment can be catastrophic for both you and the book itself. You could easily be one of the twelve publishers throwing *Harry Potter* into the rejection pile, investing instead in a book that fits all the criteria of a best seller but only ends up selling a handful of copies. So if it's easy to tell good from bad, then why is Kate Mills's job so difficult?

Perhaps it's because homing in on excellence is harder than we think. There are thousands of books in any bookstore, millions of songs available on iTunes, a vast expanse of products on the shelves of any box store. How can someone curate only the best?

Well, it helps to have friends. And if a friend recommends a book, we are more likely to give it a chance. If we hear a new restaurant doesn't live up to the hype, we go elsewhere. If our neighbor hates her refrigerator, we'll make sure to order the competing brand. In a crowded field of offerings, we often can't judge a product on its own merits. We ask, we observe, we listen. We rely on others to inform our choice. Recommendations reduce noise, steering us toward the good stuff. And they're comforting, too. A runaway best seller provides a safe, socially vetted bet. As a result, we march with the crowd toward a few books, songs, restaurants, or gadgets, leaving everything else caked in the dust our heels kick up.

But when we crowdsource our choices, are we investing our time and money in superior items, or are we simply flocking toward the flock?

•

Matthew Salganik, Peter Sheridan Dodds, and Duncan Watts—the creators of the MusicLab at Yahoo—are, in a sense, Rowling's scientific peers. Seeking to understand how popularity influences success, they asked thousands of participants to listen to songs by unsigned bands, a musical version of the slush pile that Kate Mills faces. They deliberately chose songs that would be unfamiliar to pretty much anyone outside the friends and families of the band members.

The study participants that the MusicLab recruited were young—three out of four had not yet reached their mid-twenties—and they cared a lot about music. If you're picturing your teenage daughter thumbing through your Spotify playlist with an expression of judgey amusement or downright disgust, multiply that image by 14,000. Scared yet?

Unknown to them, the 14,000 young people were steered into nine different virtual rooms. Some were ushered into the control group and given a simple task: rank forty-eight songs from best to worst. As a reward, they were allowed to download any songs they wanted to keep in their music libraries. A participant downloading a track seemed like a reliable indicator that he or she genuinely enjoyed the listening experience—at least enough, anyway, to want to play it again. The researchers

151

deemed a song "good" if it was frequently downloaded, and "bad" if it was snubbed by those who listened to it.

Of course, quality is in the ear of the beholder, and songs liked by this group of primarily American teenagers might be abhorred by 14,000, say, Transylvanian grandmothers or classical musicians. So quantifying true quality is pretty challenging. What we *can* hope to measure is a song's "fitness," which captures its ability to compete for our attention compared to other songs. And since the members of the control group were indistinguishable from the rest of the participants, they were expected to react similarly to the music they were hearing.

As if doing homework with earbuds in, members of the control group faithfully rated the songs. And then they cashed in on their reward by downloading their favorites. Simple enough. Yet only a small portion of the 14,000 total study participants ended up in that control group. The rest were sent to one of eight other identical virtual rooms where they had the same task—ranking songs and downloading their favorites—with one crucial difference. They were given a tally of how many times *other members of their group* had downloaded each song. These tallies changed as each teenager, entering the room in his own time, downloaded his favorites. Each participant saw a slightly different billboard, shaped by the choices of those who came before. And each left a slightly different billboard behind for the person who happened to enter the room next.

The download counts allowed the teenagers to tap into the collective intelligence of their social world, helping them to zoom in on the best song. And it worked: in all eight non-control groups, a song floated to the top and stayed there, with amazing consistency. In other words, each group quickly agreed on which was the best song. There was a twist, however: while the agreement within each group was swift and definite, there was a remarkable disagreement *among* the groups. If we see the eight groups as parallel universes, each universe developed a vastly different taste in music. The favorite track in one—for example, "Lock Down," by 52 Metro—was pretty much unanimously despised in another. Once the teenagers were privy to the preferences of their peers, social influence warped their tastes, resulting in astounding unpredictability in outcomes.

If fitness were the only determinant of success, the best song would always win and success would be predictable. By now we know it's more complicated than that. Since performance is bounded, we've seen how difficult it is to pick the best from the best even for experts. But the MusicLab contenders weren't all necessarily excellent—there was swill mixed in with the cru—and yet the groups *still* couldn't reach consensus. In fact, the only aspect that was predictable among the virtual worlds was, well…how unpredictable the favorite song would be. The stronger the social influence, the more unpredictable the outcome. Listeners took whatever song appeared to be the early crowd favorite and doubled down on it. The song's inherent worth appeared to have little to do with the outcome.

•

Success in the MusicLab became, in other words, a self-fulfilling prophecy, a term Robert Merton coined in 1948 to describe gaps in educational achievement. African-Americans,

Latinx, and students of other underrepresented groups, he argued, were disadvantaged from the get-go by a *"false* definition of the situation evoking a new behavior that makes the originally false conception come *true."* Twenty years later, a dramatic experiment proved how powerful self-fulfilling prophecies are.

The experiment took place at the Oak School, an elementary school in a lower-middle-class neighborhood in San Francisco. All the children from first to sixth grade were given what was called the Harvard Test of Inflected Acquisition, an official-sounding name, and each teacher received the names of the students in their classrooms who had scored in the top 20 percent on the test. These were the students expected to show special progress in the coming year. At the end of the school year, the children took the test again. Sure enough, the 20 percent for whom the test predicted the greatest intellectual growth did exceptionally well, improving their IQ scores far more than the children who did not make the list. The Harvard Test was an astounding success, accurately pinpointing the students who would excel.

Except...*there is no such a thing as the Harvard Test.* Sure, the kids did take a test at the beginning of the year, but it was a standard IQ test. Most important, the researchers never used the results of the IQ test. Rather, the kids on the lists provided to the teachers were chosen entirely at random. The Harvard Test was bogus. But what wasn't bogus was this: *The 20 percent of first and second graders who'd been labeled "gifted" did indeed excel spectacularly on the IQ test they took at the end of the school year.*

By claiming that a child showed greater aptitude on an assessment test than his or her classmates, the researchers changed the teachers' *perception* of that child's abilities. The students had no clue of their gifted status and went about their school day as always. They raised their hands eagerly or stared off into space in the back of the classroom. They handed in homework or offered excuses. They loved school or hated it. But the perception of their hidden abilities, based on false test scores, created a self-fulfilling prophecy, resulting in higher teacher expectation. The teachers expected brilliance from the selected kids, so they encouraged brilliance. The children responded by *producing* brilliance.

•

Self-fulfilling prophecies suggest that, under the right circumstances, the weakest students or the weakest songs can land at the top. But can a false belief in a person or a product's value lead to lasting success? Or are we bound to notice, sooner or later, that the emperor has no clothes? Two years after the original experiment, the MusicLab went back to the drawing board, hoping to address this precise question.

As if mimicking the Oak School experiment, the researchers deliberately deceived the new participants—some 10,000 young people. Songs that had been frequently downloaded in the control group were given low download counts, and the most unpopular ones were labeled as the top songs. In other words, they created the false impression that the least downloaded song was the peer favorite.

Now the teenagers entered a world where, unbeknownst to them, the billboard was turned upside down, indicating that everyone before them not just liked but *loved* a certain song. The hesitation they experienced in this moment is a familiar one. A trendy new gadget comes on the market—those hand-held milk frothers that were all the rage a decade ago come to mind—and despite its uselessness, everyone wants one. Or a terrible TV sitcom hooks our friends, who can't stop talking about it. "Am I crazy?" we wonder. "Did I miss something? Let me look again. Perhaps on second thought…"

The new experiment imitated, albeit on a larger scale, Rowling's experiment. Books and songs alike benefit from *reputation signaling:* If you know the author or the singer, you're excited about her book or album. If you don't, you're largely indifferent. Reputation signaling is, of course, everywhere. A high-status winery charges more than a low-status vineyard for wines of equivalent quality, despite the fact that—as Hodgson's research shows us—status in winemaking is premised on a flawed system. Notre Dame's football team, the most storied in the history of college football, nets a coveted bowl invitation virtually every year, even when the team's performance is questionable. High-status investment banks charge more for financial products no different from those of their peers. And it happens in science: when a prominent researcher is accidentally omitted from the list of coauthors, a paper is less likely to be accepted for publication.

By deceiving participants about their peers' preferences, the MusicLab could follow what happens when reputation signals get crossed. Sure enough, the flipped billboard was lethal for the good tracks, and bad songs benefited from the inversion.

Social influence is essential for human survival. It's probably what kept us from eating the poisonous mushrooms again and again, or getting too friendly with a tiger. For good reason, our judgments are cued by the views and experiences of those in our social orbit. We use our peers' opinions to evaluate everything from brands of ice cream to works of art. If a product is well liked, we assume it's superior. If it's disliked, we assume it stinks. Popularity breeds popularity, just as success breeds success.

But the MusicLab's most fascinating discovery emerges from one of the experiment's more peculiar findings: in rare cases, *exceptional fitness can defy social influence.* Indeed, the control group's favorite—a song called "She Said," by Parker Theory—made a remarkable comeback. The teenagers faced with an inverted chart saw it at the bottom initially, but then its download numbers crept up. Soon after the billboard was inverted, "She Said" began a slow but steady climb from the lowest rung on the ladder. With time, preferential attachment sent it scurrying toward the top. Like a "pulled up by the bootstraps" fable, *despite being the most penalized contender,* it got back on track in the race. "She Said" shows how strong performance can recover from adverse social influence and rise in triumph, as predictably buoyant as oil floating on vinegar.

The recovery of "She Said" tells us that preferential attachment, the engine that drives the "success breeds success" dynamic encountered in the previous chapter, does not act in isolation when it comes to success. It works hand in hand with a product's fitness. "She Said" is an example of the *Third Law of Success:*

> *Previous success × fitness = future success.*

Fitness and the rich-get-richer phenomenon don't clash but are entangled, working together to influence our choices and affect our outcomes. *Crowds can push the merely good to unearned fame, but they'll rarely get wholeheartedly behind the terrible.* A false perception of popularity can boost a bad song, but it will never become a collective favorite. And when performance and preferential attachment harmonize, as they did in the case of "She Said," they create the perfect storm for success.

•

I first encountered the Third Law of Success about seven years before the MusicLab experiments, while trying to understand how Google, an unknown latecomer to the World Wide Web, became its biggest hub. From a theoretical perspective, Google's success didn't make sense. Preferential attachment consistently predicts that the most connected Web pages are those that have been around the longest. They've had more time to collect links, which gives them a seemingly permanent advantage over upstarts. And this is true more broadly. Let's say we're looking at surgeons. All things being equal, older surgeons will have a leg up on younger ones, because they've seen more patients, so they'll have more clients to recommend them. That makes it more likely that you, too, will end up in their operating room. Younger surgeons, lacking a roster of satisfied patients, will always start out in the shadow of their more experienced peers.

There are, however, prominent exceptions to this rule, and Google is one. When it arrived on the scene in 1997, most people were using search engines like Altavista and Yahoo's Inktomi. Within three years, though, Google was far ahead. Its success was so swift and absolute that its brand became a verb. So we kept wondering—how did Google start from the bottom and defy the considerable early-bird advantage of its gigantic competitors? Looking more closely at the data, we soon discovered that there are many Google-like rampantly successful latecomers in any market, companies that acquire market share at an exceptional rate in spite of their relative youth. There's Boeing, for example, an upstart that disrupted the airline industry. There's Zantac, an ulcer drug that obliterated its competition. Sam Adams brought a microbrew taste to beer drinkers everywhere. How did each defy the first movers already turbocharged by preferential attachment?

Well, it was simple, really. They found success because their products had unique, intrinsic qualities that helped them overcome the handicap of their obscurity. A search engine that pointed users to more relevant sites. A more efficient and reliable plane. A superior drug. A better-tasting beer. Not only could they compete with the dinosaur hubs, they—spryer and more fit to the task at hand—could *outcompete* them.

So, to understand how these latecomers became the hubs they are now, we needed to assign each node an intrinsic characteristic that reflected its superiority. We named this property "fitness," borrowing a term from evolution. It was an apt choice. Because fitness doesn't exactly equal "quality," though it certainly depends on it. Instead of making value judgments, fitness allows us to capture a product's inherent ability to outcompete other products clamoring for the same buyers, audiences, or admirers. For example, few literary types see the Fifty Shades of Gray volumes as "quality" books. Yet we can't question their fitness, their ability to outcompete other, more literary options in the bookstore. Fitness helps us acknowledge that not all surgeons are equally good, just as not all websites are equally useful.

The Third Law, which tells us that future success is the product of fitness and previous success, helped us translate our instincts into the predictive language of math. The equation behind the law allowed us to foresee how a high-fitness node, arriving late to the game, would nevertheless become a major player. It worked spectacularly, accurately describing the rich competitive dynamics through which the pages on the World Wide Web acquire links.

Equally important, the Third Law showed us precisely *how* success and excellence, working in tandem, lead to dominance. The higher your fitness, the more links you'll proactively acquire each day, despite any obscurity you may start out with. A really good surgeon can perform an operation expertly, minimizing pain and improving the health of her patients. As she performs better, her recommendations grow more enthusiastic, and she attracts even more patients. The model showed us that if two nodes have the same fitness, the older nodes still have an advantage, just as a doctor with decades in practice will garner more patients than an equally good newbie. Yet, if two nodes have the same visibility, their fitness difference alone will decide who will collect more links.

If it's fitness that determines a product's ultimate success, then what happens when fitness is entwined with popularity, as the Third Law predicts? Can we ever observe a product's true value, removed from its *perceived* value?

•

The MusicLab experiment shows just how malleable our tastes are. That's not to say that we can't see the thoroughly lousy product in front of our noses, but when we're faced with multiple "good enough" options, since quality is bounded, we tend to concede our own judgment in favor of the crowd's. And once that happens, what becomes popular doesn't necessarily reflect a product's true superiority. And that's where the real problem lies. I want an *enjoyable* book, not a merely popular one. I want a *good* hotel, not a crowded one. Yet, as a consumer scrolling through Amazon, Hotels.com, or any other forum that relies on public opinion to rank products, popularity is usually all I have to go on. In the end, popularity and excellence become hopelessly intermingled, one masking the other. Could we ever hope to disentangle the two? Wouldn't it be helpful to know how good *The Cuckoo's Calling* really is, divorced from its author's reputation?

Well, it turns out that if we apply the Third Law to big data, we can.

Not long ago, I came across a paper by researchers at an Australian university that did exactly that, disentangling popularity from excellence. As I read their paper with increasing fascination, I spotted a familiar name among the authors: a Spanish network scientist named Manuel Cebrian. I'd met him years before when he applied to work as a postdoc in my lab. Though he was one of the best applicants, we didn't have the money to hire him. So he ended up across the river at MIT. There, he used network science to win the DARPA challenge, a race to locate ten red weather balloons scattered across the United States. Manuel eventually took a position in Australia, dropping out of sight for years. As soon as I realized that the paper was his, I sent him an e-mail with a long list of thoughts and questions. Given the fourteen-hour time difference between Sidney and Boston, I was hoping, at best, for an answer the next day.

To my happy surprise, a few hours later, Manuel—like a scholarly wizard in a Rowling novel—walked into my lab. He was in Boston for a few days and figured it'd be easier to answer my questions in person, he said, a big smile on his face, and then he did just that. And the more I learned, the more intrigued I became. He was showing me how to use the Third Law to boost success.

Manuel and his team had developed an algorithm to extricate popularity systematically from fitness. To show that it worked, they used it to find the gems in the MusicLab's rough. Take for example an excellent song like "Went with the Count," which had been ranked number two by the control group. But it was listed in the twenty-fifth position on the billboard when a dozen or so teenagers first came across it, a pretty low status. Despite its low ranking, a handful of them thought it was a terrific song, so they downloaded it to keep for themselves. This pushed "Went with the Count" a few positions higher on the billboard. Sometime later, as the billboard changed, another dozen or so teenagers encountered a lower-quality song in the twenty-fifth position. They dutifully listened to the song, but no one bothered to download it. The algorithm noticed the difference in download counts and boosted the fitness of "Went with the Count" while lowering the fitness of its rival. By monitoring, over and over, how many teenagers chose to download each song in its different positions on the billboard, the algorithm was collecting more and more data on every track's true fitness.

Manuel and his team could use each song's natural trajectory together with each teenager's choices to understand the herd dynamics as they played out over time, following the hoofprints in the data, if you will. In the end, their algorithm spit out a number for each song: its fitness. For example, it assigned the least downloaded song a very low fitness: 0.33. Contrast that with "Went with the Count," the number two song in the control, which had a fitness of 0.43. According to the algorithm, "She Said," the crowd favorite, had a fitness of 0.54. In other words, Manuel could set aside the volatile role of social influence, unveiling the inherent competitiveness of each track.

Once you can identify superior products, the real question is this: How should you rank songs, books, or any other products on your website so that people find what *they* want? If you do it right, displaying at the top the products that genuinely excite consumers, they're more likely to pull out their credit cards and make a purchase. So, should you rank products based on popularity? Or should you ignore social influence altogether, listing songs by their inherent fitness? The answer is unequivocal: Show us the good stuff! When songs were ordered by popularity, the teenagers downloaded about five thousand altogether. The same number of participants shown a list ranked by fitness, though, downloaded as many as seven thousand songs. That's a *40 percent increase*, reflecting just how compelling excellence is. Teenagers who encountered a list that was relevant to them were far more likely to click the download button than those shown the merely popular songs.

By looking over the teenagers' shoulders as they browsed

the MusicLab, Manuel and his colleagues could unearth the precious gems, identifying songs that would become hits. Let me say that again. *They could predict hits.* That's pretty astonishing when we think of the myriad Kate Millses out there — experts in their fields who, relying entirely on their "gut" to sift through manuscripts on their overloaded desks, regularly pass on potential blockbusters. The same goes for all of us, sifting through Amazon's infinite list of offerings, trying to find a good read. Could we use the Third Law to help us weigh our options?

Remember Dashun Wang, the graduate student in my lab whose initial project prompted our forays into the Science of Success? After getting his Ph.D., Dashun joined IBM, where he helped create an algorithm that separated each product's fitness from the herding dynamics that usually play out when we make book purchases. Talk about big data: he used 28 million consumer ratings accumulated over seventeen years of Amazon sales, untangling, in real time, the dynamics dictated by the Third Law. To put his findings into a familiar form, he translated the fitness of each product into the five-star rating that Amazon patrons use to rank products. Using an algorithm not all that different from Manuel's, he identified the true number of stars each product should have if social influence didn't play a role. Once he did this, he could look at how the stars were skewed by social influence.

His findings are deeply counterintuitive. *The more ratings a product had, the more its final rating differed from its true fitness.* That doesn't really make sense, right? You'd think that as each new person offers an evaluation, he or she would balance out both angry voices and overly positive paid ones, pushing us closer to an honest "average" response.

You know that game where kids are asked to guess how many M&M's are in a jar? The more people we query, the closer we get to the true number—but only if you don't tell the kids what others guessed. The same is true on Amazon. The more people who weigh in on the ratings, the less the result will reflect the true fitness of the product. It's social influence all over again. You bought that coffeemaker, and you have your reservations. If you're fair, it's a three-star machine. You sit down to write your review, and you see only five stars before you. Fine; it's really four stars, you decide. In an odd way, on Amazon the consensus is irrelevant. Often, it's the *first reviews*, unaffected by peers, that best capture a product's true fitness.

Dashun's and Manuel's findings could have enormous implications for online marketplaces going forward. By analyzing patterns in crowd behavior and honing methods of gauging fitness—or at least extricating it from popularity—the market can effectively use collective intelligence so that the cream always rises to the top. In time, similar models will shape success in a wide range of fields, from fundraising to electoral victories. In the not-far-off future, we'll find a new barber or hair salon in much the same way we did before, by hopping online and comparing the rankings of barbers or salons in the area. But instead of being guided toward what's popular, we'll be guided toward what's intrinsically valuable.

Once we know how significant herd dynamics are in shaping even choices that seem unimportant—which article we read, which song we listen to, which Facebook post we see—we must question the premise that popular opinion will always push us toward the best products. And we can bring that framework to the bigger choices in life—which candidate to vote for, which school to attend, which community to live in. In the end, if something really matters to us, there are no shortcuts. We need to invest the time and *make our own choices*, independent of the crowd. Because if the Third Law tells us anything, it's that popularity doesn't mean nearly as much about a product's fitness as we hope it does. Sure, this difference might not matter if we read a mediocre book or watch a low-quality TV show. But it *does* matter if we choose a college, or a doctor, or a candidate for office merely because other people seem to think they're good.

And here's one solid application for the Third Law: encourage independent decision making at your workplace. Instead of doing a "show of hands" at the end of a meeting, have people vote privately, via e-mail, on issues of importance. Remember how the first few reviews on Amazon best reflect the true fitness of a product? Those are the reviews least shaped by social influence. Let your colleagues step out of the herd, voicing their honest opinions.

•

At first glance, the MusicLab experiment suggests that Rowling's amazing career is more a fluke of history than a direct outcome of her genius. "Had things turned out only slightly different, the real Rowling might have met with the same success as the fake Robert Galbraith, not the other way around," wrote Duncan Watts, one of the MusicLab researchers. "As hard as it is to imagine in the Harry Potter–obsessed world that we now inhabit, it's entirely plausible that in this parallel universe, *Harry Potter and the Sorcerer's Stone* would just be a 'perfectly good' book that never sold more than a handful of copies; Rowling would still be a struggling single mother in Manchester, England; and the rest of us would be none the wiser."

This conclusion makes complete sense if we take the MusicLab experiments at face value. After all, in each of the eight universes, a different *Harry Potter*–like runaway success floated to the top and reinforced the dictates of preferential attachment: it's success that breeds success; fitness and performance are missing from the picture. The Third Law forces us to refine The Formula: when a product has fitness *and* previous success, its *long-term success* is determined by fitness alone. To put it in Darwinian terms, the fittest survives — the best song, the most reliable company, the superior technology. In other words, the Third Law echoes the First Law: when performance is measurable or discernible, it drives success. Working in tandem with popularity, fitness guides our choices in the long run.

The catch, though, is the part about the "long run." Sure, even in a crowded field, the best product or performer will always gain one more vote, one more buy, or one more endorsement, increasing its popularity faster than the low-fitness ones. If we wait long enough, the best will inevitably climb toward the top, just as "She Said" did. But interestingly, after the MusicLab inverted its billboard, "She Said" didn't actually reach the summit. It certainly was headed in that direction, but it would have taken more time — thousands more young people nudging it up, download by download—for the song's fitness to let it completely beat out the handicap of its obscurity.

That's also true of most products and performances: in a competitive market, time is a luxury we don't often have. A new book gains most of its readers in the first few weeks after its release; a research paper receives most of its citations in the first two years after its publication; a start-up has six months to show its worth or it will lose its angel's backing. Products, people, and ideas must demonstrate their value in an incredibly short window of time or they perish. Given these trends, wouldn't Rowling—facing, as all authors do, a minuscule window for success—be doomed to obscurity in an alternative universe?

This is where Duncan and I differ: the success of *Harry Potter* wasn't a fluke. Sure, I found all seven volumes utterly transporting, but putting my admiration aside, *Harry Potter*'s slow rise from rags to riches is one of the best illustrations of the Third Law I can think of. Indeed, even after *Harry Potter* found a publisher after a dozen rejections, it was *still* no immediate success. In June 1997, when it was published in the UK, the initial print run of the first volume was a mere five hundred copies, three hundred of which were sent to libraries at no cost. That's about as lowly a beginning as it gets. What happened next is precisely what the Third Law predicts for a high-fitness but low-visibility product: the book built an audience one reader at a time. When the first reviews came in, the read was described as "a hugely entertaining thriller." As one reviewer put it, "I have yet to find a child who can put it down." One endorsement at a time, preferential attachment began to kick in.

When the American edition was published in September 1998, we saw, once again, the Third Law in action. The media largely ignored the book. A full year had to pass for *Harry Potter* to build enough of an audience to reach the *New York Times* Best Seller list. But when the book finally reached the top of the list in August 1999, it stayed near the summit for almost a year and a half. Only when the *Times* split the list into separate children's and adult sections did *Harry Potter* finally get dethroned. The move came under pressure from publishers desperate to see their books at the top of a list that had been hijacked by a wizard child.

•

Examples of the Third Law are everywhere; enjoy the fun of how often you'll now spot them. There's an excellent one that's likely as close as your freezer. In 1977, when Ben Cohen and Jerry Greenfield opened an ice-cream shop in a refurbished gas station, making and selling ice cream was already big business in the United States. But the ice cream you could buy in the store was mass-produced paste with boring flavors, full of chemicals and corn syrup. Ben and Jerry, best friends and self-described hippies, had never made ice cream, but they were convinced they could do better. They also had an idea. Ben had trouble smelling things and relied on visuals and mouthfeel when he ate. What if they mixed chunks of interesting flavors into the ice cream, making the experience more rewarding? They agreed the notion was worth a try, so they enrolled in a correspondence course, spending five dollars apiece to learn the craft.

Then they invested $12,000 more to build the business.

They used quality ingredients, churned the ice cream themselves, and dreamed up creative flavors with unusual names. With a hand-painted sign that read "Ben & Jerry's Homemade," and handcrafted scoops, the shop's aesthetic emphasized what made the company unique: the ice cream wasn't just delicious, it was handmade. And among their initial offerings was Cherry Garcia, a pale pink ice cream studded with fruit and dark chocolate chunks that became a hit right away.

As we've seen, however, putting out an excellent product isn't enough. The founders must have sensed that when, on the one-year anniversary of their shop's launch, they chose to hand out free cones. They needed to kick-start preferential attachment. Free cones! Who wouldn't line up? And when that proffered treat was delicious, swirled with unusual flavors, the ice cream's value seemed to skyrocket.

The ploy worked, but only over time. In a slow Third Law–style development, Ben & Jerry's became a sensation in Vermont. Then in 1981, the brewing enthusiasm finally crossed the state line after *Time* magazine put a cone on its cover, calling Ben & Jerry's "the world's best ice cream."

Ben and Jerry harnessed the magic in the Third Law, channeling the same spell Rowling incanted. But, while it's tempting to focus on the deliciousness of the ice cream to explain the company's journey from revamped gas station to billion-dollar company, there's more to it than that. Fitness *and preferential attachment* were both necessary. Drop either and Ben & Jerry's wouldn't be the runaway success we know today.

Doing so would also undercut an even more important

element in the company's feats: the teamwork that generated the ice cream to begin with.

Team success is the topic of the next law. As we'll see, understanding how these laws fit into the framework of our own lives is one thing. But we rarely work alone, so examining the team dynamics behind blockbuster products is crucial. The addictive quality in a cone of Cherry Garcia? That came from a specific mix of talents suited to the task, a duo who perfectly blended preferential attachment and fitness through an ice-cream machine to achieve their dream. The melding of two creative minds is what allowed Ben Cohen and Jerry Greenfield to create a Big Rock Candy Mountain of decadence, a tie-dye swirl of strange and wonderful offerings, a Willy Wonka fantasy world we now consume by the spoonful.

While team success requires diversity and balance, a single individual will receive credit for the group's achievements.

It's a law embodied by chickens and soccer players—who show us how all-star teams are bound to fail—and by jazz musicians, Broadway hit makers, and call-center representatives, who help us strategize to maximize group success. A van driver overlooked for a Nobel Prize serves as a cautionary tale: a lot can go wrong when we let the community assign credit.

8

Kind of Conventional, Kind of Innovative, *Kind of Blue*

The Importance of Balance, Diversity, and Leadership

On March 2, 1959, five musicians handpicked by Miles Davis entered Columbia Records' Thirtieth Street Studio for an all-day session. Some were meeting for the first time. They'd had only a vague briefing of the music they were about to record. A few sketches of scales and melody lines had been provided in advance, but that was all the preparation they'd had. Once they assembled in the soundproof studio with instruments at the ready, Davis, a cigarette dangling from his lips, gave brief instructions. Then they started the track that would become "So What"—a few melancholic bass lines, soft drumming, and a piano bobbing along delicately before trumpet and sax chime in.

The product of this session, *Kind of Blue*, captured the tension that comes from spontaneous collaboration. The sound—at once cool, swingy, melodic, and emotionally

175

fraught—was thoughtfully curated by Davis. The fiftieth-anniversary rerelease of the album reveals his occasional terse feedback to his team. He was a stickler for structural precision. But he also enabled wild improvisation within the prescribed framework. Building on his own experience of playing in a range of genres from bebop to blues, Davis created an album that continues to sound fresh now, six decades later, to both seasoned jazz players and a broad audience.

Davis's thoughtfully curated group of musicians improvising under his guidance made *Kind of Blue* the most enduring jazz album ever recorded. Since its initial release in 1959, it's been rereleased 118 times. That's an unheard-of success in a niche genre. Most important, *Kind of Blue* defined jazz for generations as a point of entry, a source of continued inspiration, a gold standard. In other words, the album is a masterpiece.

There are multiple theories about why *Kind of Blue* has been such an enduring success. They always start with Davis's quiet but pointed leadership during the recording process. Bill Evans, the pianist, remained convinced that the secret was the simplicity of the charts and the vagueness of the instructions that Davis gave his band: "Play this pretty," he would say. Or he'd point to someone and say, "*You* play this note." "You play *this* note," he'd instruct someone else. But there's also Davis's left-field choice to bring an unexpected mix of musicians together, handpicking a unique sound from disparate parts. For those of us studying success, *Kind of Blue* is a fascinating experiment in team building that prompts us to ask, how can we follow in Davis's footsteps and assemble a team poised for success?

• • •

That's the kind of question that intrigues Brian Uzzi. A professor at the Kellogg School of Management at Northwestern, he studies team dynamics and the roots of group creativity. If you ran into him in a bar, you'd probably never guess he's a star professor at one of the top business schools in the world. With long, unruly hair, he typically sports a leather jacket and multiple large silver rings on both hands. He looks like a rock star who would be more comfortable on a Harley than in a buttoned-up suit in a corporate boardroom. A master of messaging, he's not sending mixed signals, though—he *does* own a Harley, and he plays bass in a rock band. But wait until he starts sharing his research in an unmistakable New York accent and you'll realize how deceiving appearances can be. He's the most persuasive lecturer I've ever encountered.

Over the past decade, Brian has energized the Science of Success with his relentless investigation of how teams work, when they excel, and when they are doomed to failure. He calls his work "team science," and it's a journey that started with an unlikely topic: Broadway musicals. Like jazz, the musical is a distinctively American art form, full of complex collaborative artistry. Brian examined the public's response to musicals by using both profit and critical reception as his metrics. In studying the creative networks behind every Broadway production, he located the sweet spot for team success.

When we watch a show, we tend to focus on the stars. After all, they're doing all the work as they embody the characters and tell the story. But the truth is, the stars are largely irrelevant to the success of a Broadway musical, as their ever-evolving casts can attest. Rather, a show's success depends on

177

six key collaborators: a composer, a lyricist, a librettist, a choreographer, a director, and a producer. They work in tandem to build the story, music, and dance elements; they choose the actors and the venue. A musical might start with a choreographer like Martin Hamlisch, who envisions the dance elements, as happened with *A Chorus Line*. Hamlisch then recruited the five other indispensable team members who together created a box office hit that won nine Tony Awards. Or it might start with a librettist like Mel Brooks, who writes the dialogue and plot, as happened with *The Producers*. Brooks then brought in a director, a producer, and his counterparts in music and dance to develop the show. *The Producers* was another blockbuster, running for 2,502 performances and winning a record-breaking twelve Tony Awards. If any one of these elements misses the mark—if the script stinks, or the songs aren't catchy, or the dance numbers don't wow—no matter whom you put up onstage, it flops.

"There's no business like show business," goes Irving Berlin's famous song, reminding us that musicals are commercial undertakings. A successful hit can rake in millions for its investors. Yet if a show is too "out there," straying too far from the mainstream, it doesn't sell tickets. And if the result is too conventional, it's panned by critics, scaring the audience away.

The Broadway data that Brian and his colleagues analyzed was fascinating and conclusive. They looked at the careers of over two thousand creative contributors who were collectively responsible for 474 musicals, just about anything you've seen on Broadway. Roughly fifty of these musicals died in preproduction. And more than half were flops, failing to turn a profit. In fact, only 23 percent made money. But, in classic Second Law style, those that did turn a profit saw unbounded success, raking in both recognition and money.

A hit requires convention *and* innovation. Teams must elaborate on familiar themes and approaches in order to create something new. Here's an example. When Rodgers and Hammerstein developed the music for the 1945 hit *Carousel*, they were adapting the 1909 Ferenc Molnár play *Liliom*, which was an utter failure when debuted in its original Hungarian. Rodgers and Hammerstein not only transported the show from Budapest to the Maine coast, they did something wholly new in the context of musicals. Instead of waiting until the lead characters fall in love to introduce a memorable romantic song, they included several love songs right from the start, an innovation that worked within the constraints of the genre. In *Carousel*, even before meeting each other, the characters sing wistfully about hoped-for love. With that simple innovation, the duo maximized the kind of wide-eyed romance that audiences sought from a Broadway show. And the tweak worked. While Molnár's *Liliom* was a failure, *Carousel* was an immediate critical and box office hit, running for 890 performances and multiple revivals. In 1999, *Time* named *Carousel* the best musical of the twentieth century.

In working collaboratively, Rodgers and Hammerstein struck an important balance, too. Rodgers was a cynic about love, bringing acidity to tunes that could have been sweet. Hammerstein was a romantic, and his solo writing could occasionally be too saccharine. Together, the duo harmonized their talents. It was a collaboration helped by their friendship. A few years prior, while working on *Oklahoma!*,

179

they'd developed a deep personal trust that they brought to their shared creative work.

Brian discovered, though, that a Rodgers and Hammerstein musical would be doomed to failure if the other members of the creative team were as closely bonded as the two composers. Such tightly knit "small worldiness" usually resulted in shows that critics found derivative and audiences avoided. The other extreme was just as bad: if creative teams were too loosely linked, they struggled to produce crowd-pleasing material. Success on Broadway, it turns out, requires a careful balance between convention and innovation, which is best offered by a specific mix of collaborators.

•

Balázs Vedres, a Science of Success researcher and my colleague at the Central European University in Budapest, is as passionate about jazz as Brian is about musicals. Just like Brian, he plays the bass in a band. And like Brian, he is a sociologist, bringing a similar perspective to the study of how collaborations shape success. In examining the entire history of jazz—or more than 100,000 published sessions from the 1890s to 2010—Balázs found a direct relationship between the diversity of contributors to an album and its success, measured by the number of times the album is rereleased.

Balázs identified comparable dynamics in video game development, where teams work in ever-evolving configurations to produce innovative material. Like Broadway musicals and jazz tunes, video games must strike a careful balance between innovation and conformity. They need to be familiar enough so that they're navigable. But they must also bring something new to the table to attract an audience. For these reasons, teams that produce successful games tend to combine career histories that span pretty much every area of game development. Crucially, though, for a team to succeed, some of its members must overlap, bridging diversity with shared experiences and close-knit relationships. Multiplicity — of newcomers and incumbents, tried-and-true friends and distant acquaintances collaborating for the first time — is crucial for team success.

These are concepts I use every day to move science forward in my lab. Indeed, the challenges facing science are too complex to be solved by a single individual. As Brian Uzzi has shown recently, the highest-impact papers in science are produced not by solo geniuses but by teams. That's information I take to heart, and it's not unheard of that I invite ten or twenty researchers to help advance one of our projects. Some do analytical calculations, others perform numerical simulations, and a dozen or so may work on the experimental confirmation. Diversity is there by default — students, postdocs, and professors must seamlessly collaborate to bring a project to fruition.

But diversity is not enough. The strong bond aspect is equally crucial. I try to pair a trusted hand — usually a postdoc who has written a paper or two with me — with a novice new to the lab. And there are always a few weak ties — outside experts whom we haven't worked with before who offer key insights or experimental support.

Still, no matter how I look at it, there's an issue here that isn't addressed in team research: leadership. It's my job to *lead* a lab. I can't just put the right people together and head off to Hawaii, keeping fingers crossed the team's genius will manifest itself. The team I assemble looks to me to decide what next steps to take and to establish what other evidence we need. Like it or not, I can't take myself out of the equation — I'm the final arbitrator of our progress. Which makes me wonder: How much is our success about my letting everyone improvise freely? How assertive should I be in my own role?

•

My understanding of how leadership plays out in a team setting was enriched by research done by James Bagrow, who was once a postdoc in my lab and now runs his own research group at the University of Vermont. Jim, as we called him, was a gentle master of dark humor who was quick to spot the half-empty glass. That made him ideally suited to disaster, the subject of the notorious project that was supposed to launch Dashun's career. Jim was, in fact, the first author on that infamous paper, and Dashun, new to the lab, served as his apprentice. And when the disaster paper went nowhere, Jim, too, was able to shrug and move on. He made a spectacular recovery, joining forces with two other postdocs and writing a brilliant paper on network communities. After a stint with Brian Uzzi at Northwestern, Jim's now a rising star in the burgeoning field of team science.

In a particularly interesting project, Jim explored an enormous data set from the computer-programming site GitHub, which allows users to collaborate on software projects. GitHub is a social-networking site for geeks, allowing software developers to follow one another's projects. It also collects rich layers of information on the activities of its members, including when new teams form, when members join existing teams, and when someone contributes a piece of code to a joint project. These collaborations evolve in an entirely self-organized manner, with team members often never meeting face-to-face. GitHub also offers tools that help users to discover relevant projects. Users, seeing the work of a particular team, can follow it if they find it interesting.

Jim gauged a team's success by counting how many other people follow a project. Like scientific citations, the follower counts captured how the larger community responded to the work. Jim deemed a project with a lot of followers successful, a project with only a few less so. Once again, success was highly lopsided: The vast majority of teams produced work that gathered little interest. Now and again, though, a rare team attracted enormous numbers of followers. In other words, GitHub followed the dictates of the Second Law, bestowing unbounded visibility on a few projects and virtually ignoring everyone else.

On GitHub, working in teams had clear advantages. Team projects were much more successful than solo projects. The larger the team, the more followers it had. Because GitHub also tracks the number of contributions each team member makes to a project, Jim could see who on a team was doing the bulk of the work. In other words, he could measure *individual performance*. When he analyzed the data, he saw something striking: Balance was nowhere to be seen. Instead, in many cases, the lion's share of the programming was being done by a *single team member*. And the bigger the team was, the harder that major contributor worked. In other words, each team had a naturally emerging leader. And as the number of team members increased, the more the leader dominated the team's output.

Such lopsided contributions are not unique to GitHub. Take, for example, the dozens, often *hundreds*, of editors who contribute to a single Wikipedia page. Just like GitHub, Wikipedia tracks the contributions of each editor, allowing us to see how evenly the work is distributed. Once again, effort is lopsided: Most editors do little, changing a word here or there, or maybe adding a snippet of new information. A few, however, do the heavy lifting, single-handedly creating and tirelessly editing most of the content. And we saw the same dynamic when we tracked how teams consisting of high school students conduct research in synthetic biology, aiming to engineer new functions in living organisms. They could make bacteria smell and yeast cells do math. But the bigger the team was, the more lopsided were the individual contributions to the final product.

Most important, in the case of GitHub, Jim found that the degree to which leaders were engaged with their team played a key role in the team's success. Those rare, runaway successes all had something in common, regardless of their programming aims: *The more they were dominated by a single leader, the more successful they were.*

•

"No grand idea was ever born in a conference," F. Scott Fitzgerald famously quipped. Jim's findings tell us that Fitzgerald wasn't quite right — grand ideas can be born from teamwork, but they must be sharpened and directed toward their best route to action by a single visionary. Diversity creates the best mix for success, but for that mix to be potent, it needs a leader. Indeed, the more successful a team is in the programming universe, the more lopsided the contributions are to the work. A single leader emerges who calls the shots and does most of the programming. To be sure, his fellow contributors also play a vital role, offering key expertise and filling in the holes. But it's the leader who makes the project whole, correcting individual errors, rejecting pieces he considers subpar, and ensuring that the final product matches his vision and standards.

But how much leadership is too much? If a single superstar like Davis can make such an enormous difference to a collaborative project, how much better would two, or even five, superstar talents do? At what point are there too many Julia Childs in the kitchen? That's a tricky question to answer if we're talking about human superstars. But it's a breeze with chickens.

William Muir studies animal breeding, specifically, how genes and selection work together to generate behavioral traits. He's a scientist and a professor, but he's also, basically, a chicken farmer. And, despite the colorfully illustrated children's books that lend a kind of kid-lit romance to the job, chicken farmers have one goal in mind: maximizing the egg-laying productivity of hens. Muir had cages and cages of birds to work with, and he took a passionate interest in how to selectively breed them. Some hens were just better layers than others. So Muir decided to use the most straightforward method he could think of: Take the best-laying hen from each cage, group them together, and breed them. In a few

185

generations, he presumed, he'd have a coop full of super chickens sitting on mountains of eggs. He'd have, in other words, an all-star team.

For the sake of comparison, Muir also identified his most productive cage. Not every chicken clucking away in this particular cage was a standout layer, but as a team they produced an impressive number of eggs. He put these hens in a cage side by side with his super chickens, and bred and rebred each group. The question was, of course, over time how much better would the super chickens do than the control group? So Muir let the hens breed for six generations—a standard procedure in animal science—and then, using the great-great-great-grandchildren of the original groups, he began tallying eggs.

When Muir presented his results at a scientific conference for the first time, he started with the control group. Six generations in, they were thriving. The chickens were not only plump and healthy, their collective egg production had increased by 160 percent. The experiment, in other words, was already a success: Muir demonstrated that by isolating and selectively breeding his best accidental team, that is, his most productive cage, he could dramatically increase the number of eggs his chickens laid. It also meant that his super chickens, selected for individual productivity, had a really high bar to reach.

When he got to the slides showing his superstar cage, though, the audience gasped. Six generations in, the descendants of his superstar hens didn't look at all like superstars. They looked like they'd been through hell and back. For starters, out of nine hens, only three remained. The missing six had been murdered by their surviving cage mates. And the three survivors were certainly not thriving, either. They were missing most of their feathers. Their tails were bouquets of broken quills. The exposed skin on their wings was pocked with scars. The cage had become a war zone. As far as Muir's experiment went, egg production was the least of their worries. Maimed and in distress from constant in-fighting, these hens didn't lay eggs.

Recalling examples from our own lives in which too much leadership results in the kind of bickering and backstabbing and bullying that brings out the worst in both avian and human nature is likely not difficult. There's the infamous example of Duke University, which in the late 1980s and early '90s, in hopes of creating the best English department in the world, decided to hire every literary superstar they could get their hands on. Needless to say, the result was far from what was envisioned. The department unraveled, a victim of warring critical theories, vastly different approaches to curriculum, and colliding personalities.

A 2014 study that examined the "too-much-talent" effect in professional sports found that in soccer and basketball, talent benefited teams, but only up to a point. Unsurprisingly, access to better talent resulted in more wins. Yet, when composed of too many outstanding players, teams suffered. In soccer and basketball, players heavily rely on one another, so having too many divas hurts cooperation and performance.

Chickens, English professors, and soccer players all tell the same story: when we handpick for talent, prioritizing individual accomplishment over team achievement, we rarely get the results we hope for. In fact, this approach to teamwork is counterproductive regardless of species: derailed by a desire for dominance, no one can focus on the task at hand.

As Jim Bagrow's research showed, leaders and heavy lifters are essential for team success. But too much leadership can be detrimental. Sometimes the reasons for failure are obvious. Egos clash and the eggs don't get laid. But perhaps more often, the roots of the failure are far subtler. Like whether a group of people can work intelligently as a team.

•

Intelligence tests, even with all their controversies, remain some of the most consistent predictors of academic and professional success. Measuring how well people memorize, retain, and process new information, these tests gauge a person's "general cognitive ability," or IQ. Nudging a neighbor for help would, of course, be cheating. Yet it would probably better reflect how we solve problems in the modern workplace. So Anita Williams Woolley, from Carnegie Mellon University, along with several colleagues at MIT, set out to answer a simple question: Could they measure the intelligence of a group of people working together? That is, can we measure "collective intelligence," capturing a team's ability to perform tasks as a whole?

They asked triads of strangers to complete simple tasks together: Generate a list of uses for a brick. Plan a trip to a grocery store. Play video checkers. Researchers recorded each member's actions as the groups searched for solutions. And their results debunked many expectations. For one, team members with high IQs didn't do any better on collective intelligence tests than their lower-IQ peers. In fact, individual intelligence didn't seem to matter much in the context of group performance. Neither did factors like the motivation level of group members or their individual satisfaction.

What *did* matter was how the test takers communicated. First, teams tended to do well if individuals in the group had higher-than-average ability to read emotional cues. Second, groups where a few people dominated the conversation had a lower collective intelligence than those with more equality among group members. In other words, the best teams were those whose members shared discussion time and listened to one another. The third key factor was a fascinating offshoot of the other two: teams with female members had higher collective intelligence.

Collective intelligence tests provide hard evidence that the ability of individual group members is not a key determinant of a team's performance. And since, these days, most consequential decisions are made by groups—whether to launch a new product or to pass a new law—there is clear benefit in harnessing collective intelligence effectively. A lot can go wrong when we don't. There's the Kennedy administration's Bay of Pigs fiasco. There's the Bush administration's painfully drawn-out and inadequate response to Hurricane Katrina. Or there's the 2002 collapse of Swissair, caused by a management team that believed so much in the company's financial stability that they nicknamed it "The Flying Bank." They're all examples of what I'd call collective stupidity. My colleagues call it groupthink, which, I'll grant, has a nicer ring. No matter how you brand it, groupthink emerges when teams become too cohesive and cliquish, striving for consensus around a single, flawed plan when they should be seeking

189

alternative solutions. Spotting collective stupidity after the fact is easy. Far more useful, however, would be to thoughtfully create teams that perform well, using science to avoid the pitfalls that can come from collaboration.

•

So, when we throw these insights into the mix, we see an important split in the way teams work. *Successful teams require balance and diversity. But they also need a leader.* In a world where teams are increasingly big and increasingly distant, team science offers precise recommendations for how to maximize their success. Trust someone to be in charge and build an expert, diverse support group around him or her. Without singular, visionary leadership, a team might do its job. But it's unlikely to experience the kind of breakthrough that will put a project on the map in indelible ink. Especially in areas where audience reception matters, the Miles Davises, the Oprah Winfreys, and the Jeff Bezoses are essential.

But let's remember that leadership alone won't suffice. Nor will the right mix of collaborators who bring diverse experiences, perspectives, and insights to the project. We need them both. Collective intelligence depends on team players who, working with the visionary, discuss and listen, allowing diverse perspectives to rise to the surface. The data shows us again and again that assembling and managing teams is a delicate science that can make or break a project.

In other words, for a team to succeed, it's not enough to have the "best" individual team members. In fact, as we've seen, an all-star team can put a project on a quick path to failure. What matters is that people are offered opportunities to build rapport and contribute in equal measure.

My colleague Sandy Pentland, a researcher at MIT's Media Lab, proved this unequivocally when, for six weeks, he turned a bank's call center into his laboratory. In addition to their regular headsets, employees now donned Sandy's specially designed electronic badges, which gathered information on everything from an employee's tone of voice to how often he or she spoke. The content of the conversations wasn't the point—in fact, it didn't matter at all. What the badges captured were underlying patterns of communication that aren't easy to measure otherwise.

The data showed that face-to-face communication between team members mattered tremendously to team performance. We're talking about the old-fashioned, informal kind of chit-chat, when people make eye contact, speak animatedly, share stories, take the time to laugh or ask questions or listen. E-mails and quick announcements at the start of a shift might be "to the point," but they provided little opportunity for discourse, gossip, and spontaneous problem solving. In fact, e-mail turned out to be the least valuable form of communication. It was *too efficient*. Chatting by the proverbial water-cooler—lost time from the manager's perspective—is what really mattered. What looked like wasted time was actually employees doing important work, strengthening rapport through fluid communication. Odder still, given the strict edicts of middle school teachers everywhere, the research suggested that managers should *encourage* side chat and back-channel conversations during meetings. This helped build harmony between team members, helped people quickly clarify issues, and created space for creativity to flourish.

Remember, this is a call center where we, the impatient callers-in, demand extreme efficiency. If a team could successfully shave even *thirty seconds* off every call, those of us on the other side of the line would greatly appreciate it. And the saved time would mean huge savings for the bank, too. So, on Sandy's recommendation, the bank manager defied his industry's practice of staggering breaks to maximize efficiency. Instead, he provided collective breaks hoping that, while sipping coffee and chatting, employees would increase the number of interactions they had with other team members, diversify whom they communicated with, and feed off one another's energy and experience.

The idea worked, spectacularly. These more "human" person-to-person moments *improved the average call-handling time by 8 percent overall and by an astonishing 20 percent in lower-performing teams.* The approach flew in the face of conventional business practices, yet it made a tremendous difference to everyone waiting out in the world as the minutes ticked by. An added benefit was the creation of a work environment that was measurably more collegial.

Taken together, the new approach made a tremendous difference to the bank's bottom line: these minimal adjustments, implemented across all teams, led to an estimated $15 million a year in productivity increases.

The importance of balance and diversity goes well beyond call centers. Indeed, Sandy went on to document the same dynamics in groups of innovators, post-op staff in hospitals, bank tellers, marketing departments, and backroom operations crews. Teams that communicated with true esprit de corps tended to be more productive, and those that found a balance between engagement within their group and engagement with parties outside their group were more creative. Seeking fresh perspective and insight from diverse individuals appears to be crucial for team performance.

And here's one more surprising finding: Instead of hosting an out-of-work happy hour to encourage team building, invest in longer lunchroom tables. Sitting next to someone unexpected halfway through the workday offers an opportunity to recognize common challenges and to engage fresh perspectives. Apparently sharing a beer with colleagues after work doesn't have the same impact, since people remain glued to familiar cliques at the bar.

Perhaps most important for managers and administrators interested in maximizing teamwork, the researchers consistently found that making people aware of their communication dynamics leads to measurable improvements. By mapping the network of interactions visually, bosses might realize that they're dominating meetings, introverted employees can realize that they're not stepping outside their comfort zones, and team members can recognize that they're not using one another thoughtfully. And in a culture where many employees dislike their jobs, improved communication is a win for everyone.

•

It's not a coincidence that Davis's undisputed masterpiece was recorded by experienced musicians who had never before played as a team. When Balázs Vedres mapped the relationships between the players on the album, he discovered that Davis was not just a brilliant musician, he was also a brilliant team builder. He intuited everything that team science was to discover a half century later: That assembling a group of players required deft balance. That when musicians were too close-knit or too disparate the albums they produced were consistently unsuccessful. The diversity necessary for positive reception was about relationships. Simply throwing a bunch of unexpected instruments together in an effort to create an experimental sound, for instance, actually hampered success. Instead, Balázs showed that stylistic diversity achieved through diverse collaborations mattered to an album's reception more than anything else. Difference made a difference.

Orchestrating success is a delicate balancing act, one at which Davis was exceptionally good. He brought together "forbidden triads," a network science term capturing when two people share a common, strong tie—like your sister and your boss, who both have a strong tie with you, but who aren't directly linked to each other. When Davis invited the pianist Wynton Kelly to record on the track "Freddie Freeloader," he'd never played a session with Kelly before. It might have been fatal to take on an outsider. But Kelly had played several sessions with at least two other musicians in the group, so his presence brought both familiarity and freshness to Davis's carefully curated mix.

Kind of Blue and Balázs's comprehensive study of jazz albums tell us there's a "sweet spot" for team success: spontaneous contributions of a group's diverse contributors, yet with the direction of a singular leader. If Davis had given each of his band members an equal share in the album's direction, for example, *Kind of Blue* would almost surely not have become jazz's most iconic record. Like chicken coops crowded with dominant egg layers, given free rein our talented jazz musicians would have left a mangled carcass behind in the recording studio.

But here's the strange part: You'll recall Miles Davis as the standout name, as the owner and maestro of the album. Fair enough. His genius put the whole thing together. But isn't that...strange? Because *five other world-class talents* played with heart and soul, helping make *Kind of Blue* a runaway success.

Remember that guy who'd show up late to meetings and yet somehow managed to become the boss? Time to reckon with him and his lot.

9

The Algorithm That Found the Overlooked Scientist

It's About Perception, Not Performance

I first learned about Douglas Prasher three years ago, when an algorithm we'd just developed made an unpredictable prediction: he should have been a recipient of the 2008 Nobel Prize.

Instead, the award had been given to three other scientists. Even more surprising was our inability to find Prasher anywhere. He wasn't on the faculty at any university. We couldn't locate him at an industrial research lab. In fact, as we started digging for him, we realized that he hadn't written a research paper in nearly a decade. It was truly puzzling. This fellow, who, according to our algorithm, deserved a *Nobel Prize*, had seemingly disappeared off the face of the earth.

We often view science as the quest of the lonely genius, with Marie Curie laboring long nights in the lab, or Newton and Einstein mulling deep thoughts under an apple tree or in a lonely patent office. But today research is typically done in teams whose members work in collaboration, with each member offering his or her unique expertise. That makes our habit of honoring exceptional scientists antiquated. Major prizes like the Nobel are oriented toward individual accomplishments, twentieth century–style. A Nobel Prize can be awarded to no more than three recipients, complicating credit allocation in an era when solo papers are basically unheard of and collaboration is increasingly important. As we mentioned in the previous chapter, since the 1990s, the highest-impact discoveries have not been made by solo geniuses but rather by large teams. So how does the Nobel Committee decide whom, among myriad contributors, to honor with a prize?

That's a question that's not limited to science, of course. In most situations involving teamwork, bonuses are given to some, promotions and raises to others, while most team members go unnoticed. Especially when we take an egalitarian approach to teamwork, as we increasingly do, we risk blurring the roles of the contributors and confusing how we dole out reward.

●

In 2013, Hua-Wei Shen, an accomplished computer scientist from Beijing, joined my lab. Though new to the team, he was intimately familiar with our work. In addition to running a network science lab at his own university, he had also translated my previous book, *Bursts*, into Chinese. He eagerly joined our small but growing "success group." Each time we begin a new project, we start with a journal club—a reading group that surveys the current scientific literature to understand what is being done in a particular area. Each of us reads a batch of papers and summarizes key findings for the rest of the lab. Given that a million papers are published each year, this is the only way we've found to explore the vast body of knowledge out there.

At one of these journal clubs, Hua-Wei presented a sociology paper that investigated credit allocation in science. As we discussed the issue, we realized how bizarre our profession's credit protocols are. You have to be an insider to understand the nuances. Take, for example, the paper that reported the discovery of W and Z particles, which was authored by 137 scientists. Who walked away with the Nobel? The 105th and 126th authors, Carlo Rubbia and Simon van der Meer, of course. Somehow, the Nobel Committee manages to sort out who did what and who deserves the lion's share of the credit, no matter where an author's name lies. But how exactly?

As we discussed our profession's strange process of credit allocation in our journal club, I challenged Hua-Wei. If the Nobel Committee could select the deserving scientist from among more than a hundred authors, why couldn't we?

Hua-Wei jumped on the problem, and within a few weeks, he'd developed an algorithm that, like a compass pointing north, located every Nobel Prize winner from extensive lists of contributing scientists with an ease that seemed almost magnetic. Regardless of whether the winner was in physics, where authors are sometimes listed alphabetically, or in biology, where a team's leader is usually the last named, we could correctly foresee who would win. We were amazed by the algorithm's accuracy. With remarkable ease, the program not only agreed with the Nobel's decision to select Rubbia and Van der Meer from among 135 authors, it was also able to do the same for all Nobel-winning papers in the past thirty years, without having to read any of them.

There were only a few cases where our algorithm and the Nobel Committee disagreed. And they were all juicy cases, stories of misallocated credit that created discord in the community and prompted concerns from the prizewinners themselves. One of those cases was particularly intriguing: Mysteriously, the algorithm kept insisting, like a GPS gone haywire because of a road closure, that the 2008 Nobel in chemistry should go to Douglas Prasher. The problem was, Douglas Prasher appeared to have disappeared off the face of the earth.

Until…we found him. No, he wasn't hiding out in a clandestine government facility. Nor was he behind the firewall of a secretive, high-tech company. He was living in Huntsville, Alabama, driving a courtesy van at a Toyota dealership. The van that, you know, gives customers a ride back to work when they drop their cars off for a day in the shop.

What happened? Finding the answer required some detective work.

Prasher was the first scientist to clone GFP, a luminous protein that makes jellyfish shine in the dark depths of the ocean. In essence, GFP is a tiny flashlight that researchers can attach to any protein, so when we inspect proteins under the microscope we can see exactly when they are produced, where they travel in a cell, and how and when they disappear. GFP is "a guiding star for biochemistry," claimed the Nobel Foundation when it announced its award.

Prasher was the first to see GFP's potential. He had been

elbow-deep in the gelatinous muck of jellyfish carcasses as a young researcher, long before anyone considered them worthwhile to study. He didn't just get his hands dirty, capturing the jellyfish using pool-skimming nets and extracting their bioluminescent proteins by the bucketful. He also built vast libraries of jellyfish DNA from frozen hand-harvested tissues. Most important, he was the first researcher to identify the gene encoding the particular light-emitting proteins that are used today in medical research. And, fully aware of the enormous potential of the fluorescent gene he'd discovered, Prasher even figured out a way to extract the material from the jellyfish and then clone it.

Today, virtually all molecular biology labs depend on his discovery. If you want to explore how tumors grow cancerous tissues, if you want to understand how the brain of a mouse works when it navigates a maze, or if you want to develop the next drug for diabetes, you need to use GFP. Few tools have had such an enormous impact on modern biology and medicine. So it was no surprise that the Nobel Committee wanted to honor someone for the discovery of the fluorescent protein. What *was* a surprise, though, was that the recipient wasn't Prasher.

Our algorithm, applied to dozens of prizewinning discoveries, proved that the Nobel Committee rarely made mistakes. So what exactly went wrong in 2008? To find the answer, we needed to examine how credit is assigned to teamwork everywhere.

•

Two years ago, a text popped up on my phone from Ákos Erdős, my neighbor in Boston. "I've got tickets to see my favorite singer on Sunday, but I'll be out of town," he wrote. "Maybe you can use them?" I was free and alone that night, so I said yes. When Ákos gave me the details, though, I was giddy. *He was handing over tickets to see Norah Jones.* I've been a super-fan since she released her first album, *Come Away with Me*, in 2002, adding each of her new albums to my music library ever since. And I turn to her every time I need peace or a clear head—in fact, I fall asleep to her voice almost every night.

Four days later, I was at the Orpheum Theater in down-town Boston, listening to her soothing voice in person for the first time. To my surprise, despite her big, confident, and deeply familiar voice, she had an unassuming presence. The music was as organic and full-bodied as I remembered, but Jones, a mere five-foot-one, seemed lost in her own crowd. Between songs, she took the time to shout out her team—her bass player, her guitarist, her drummer, her organist—thoughtfully identifying each musician by name. We politely clapped, of course, but I can't recall a single one of their names now. I can barely remember which instruments backed her up, except the piano, which she occasionally played her-self. And when people asked me what I did over the weekend, I told them I was at a *Norah Jones* concert, not a Norah Jones *and* Jason Roberts *and* Greg Wieczorek concert, even though a quick Google search tells me she did share the stage with them and several others. Her famous name calls up a singular famous face and familiar voice. Everyone knew immediately whom I was talking about. If I'd said I went to see Jason Rob-erts or Greg Wieczorek or even Puss n Boots—one of three other bands that Jones sings in—I would have been met with confusion.

Invisible players like Jason Roberts and Greg Wieczorek are everywhere. In 2009, Michael Lewis, the author of *Moneyball*, wrote a fascinating profile of one of them, the basketball player Shane Battier, for the *New York Times Magazine*. Conventional statistics showed that Battier, who played for the Houston Rockets, was pretty mediocre by NBA standards. He was a poor dribbler, seldom attempted shots, and grabbed few rebounds. He was slow and lacked flash. His scoring record was unimpressive. Basketball fans seeing his game and stats were quick to dismiss him. While he played defense aggressively, the players he guarded seemed to regard him as more of an annoyance than a threat. He was like a six-foot-eight mosquito they needed to incessantly swat away.

And yet, there was something unique about Battier: his team was far more likely to win when he was on the court. Battier studied other players' weaknesses and used that knowledge to subtly overpower them. His style was quiet, and while he worked the whole court, weakening his opponents in unexpected places, he flew under the radar, everywhere and nowhere at once. He'd blend in so much he might disappear if not for the conspicuousness of his white-and-red jersey. Still, statistics show that when Battier guarded Kobe Bryant—considered by most to be the best player in the league—the Lakers' offensive play was actually worse than if Bryant had taken the night off. In other words, Battier—a middling player by most metrics—rendered Bryant, a basketball god, a "detriment to his own team." Yet Battier got almost no credit for the Rockets' success from 2006 to 2011 from sportscasters, fans, other players, and even his own teammates.

Harry Truman once said, "It's amazing how much can be

accomplished if no one cares who gets the credit." Shane Battier is certainly living proof of this assertion, demonstrating on the court just how far an unselfish and unassuming attitude can go. It's apt, then, that Truman's famous quote is also attributed to the UCLA basketball coach John Wooden, who understood well before Battier how valuable true team players were to the sport. But then again, maybe the idea actually belongs to Charles Montague, the English novelist, who wrote: "There is no limit to what a man can do as long as he cares not a straw who gets the credit for it." Ironic that a quote about shared credit can be attributed to so many different people, huh?

But the many invisible Shane Battiers and Jason Robertses and Greg Wieczoreks around us beg the important question, *if no one claims credit, who gets it?* Anyone working in a team setting—whether you're a programmer writing code for Facebook, or an engineer helping to launch the next satellite, or even a doctor assisting with a liver transplant—must wonder who will ultimately be recognized for these collective achievements. I certainly did. Luckily, our research on credit allocation provided an answer.

•

The mechanism behind Hua-Wei's algorithm was simple: citation patterns—not only for the paper of interest but for all papers written by the coauthors—leave a trail of impact. We can map this trail to gauge a community's perception of who deserves credit for a discovery. If a scientist was key to an insight, his prior work was likely connected to it. And having struck gold, he typically continued to explore ideas in the same vein. Hua-Wei and I found that if we traced the career path of each member of a scientific team, we could accurately pinpoint the presumptive "owner" of a given discovery, which was almost always the researcher with the most consistent track record in that area.

Here's a left-field example. If I coauthored a paper with the pope, who would get the credit? Well, it depends. If the paper probes a deep theological question, and my contribution merely helps him use tools of network science to address the issue—which is the only way I could see contributing to a theological debate—then it's obviously the pope's paper. Theologists will cite our joint paper with other documents attributed to the papacy, and I'd just be some random name hitching a ride on the list of contributors. On the other hand, if the paper primarily addresses network science, the result would be entirely different. Then—forgive me my blasphemy—the paper is mine. The pope may have access to divine powers that offer him unique insights, and some of these insights may even have contributed the key idea to the paper. But because he has no track record in network science, I'm the relevant name. A Francis-Barabási or a Barabási-Francis paper on network science isn't really a shared paper. It's my paper.

For me, the most unexpected message behind the algorithm was this: when we allocate credit to the members of a team, who gets the credit has nothing to do with who actually did the work. We don't dole out reward on the basis of who came up with the idea in the first place, who slaved for weeks, who showed up to meetings to graze the coffee and doughnuts, who jumped in at the last minute with a crucial suggestion, who had the eureka moment, or who yammered on and on but didn't really contribute anything. The algorithm accurately selected Nobel Prize winners and handed them the win not by figuring out who did what. Rather, it did so by detecting how peers in the discipline paid attention to the work of some of the coauthors and ignored the work of the others. The predictive accuracy of the algorithm led us to our next insight about teams: *Credit for teamwork isn't based on performance. Credit is based on perception.* Which makes perfect sense if we remember that success is a collective phenomenon, centered on how other people perceive our performance. Our audiences and colleagues allocate credit based on their perceptions of our related work and the body of work produced by our collaborators. Combining this insight with the findings of the previous chapter—which acknowledges the importance of diversity and balance in team settings—we arrive at the *Fourth Law of Success:*

> *While team success requires diversity and balance, a single individual will receive credit for the group's achievements.*

Understanding this is essential for success, helping us turn the Fourth Law into a tool for both getting the most out of teamwork and collecting the credit we deserve.

•

I'll never forget the devastating photo of the Syrian toddler facedown in the sand that surfaced in 2015. Half submerged in a gentle surf, his weary pose was not altogether different from that of most children who've had an exhausting day outside. But instead of a parent's embrace, the strip of beach is the shoulder he rests his lifeless body on. And he looks cold in his thin T-shirt, a wedge of belly exposed.

He was only one of the thousands who drowned that year as they desperately tried to leave a war-torn homeland, but his image is branded into our collective brain. When we hear the statistics about the refugee crisis, we tune out. The numbers don't connect with the true horror of the events, so they don't resonate. They don't move us to action. But then a face, a person, a photo comes along and the horror of the circumstances suddenly hits us. Briefly, for millions of people around the world, that little boy became the reason to do something about that terrible war. After his photo surfaced, funding for refugee-related causes jumped a hundredfold.

Survival shaped our brains to ignore millions of data points and zoom in on the bear that threatens us or the berry that keeps us alive. Evolution also shaped us to create relational bonds. And in the modern world, this remnant of our biology affects our decisions in ways we don't often even recognize, like deciding whom to reward for a job well done.

That tendency—to focus on individual accomplishment over team achievement, to seek unique faces or heroes—is deeply ingrained in our language. We refer to major work as belonging to a single creator: Darwin's theory of evolution, Freudian psychoanalysis, a Frank Gehry building design, a Julia Roberts movie, or a David Lynch TV series. We also hire, promote, and make tenure decisions based on an individual's body of work, despite how rare solo work is in this day and age.

In some cases—think Warhol's soup cans or Elon Musk's electric car—those toiling in the background aren't even acknowledged, a rude oversight in many success stories. Yet even in cases like movie credits and science authorships, where each team member is carefully acknowledged, doing so has little effect. When we skim through a full list of contributors, the many unfamiliar names are essentially irrelevant to us. On the other hand, the rare name we've seen before will stand out like a protein lit from within with Prasher's GFP. The instinct is almost an unconscious response, a way for our brains to filter out irrelevant trivia.

Credit allocation is guided by the same rich-get-richer phenomenon we see in every other area of success. Preferential attachment, the mechanism behind the Third Law, is not limited to earnings, visibility, and citations. The term also applies to credit. As an apologetic banker is quick to remind the loan applicant who wanders into her office with no borrowing history: We only give credit to people who already have credit.

And that means there are dangers to collaborating. For example, if I contributed to a paper by a postdoc in my lab—someone like Burcu or Dashun—including myself in the author list makes sense in theory. With a three-decade track record, my more recognizable name will stand out to colleagues outside the lab, increasing the odds that they'll pay attention to the research. But there's also a downside to this: Despite the years of heroic work that Dashun put into the papers we wrote about success, for example, once my name is on the author list, people will associate his discoveries with me. They will misdirect the lion's share of credit on the paper simply because they're more familiar with my work. That's a problem that extends well beyond science.

You might think you're in luck when offered a job working for a recognizable name in your field. Not only will you have the chance to rub elbows with a luminary, you'll be able to collaborate on important projects, boosting your résumé. Each team member involved in an important endeavor can lay claim to the resulting product. You can learn from the best, even potentially make your way up the ladder to a position of leadership. And you can use this association to your advantage when you seek other gigs. Imagine getting a letter of recommendation from a leading figure in your profession, someone who can legitimately attest to your abilities.

As a tried-and-true method, recommended by grandparents everywhere, there are clear benefits to apprenticeship. Yet it can fail in the long run. Think of the thousands of engineers and designers whose tireless work allowed Steve Jobs to "invent" the iPhone. Or of the fifty artists, craftsmen, and engineers who helped the conceptual artist Olafur Eliasson conceive and build a waterfall under the Brooklyn Bridge. Or of Norah Jones's backup band members, who spend their careers playing on major stages but are *always* overshadowed by their infinitely more visible singer. Of course, every band needs a bass player, and each new iPhone release requires the creativity of countless engineers. But if you want to be Steve Jobs or Olafur Eliasson or Norah Jones—superstars in their respective realms—you can't be backup forever. You need to kick-start preferential attachment, building your own credit.

I tell my students that working with a recognized name is the best way to build a reputation in science...initially. At some point, though, you need to break out on your own. This advice isn't just gleaned from my experience as a scientist. It's actually *based* on science. For example, our algorithm showed that when it was first published in 1985, the paper that led to the 1997 Nobel Prize in Physics "belonged" to Arthur Ashkin. Of the five authors, he was the senior scientist, far better known in the field than his up-and-coming coauthor, Steven Chu. In fact, the algorithm gave Ashkin 79 percent of the credit, since the paper was frequently co-cited with other papers Ashkin had published earlier on optical tweezers. Steven Chu, on the other hand, initially got only 5 percent of the credit. Yet, over time, ownership of the paper shifted because Chu continued to publish other high-impact papers on the same theme and Ashkin didn't. Slowly people began to associate Chu with the groundbreaking research. Our algorithm captured this momentum, shifting the credit over to Chu. So by 1997, when the Nobel Committee doled out its awards, Chu took home the prize.

In other words, too much time spent in someone else's shadow eclipses our contributions. We get relegated to the periphery when we pursue piecemeal projects, hopping around between various lines of inquiry. A better approach: stake a claim in uncharted territory, like one of my former postdocs, Marta Gonzalez, did. Marta began analyzing human mobility as a postdoc in my lab. When our first joint paper was published, I walked away with the bulk of the credit. Yet, in the ten years since, she has become the expert on the topic, utterly usurping me. Today, her name comes up when human mobility is discussed. I might have served as an ambassador for her, coauthoring her first papers, but she ultimately owned the topic, building a name for herself in the field.

Frankly, it's not always easy to do what Marta did. But she

isn't alone. As we'll see next, other women have learned how to move from the shadows into the spotlight, and, by taking control of their own credit, ultimately seeing their just reward.

•

Darlene Love was on her hands and knees in a bathroom when she heard her own voice on the radio singing a Christmas song. The tune, called "Christmas (Baby Please Come Home)," appeared on a seasonal album produced by Phil Spector in 1963. A buoyant call-and-response number, the now-classic song filled her with the bittersweet longing evoked by the lyrics. Not for a faraway lover, but for a faraway life. The luxurious bathroom where she found herself in the early 1980s, after all, was not her own—a reward for the many musical hits she'd belted out on famous records. She was scrubbing toilets for rich people to pay her bills.

Love has been singing since birth, practically, starting in the choir at her father's church. She began singing professionally at sixteen, in a trio called the Blossoms. They sang backup for a slew of bands in the 1950s and '60s, imbuing records by Elvis Presley and other white musicians with a black gospel sound. If there's a "shoo-op" on an oldies tune, Love probably crooned it. *Da doo ron-ron-ron, da doo ron-ron?* That's pure Darlene Love. Her voice is effortlessly youthful on these recordings, as clear as a mountain stream.

During that era, Love was also the lead singer on a few tracks, but as a black woman in a music world dominated by white men, she had no control over the production or distribution of her music. In fact, she signed a deeply exploitive contract with producer Phil Spector that treated her like a disembodied voice that could be employed for others' benefit. In a stunning example, the hit "He's a Rebel," featuring Love's crisp voice, was intentionally misappropriated by Spector for the Crystals, another group he managed. Teens across the country watched the Crystals passionlessly lip-synch the track on TV, unaware of who the true singer was.

By the early 1980s, Love had given up. She continued to sing backup for a few big names, occasionally stepping into a recording studio or onto a stage, but she also had to take on cleaning gigs to make ends meet. So when the sound of her own voice echoed across the tile in the bathroom, she decided to try something different. "I just looked up and I said, 'Okay, all right, Darlene. This is not where you're supposed to be,'" she recalls in the 2015 documentary *20 Feet from Stardom*. "'You're supposed to be singing. There's a whole world out there that wants to hear you sing.'"

Breaking through to that world wasn't easy. Love had been a team player for most of her life and hadn't cultivated the support network of professionals that push stars forward. Never mind that back then there was almost no precedent for successful black female solo singers. Once she decided to change course, however, she began to slowly emerge from the background. First, she managed to book an annual appearance on *David Letterman* to sing "Christmas (Baby Please Come Home)," breathing life into an old classic and making it famous again. Next, she landed a role as Danny Glover's wife in *Lethal Weapon*. Continually trying to get her face and name out there, she then sang a duet with Bette Midler and released several solo albums.

Eventually the night arrived when, just shy of seventy,

Darlene Love took front-and-center stage, her coppery hair gleaming in the spotlights, her smile radiating. With her maid days long gone, her voice soared, reaching every corner of the large room, where it was greeted by the most thunderous applause she'd ever received.

This time, however, she was not singing backup. Bruce Springsteen, grinning as he played guitar, was the one backing *her*, as she hit the notes, high and low, that surely brought many to tears. The stage she now commanded was at the Rock & Roll Hall of Fame. Darlene Love was there to be inducted for her lifetime contribution to music.

Love's story is one of triumph against enormously formidable odds. She succeeded because, guided by the strength of her own voice, she fought to rectify the credit that had been deliberately snatched from her as a young woman. But crucial to her success was an approach that makes a lot of sense in light of the Fourth Law. At a certain point, Love refused to be a nameless team member any longer. By stepping into the spotlight and utilizing the relationships she'd built in the industry, she made sure that each of her projects could be directly linked to her. Instead of working for the many stars she'd sung backup for, she worked *with* them.

Sadly, not all of her contemporaries had her foresight or her doggedness. The Fourth Law affirms that credit decisions are based on perception, not performance, and our perception of who deserves credit is often riddled with sexist and racist prejudices. The fact that women earn roughly seventy cents to their male counterparts' dollar—even in an evolved country like the United States—speaks to some of the many injustices implicit in the Fourth Law. After all, earnings are one of the most tangible ways that our society allocates credit. We're supposedly paid in proportion to our contribution. And yet, as the gender pay gap reminds us, we clearly aren't.

Gendered pay, of course, isn't the only manifestation of credit misallocation caused by sexism. There are examples of it everywhere, in every professional realm, in every country. Here's one shocking example that I came across recently. Female economics professors are *twice as likely* to be denied tenure as their male colleagues. We suspected this, since a "tenure gap" is just one component of a long data trail that documents the obstacles women face in science. The most unexpected aspect, though, was the reason behind the tenure denial. It turns out that the disparity can't be explained by differences in productivity, quality, confidence, or competitiveness between men and women. Nor can it be explained, even, by the professional penalty some women pay for their family commitments—though that does affect how long it takes to be considered for tenure. What, then, could explain such a troubling disparity?

The data shows that women economists who exclusively work alone are just as likely to receive tenure as men. Regardless of gender, every solo paper an economist writes increases his or her chances of tenure by 8 or 9 percent. Yet a gap suddenly appears once a woman coauthors a paper, and the chances only widen with each collaborative project she participates in. Instead of increasing her odds, every coauthored paper she contributes to *lowers* them. The effect is so dramatic, in fact, that women who exclusively collaborate face a yawning tenure chasm. The research shows that when women coauthor, they're accorded far less than half the usual benefits of authorship. And when women coauthor exclusively with men, they see virtually no gains. In other words, *female economists pay an enormous penalty for collaborating.*

To be clear, men pay no price for collaborative work. They can work alone, in partnerships, or in groups, and their chances of tenure will remain the same. Women, on the other hand, collaborate at their own peril. From a tenure perspective, *if you're a female economist publishing with men, you might as well not publish at all.*

It's a stunning finding, isn't it? Especially since there's extensive research showing that teams containing women have higher performance. Yet hardworking women, already facing difficult odds in a male-dominated field, are less likely to be given institutional support, are less likely to further their careers, and are less likely to advance within the community, *because, essentially, they're team players.*

While this issue, of course, isn't limited to economists, the example perfectly illustrates just how entrenched the Fourth Law is, especially in groups already disadvantaged by racism and sexism. Because bounded performance allows biases to determine our success more than we'd like to admit, the Second Law compounds the Fourth Law, allocating credit to people who've had the credit to begin with. That suggests people who want credit for work simply have to take it. Not in the disregarding, unfair way that Phil Spector took credit for Darlene Love's achievements. Rather, in the way that Darlene Love wrested credit back from Phil Spector.

•

Douglas Prasher, on the other hand, should have borrowed Love's entire instruction manual. Not to single him out unfairly, since he's familiar with unfairness already. Besides, all of us could learn a lot from Darlene Love. But Prasher wasn't just passed over. He was passed over for a *Nobel Prize.*

Prasher, a young scientist pursuing an esoteric subject, did what most high-achieving scientists do early in their careers. He had a fantastic idea that he followed doggedly. Never mind that his subject attracted little encouragement from his community. But then again, no one paid attention to Albert Einstein, a patent clerk, when he was in his most productive period, either. In Prasher's case, very few of his colleagues took his work on GFP seriously. A presentation that he'd given just before his tenure review at the marine biology lab where he worked in Woods Hole, Massachusetts, had gone badly. Then his grant proposal was turned down, which meant he couldn't raise the funds to continue his research. The stress was so grating that his three-year-old daughter said to his wife, "Papa doesn't smile anymore." Breaking in a moment of career-crushing despondency, Prasher told the tenure committee to suspend his review. He quit. But before he took a job at the Department of Agriculture, he did something unusual. Hoping that his work would not be in vain, Prasher mailed the cloned GFP gene—the product of his lonely toil—to two other researchers. The gesture was a genuinely friendly and unselfish one. The names scrawled on the padded envelopes belonged to the only scientists who had contacted him expressing interest in his research.

Sixteen years later, the recipients of Prasher's envelopes, Martin Chalfie and Roger Tsien, were in Stockholm accepting the Nobel Prize. Using the gene Prasher cloned, Chalfie had gone on to show the medical world that Prasher's vision had been correct all along: you could indeed use GFP in living organisms. By inserting GFP into a roundworm, Chalfie made proteins fluoresce, a trick now used by thousands of biologists. This was what Prasher planned to do next, had he had the money and opportunity to pursue the research. Tsien took Prasher's gene and mutated it, creating new strains of GFP that glowed in an array of vivid colors. And so, by utilizing Prasher's discovery in innovative ways, the inheritors of his gene published a series of groundbreaking papers about its application, slowly stepping into the role of "discoverers." With Prasher gone, they became the face of GFP.

Seventeen years after leaving academia, Prasher was in his Huntsville kitchen one morning when he heard the news about the Nobel over the radio. A local newscaster, speaking in the region's melodious drawl, mispronounced Tsien's name. Prasher decided to call the station. He did so not to claim credit. In fact, he said nothing about the key role he had played in the discovery. Ever meticulous, he was calling to correct the newscaster's pronunciation. Then he finished his breakfast and headed off to the dealership, wearing his required uniform, a blue polo shirt and khakis. Balloons adorned the dealership lot, floating above a horizon of shiny cars. Sitting in the dilapidated office, working a job that didn't pay enough, Prasher was flooded with disappointment. Not so much for missing out on the prize. More because he felt like his obscurity was his own fault. It wasn't in his personality to thrive in the spotlight, and he wasn't comfortable reaching out to the people who might have helped him. His story is a cautionary example of how the Fourth Law can dictate our fates.

When we look at the product of teamwork, we have no precise way of knowing who did what. So we assign credit to one or a few team members, typically those with the most consistent track records or the ones we recognize. While this can be a fair way to give credit where it's due, occasionally the approach—as in Prasher's case—is glaringly wrong. We're incredibly productive when we work in teams, but, as Prasher knows too well, collaboration can also be the adult version of everyone's middle school group project nightmare. You can find yourself sitting in a dazzling banquet hall, clapping along in stunned disbelief, while one of your collaborators gratefully accepts credit for your labors.

•

For me, the Fourth Law isn't about missed opportunities or credit not allocated. Instead, the discovery offers me actionable insight into how reward is doled out by our society. I invoke it nearly every time I talk with my students, aspiring scientists starting out in the field, who need to think strategically about how to "make a name for themselves" as they pursue the projects that excite them. I use it when considering possible collaborations or a new position or responsibility. Ignorance of the laws governing credit allocation and human nature can make all the work we put into a project vanish. Understanding the processes behind the Fourth Law helps us counter its injustices.

Credit is often assigned, as the First Law dictates—by invisible networks, not by individual arbitrators. Above all, the vast and fluid tangle of relationships we're embedded in determines our success. Just as Prasher's gene can highlight the nerve cells of a brain, we can now illuminate some of the invisible threads that dictate our fates.

The laws we've covered so far are based on the principle that success is a collective force. Knowing this, we've been able to examine how communities respond to products and stories, seeing how bias shapes reward, how success breeds success, how fitness matters, how credit is allocated, and how teams succeed. There are elements in each of these laws that we can harness as we seek recognition for the work we do.

The final part of this book will be dedicated to a single law, one that proves the value of Darlene Love's approach, and marks a key difference between her story and Prasher's. Not only does Love embody the Fourth Law, her persistence in the face of difficult odds shows us how to take talent and transform it into a meaningful career. Just as Love's revelation in the bathroom shaped her success story—and landed her center stage—we must urgently heed the lessons of the fifth and final law. After all, the next overnight success might be you. Your highest-impact work might be something you've currently left simmering on the back burner. Get going. Hustle. Let science be your motivational speaker. Because, as we show next, *success can come at any time.*

THE FIFTH LAW

With persistence
success can come at any time.

The Fifth Law explains how it's possible to do Nobel-winning research after retirement and why it feels like some people are playing the success game with loaded dice. We'll encounter the Q-factor, which allows us to reduce innovation to an equation. The Fifth Law tells us that while success melts like a snowflake, creativity has no expiration date.

10

Einstein's Error

Why Hard Work, Combined with Skill, Wins in the End

Inevitably, I try to examine my own failures and successes in light of the research I do. On dark winter days in Boston, as I walk to my lab, dodging icy patches of pavement, I'll find myself mentally running *my* numbers and counting *my* odds. To be sure, science has taken me on an ever-meandering, unexpected journey, propelling me from physics to networks to the Science of Success in two short decades. Yet, with their careers still ahead of them, my students and postdocs brim with possibility. Working with them is heartening, a reminder of why I chose academia in the first place.

In matters of my own fate, though, the briskness that radiates in the city air feels reinforced by what I know to be true from countless studies. Simply put, innovation and discovery seem to be a young person's game. It's a phenomenon that Einstein, who discovered relativity at the tender age of twenty-six, bluntly observed: "A person who has not made his great contribution to science before the age of thirty will never do so."

That "deadwood" feeling that looms in the background as

each year passes, and as a new cadre of bright young researchers replaces the last, can cause even us scientists to wax a bit poetic. Paul Dirac, who, like Einstein, won the Nobel Prize for a discovery he made in his twenties, summed it up in this dismal verse:

Age is, of course, a fever chill
That every physicist must fear.
He's better dead than living still
When once he's past his thirtieth year.

While Dirac failed to follow his own dictate, publishing his final paper at eighty-four, the year he died, his point holds up. Both he and Einstein were generally correct, as the data tells us that scientists tend to publish their breakthrough work at the beginning of their careers. Studies of recognized geniuses show this. Psychologist Dean Keith Simonton, for instance, analyzed the career trajectories of more than two thousand scientists and inventors from ancient times to today, everyone from da Vinci to Newton to Edison. Most of them made their mark on history before or around the age of thirty-nine, he found, evidence that underscores the widely held assumption that creativity is the purview of youth, or at least early middle age. And when Simonton turned to the careers of artists and writers, he found that they, too, experienced early primes. Regardless of field or genre, innovation, the fuel that gets me out of bed and into the lab each day, appears to be less potent for those of us who, being creakier and more jaded, probably need it most.

Must we inevitably lose our mojo as we age? I often pondered this question. Watch me try to take a day off and "relax," and you'll get a feel for why I found the prospect worrisome. Luckily for me—and anyone who'd have to tolerate my antsy early retirement—our research reveals a deeper paradox that offers true hope: we older folks don't have to assume we're has-beens. That's because *creativity itself has no age*. While Einstein and Dirac weren't exactly wrong about the fact that most discoveries have been achieved by the young, we can have a career-defining breakthrough at any moment.

If you're confused, don't worry. So was I. In fact, reconciling what seems, at first, to be a tremendous puzzle about innovation and age took me five years.

•

As fascinating as Simonton's studies are, I have a fundamental problem with them. His work focuses on geniuses, a tiny segment of the creative population—admirable, exalted people who, come to think of it, are pretty rare birds. Which raises some important questions: Are Simonton's findings relevant to ordinary scientists like me or my graying colleagues and collaborators who may never earn the genius label? Do these conclusions pertain to those in other professions with whom I interact every day? Should I fire my general practitioner simply because he's past his intellectual peak? Should I bypass an experienced architect for a young one, in hopes that the upstart will bring new, disruptive ideas to the drawing table? Should Silicon Valley start-ups stick to their tacit rule, hiring fresh-faced near-teenagers in lieu of the experienced but elderly? That is, does the extensive literature on geniuses mean anything to us mere mortals?

These were the questions that Roberta Sinatra and I

started to ask soon after she joined my lab in 2012. A young Sicilian postdoctoral researcher, Roberta started her career as a physicist, eventually meandering into network science. As soon as she arrived, it was clear that she had what it takes to translate performance into success. The enthusiasm she had about her research was infectious, motivating multiple lab members to solve difficult problems. An amazing cook, she was also a natural networker, bringing people together around her dinner table. It is certainly easier to discuss the nuances of network theory over a plate of spaghetti made from an old family recipe than in a conference room. In the kitchen or in the lab, she had a way of making deeply complicated problems appear deceptively easy.

Roberta and I were curious about the effect age has on creativity in non-superstar careers. Given the trends we saw in the career trajectories of exalted scientists, could we predict periods of innovation for everyday Joes and Janes making small but crucial contributions in fields ranging from biology to computer science? We started out with a simple question: At what stage in our careers do we write our highest-impact papers?

Sometimes simple questions are the hardest to answer. Ours was like that. It required us to reconstruct accurately the careers of tens of thousands of researchers, determining which papers belonged to which scientist from a list of roughly 40 million publications. The process took about two years, with quite a bit of help from Pierre Deville, a computer scientist working on our team. But when we were finally done and could analyze each individual career, a consistent pattern emerged.

Successful research typically came relatively early in a career—within the first two decades after starting out in the field. To be precise, it appeared that a scientist had roughly a 13 percent chance of publishing her highest-impact work in the first three years of her career. And about the same odds held true for the following three years. In fact, each year for two decades, she had a similar chance of hitting the jackpot. But, after twenty years, something changed, and her odds sank dramatically. The chance she'd publish her most-cited paper in year twenty-five was only 5 percent. And her odds continued to free-fall after that. I'm nearing the thirtieth year of my career—and according to our graph, the likelihood I'll now make a discovery that will overshadow my previous "best"? Less than 1 percent. In other words, I might as well stop trying. A quick glance at the data tells me I'm deadwood. Forget tenure; my provost should send me off into the sunset.

So Simonton was right, and his findings do apply to nongeniuses, too, those of us who follow our love of science and keep at it, day in and day out, without expecting accolades. What we found was simple: When it comes to their patterns of creativity, geniuses are no different from us. We, too, peak out early in our careers. We, too, let our guard down once that wave of creativity wanes. Geniuses or not, we mostly conform to the same fundamental patterns.

•

To my relief, though, this conclusion—that I might as well buy a bunch of Hawaiian shirts, move to Florida, and take up golf—turned out to be an incomplete reading of the data.

When we examined the reasons behind early creative innovation, we stumbled across something unexpected. Sure, the
chance of a breakthrough drops precipitously after twenty
years. But, importantly, so does *productivity*. When we looked
at the number of papers that scientists publish over the course
of their careers, we saw that, overwhelmingly, they're far
more productive at the outset. The graph showing the chance
of publishing one's highest-impact work and the graph showing the chance of publishing *any* paper mimicked each other
to such a strong degree that we couldn't tell one from the
other. This couldn't have happened by accident. There was a
deeper message here and we needed to decode it.

For months, we puzzled over how to untangle the connec-
tion between productivity and the timing of success. I'm an
early bird and tend to do my best thinking in the morning, so
I'd get up at dawn to reflect on the latest plots and send an
updated list of questions to Roberta and her team. We'd meet
in the afternoon to discuss the data, and I would ask, again
and again, "What does this really mean for me? Am I brain
dead?" Roberta, a night owl, found herself puttering around
on Google Scholar during the same period, staring at the citation histories of various scientists she admired. Everyone she
searched, from Nobel Prize winners to relatively unknown
scientists she'd rubbed shoulders with, had one thing in
common—their impact increased over time. With each passing year, each of them gained more and more citations.

Even, come to think of it…Newton, Curie, Einstein, and
Dirac, and they were *dead*. Still their work continued to
acquire citations as if they were alive and kicking. And then a
light bulb went off in Roberta's head: What, she asked

herself, was the difference between the success of living scientists and those who've already passed away?

The answer: living scientists continued to be productive. Newton, Einstein, and Curie couldn't transmit new science from the afterlife. They hadn't contributed ideas for decades or centuries. Instead, the body of work they produced during their lifetimes continues to garner our admiration. Despite their stymied productivity, which died with them, their impact, measured in citation counts, keeps growing every day. If we wanted to uncover the interplay between productivity and success, Roberta mused, we needed to compare apples to apples, not live apple trees to dead ones. So we refocused on scientists who had already retired, allowing us to inspect their full careers, not just the beginnings of them.

Roberta's late-night "aha" moment broke open a crucial new take on the data. We found that we could untangle the relationship between productivity and success by arranging each scientist's published papers in chronological order. Instead of tagging each paper with the age of the scientist who authored it, we simply labeled each paper as the first, second, or twentieth in a career. By doing this, we saw each paper for what it was: another in a series of attempts at a breakthrough.

We expected to see that a scientist's highest-impact paper would be among the first of her career. That's what decades of research on geniuses insinuated. To our bafflement, though, this wasn't the case. Rather, each paper—whether it was the first, the second, or the last on the list—had exactly the same chance of being her most important. When we saw the data arranged this way, we were stunned. *Age didn't seem to matter.*

Which created another puzzle. If my creativity has no age, and each of my papers has the same chance of being a breakthrough, then why do all of us—geniuses and everyday Joes and Janes—peak out early in our careers?

Productivity.

There's a simple analogy to explain this seemingly contradictory find. Let's say that for thirty years you buy a lottery ticket annually, always on your birthday. Your chance of winning a prize doesn't improve as you age. Nor does it decline. It's the same now as it was five years ago, and it will be the same ten years from now. But if you buy thirty lottery tickets on your thirtieth birthday? Well, if you're ever going to win the lottery, the odds are it'll be in your thirtieth year. Our measurements showed that research papers are like lottery tickets in a scientist's life. Each has exactly the same odds of becoming a breakthrough. So, in the period when a researcher publishes at his or her best pace—finishing project after project in rapid-fire succession—they tend to experience their greatest success. Not because they're more creative during this burst of activity. They succeed because they try more often.

It just so happens that for most scientists, this burst of productivity comes during the first two decades of professional life. Eager after our studies, we spend our initial years churning out projects in a flurry of motivated activity. Then, after a decade or two, our output slowly tapers off. It's the same in all creative enterprises. New opportunities open up that take us out of the office or the studio or the lab. We deal with midlife crises. Our children get into trouble; our frail parents absorb our attention. We burn out. We get distracted, our priorities

228

shift, and our pace lags. In other words, late-career professionals tend to buy fewer lottery tickets, so they inevitably have fewer wins.

And so, by analyzing the data differently, we discovered that fresh-faced thinkers disproportionately break through not because youth and creativity are intertwined. They do so because on the whole, they're more *productive*. Undeterred by disinterest or failure, young people try again and again. That's why scientists write most of their breakthrough papers in their thirties, why many painters produce their most revered canvases in their twenties, why composers and movie directors and innovators and fashion designers tend to be youthful upstarts when they make it big.

Counterintuitively, this is good news for those of us with wrinkles now and those of you who will have them in the future. Innovation itself has no age limit as long as we continually buy our metaphorical tickets and get our work out into the world. The message here, which we came to call the *Fifth Law of Success*, is simple:

With persistence success can come at any time.

Thinking about the data, I could barely contain my happiness. In fact, walking home from the lab as we began to piece together the relationship between success and productivity, I was swimming with ideas and energy. It helped that we were making progress during early summer, when the sun seemingly never sets — and when it finally does, sheds sultry colors across the languorous horizon. My joy in the discovery was personal. Productivity has always been my strong suit. Now I was able to recognize just how valuable an asset it was. With the Fifth Law as my mantra, I have a reason to double down on my research, outpacing even my younger self. I now know that each of the papers I write represents a new ticket, and each ticket is an opportunity for a breakthrough. We had to analyze thousands of careers to finally understand mine, but it really was as simple as that.

•

When, at the age of fifty, John Fenn joined the faculty at Yale, he was already old by academic standards. But then again, he was an inveterate late starter. He published his first research paper at thirty-two, a decade after finishing graduate school, a rarity among academics and hopeless as a bid toward scientific stardom according to Einstein. He was thirty-five when he got his first academic appointment, at Princeton, where he started working with atomic and molecular beams, an esoteric line of research that he continued to pursue at Yale when he moved there fifteen years later. Though Fenn was hardworking and diligent, he remained a low-impact scientist for much of his tenure. His department chair at Yale must have felt some relief when Fenn turned seventy and they could finally force him to take mandatory retirement. After all, he'd been puttering around for two decades without much to show for it.

Yet Fenn had no interest in stopping. Three years earlier, at the age of sixty-seven, he was already semiretired at Yale, stripped of his lab space and technicians, when he published a paper on a new technique he called "electrospray ionization." He turned droplets into a high-speed beam, allowing him to measure the masses of large molecules and proteins quickly and accurately. He saw it as a breakthrough and felt he was finally on a roll. And he was right—with the exploding interest in the molecular constituents of cells, his technique quickly turned into a must-have tool in labs around the world. So, after idling reluctantly as an emeritus professor at Yale, he relocated to Virginia Commonwealth University, which apparently had no problem with his ripening age. He opened a new lab and continued undeterred.

What he did in these later years was revolutionary. Improving upon his initial idea, he offered scientists a robust way to measure ribosomes and viruses with previously unbelievable accuracy, gaining knowledge that transformed our understanding of how our cells work. And his late-life push had a serious payoff. Fifteen years later, in 2002, by then a wizened man in his mid-eighties, he was awarded the Nobel Prize in Chemistry.

Fenn's story is a happy one, reminding us that the Fifth Law works in our favor if we follow its dictates. In a eulogy from his friend and mentee Carol Robinson, he's remembered as a relentlessly passionate scientist. "He believed that science should above all be fun and when it ceases to be so you should give up," she wrote. "But Fenn never gave up, continuing his research and coming into the department almost every day until just a few weeks before his death. His final paper on the mechanism of electrospray was published when he was ninety." Not a bad life lived.

Fenn embodies the Fifth Law's simple message: *Your chance of success has little to do with your age. It's shaped by your willingness to try repeatedly for a breakthrough.* Realizing this was transformative for me. I started seeing Fenns everywhere.

There's Alan Rickman, whose first movie role came at forty-six; Ray Kroc, who joined the McDonald's franchise at fifty-three; Nelson Mandela, who emerged after twenty-seven years in jail as eager as ever for political change, becoming his country's president at seventy-six. There's Julia Child, who was fifty when she hosted her first TV show, her giddy excitement for cooking trilling in her voice.

These late-in-life successes, textbook examples of the Fifth Law, had something else in common besides tenacity. Their pathways to success were guided by a hidden factor that unveiled itself throughout their careers. We named it the Q-factor, and it finally helped us answer the million-dollar question: Where do high-fitness ideas and products come from?

•

New projects always start with an idea. It's the same no matter what creative field you're in: a light bulb goes off, and you start thinking about how to bring your bright idea into the world. But the inherent importance or novelty of the idea isn't something we always know in advance. So let's call it r for "random idea," letting r stand for a number that captures its value. Opening another fast-food joint in a strip mall where five are already fighting for survival? Give it an r close to zero. Building a working teleportation machine? That could have a huge r...if you can pull it off. Of course, the better the idea—that is, the larger its r value—the more likely it is to have a strong impact.

But a good starting seed isn't the only factor. Ideas are cheap, a truism often parroted by venture capitalists. Your

232

ability to take that idea and turn it into a useful product determines the size of the check an investor is willing to cut for you. The same is true in any occupation: A terrific idea in clumsy hands rarely leads to an important outcome. Your *ability* to turn an idea into a discovery is equally important, and that varies dramatically from person to person.

We called this ability a person's Q-factor, which allowed us to reduce the process of innovation down to an equation. Each of us takes a random idea, with value r, and using our skill, we turn it into a discovery or "success" S, which captures its impact on the world. If we want to predict this impact, we need to establish how these two factors—the as-yet-unknown merit of the idea, or its r, and one's Q-factor—work in tandem to determine a project's ultimate success, or S. The simplest model we could think of also ended up being the most accurate. Multiply your Q-factor by the value of your next idea, r, and you get a formula to predict its success. Or, written as a formula:

$$S = Qr$$

In other words, the success of a product or a deal, or the impact of a discovery, will be the product of a creator's Q-factor and the value of idea r.

So, if an individual with a low Q-factor comes across a great idea with a huge r value, the impact will, sadly, be mediocre, as the resulting product—or Qr—is diminished by the small Q-factor. Fantastic idea, poor execution. Think Apple's first handheld Newton, with its inept handwriting recognition, a product Steve Jobs was forced to cancel. The reverse also happens: A creative person with a high Q-factor can put out multiple weak or mediocre products. Think AppleLisa,

NeXT, the G-4 Cube, MobileMe. Never heard of them? They're in the graveyard of Jobs's many failures. If an idea has a small r value, no matter how high the Q, the Qr product will be cheapened. Great execution, poor idea. And then there are those perfect-storm instances where the idea and the creator both shine. When the Q-factor and r are both high, they enhance each other, inevitably leading to a career-defining breakthrough. Think of the iPhone—a fantastic idea with brilliant execution, resulting in the product that defined Jobs's legacy.

This career model defied many of my expectations regarding how innovative people work. I'd been convinced that as we advance in our careers, we become better at translating our ideas into high-impact outcomes, whether that means turning an idea into a product, following a hunch about a fantastic business deal, converting that melody into a song, or translating glimmering afternoon light into a masterpiece on canvas. In other words, surely our Q-factor must increase over the course of our career. But this is where the real shock hit. Once we figured out how to measure a scientist's Q-factor, we learned that *it remained unchanged* throughout her career. The data was clear: we all start our careers with a given Q, high or low, and that Q-factor stays with us until retirement.

Now, I had a hard time believing that I was as good a scientist when I wrote my first research paper at twenty-two, the one with absolutely zero impact, as I am now. And you might have the same emotional reaction to this finding that I did. You probably feel you weren't anywhere near as good a teacher, writer, doctor, or salesperson in your twenties as you are now, whether that's a few years or decades later. As my twenty-two-year-old son gets ready to start his Ph.D. studies, how can I tell him that he already *is or isn't* a good scientist? What about growing in a career, learning more, working hard?

I just couldn't buy that the Q-factor of creative individuals doesn't change over time. Neither could the editors of the top journals where we sent the paper describing our discovery. Neither could the eight referees the journals asked to weigh in. Everyone was baffled. They asked us to recheck our findings and demonstrate their validity in all fields of science. We spent six months doing so. And we came to the same conclusion. So, as a scientist, I have no choice but to accept this at face value. Yet I continue to wrestle with the results as I try to understand what they really tell us about success, talent, and ability.

Does this finding apply to those outside the sciences? We could only answer that recently, after we figured out how to measure the Q-factor in another domain: communication. Onur Varol, a new lab member, looked at Twitter users, measuring how good they are at putting out tweets that resonate with their user base. Obviously if you have millions of followers, chances are high that thousands will retweet your messages, and a comparison with someone with only a handful of followers won't work.

When we compared individuals with the same number of followers, though, major differences greeted us. We found that some were much more talented at engaging with their audiences than others. There seemed to be no systematic growth or decay as Twitter users honed their communication skills. The high-Q-factor performers stayed that way, and the low ones didn't budge. The minute anyone joined Twitter, a Q-factor was set and stayed roughly the same for months and years.

I explained my dilemma with these findings to my neighbor, a successful businessperson. I asked if he felt he'd evolved into a better practitioner of his profession over time. How long did it take to claim one success after another? Didn't he develop a golden touch after a while, knowing when to avoid bad deals?

Far from it, he said.

His career, too, was littered with random failures blended with a few major hits. No different from the spotty record of one of the most successful entrepreneurs of our age, Steve Jobs, whose huge Q-factor allowed his many phenomenal failures to vanish behind the standout blockbusters.

•

If you feel as if there are a few people in every professional arena playing the success game with loaded dice... well, they are. But it's the Q-factor they bring to the table—the talent or knowledge innate in them—that stacks the odds in their favor. There's a John Lennon, a Steven Spielberg, a Toni Morrison, or a Marie Curie in every creative realm. Because they have towering Q-factors, the impact of their projects will loom large, even when they're working with an idea that has a modest r. A strong Q-factor will boost even a flimsy project, creating respectable impact, which, in less deft hands, would constitute a miss. These high-impact projects are separated by many obvious flops in every career, which represent numerous low-r ideas. Still, for high-Q individuals our model predicts success after success after success.

But what if our Q-factor is low? Just as we can all immediately call to mind the people in our lives with towering Q-factors, we can just as easily think of those with limited ones. This was supported by our data, whether we looked at scientists or Twitter users. Many kept at their pursuits despite a low Q. Since Q-factors don't change over time, there's some hard advice I can offer to anyone: if you are repeatedly failing at breaking through, you may very well be pursuing the wrong vocation. I've experienced this myself. In high school, I was preparing to be a sculptor. But I wasn't good, to be honest. Even back then, I was better at physics. So I followed my Q-factor, abandoning the art studio for the research lab. Or maybe you're stuck in a deeply solitary field. I've been there as well, working for years on quantum dots, an obscure discipline where even the biggest discovery gets little traction. I eventually switched to networks, an area where my work could reach a wider audience. The point is that if our Q-factor isn't resonating with our job, we must take a moment to decide if we've pinned our hopes on the wrong career path.

Once you find that perfect fit, however, that area or profession where your Q-factor shines, there's really only one more thing you need to do: not give up. Don't count on chance to deliver your success. Find the vocation where your Q-factor matches your dreams and you will have a much better chance at succeeding.

•

By now I hope I've convinced you that creativity has no expiration date.

But success does. Which is strange, given our earlier

discussions about how success can kick-start even bigger success. According to preferential attachment, as we've seen, once a project is successful, it will grow indefinitely, in proportion to previous success. Consider that for a moment, though. This is where common sense must prevail. At that rate, we'd be far too big for our britches, riding unchecked on the ever-widening wave of our individual accomplishments. All we'd have to do is achieve recognition once, and that attention, fueled by preferential attachment, would set us up for life. A single best seller would always leave its author swimming in fame and royalties. One successful patent would give an inventor the kind of endless wealth common only in fairy tales. A discovery would earn a scientist millions of citations. This is true, sometimes. A single act can provide a boost lasting the rest of a creator's life. Still, if preferential attachment is *always* unerringly unchecked, the disparity between the haves and the have-nots would be even more monumental.

Success can be unbounded, as the Second Law dictates, but there are limits. As happens with so many things in life, success is limited by time.

Mortality, after all, is intrinsic to its nature.

Success wanes because *everything ages*, falling victim to an "attention economy." Regardless of the attractiveness of the shiny object currently dangling in front of our noses, we'll eventually scan the horizon for something shinier. The same is true for our "teenage" projects. Much of the attention paid to discoveries, videos, or iPhones happens at their release, followed by a fast and universal loss of interest as time passes. Success melts like a snowflake.

• • •

The good news is the Q-factor reminds us that we're in luck if we're persistent and talented. While all projects have a shelf life, creative people don't. So the key to long-term success from a creator's perspective is straightforward: let the qualities that give you your Q-factor do their job by giving them a chance to deliver success over and over. Successful people engage in project after project after project. They don't just count their winnings; they buy more lottery tickets. Publishing serial novels, as Rowling did, for example, allows a writer to exploit the Fifth Law the only way she can. Each time she publishes a new book, her new fans will go back and read the older volumes as well. Each new book, then, breathes life into her career, keeping her whole body of work present and relevant.

Success fades with time, but the Q-factor doesn't. Since it remains constant, truly successful people are able to produce high-fitness products consistently by picking new r numbers over and over again. A high Q-factor, combined with Fenn-like persistence, helps us turn the Fifth Law into an engine for career-long success. People like Shakespeare and Austen, Musk and Edison, Curie and Einstein, are not remembered for a single work that changed everything. They tower over the intellectual canon thanks to their exceptional Q-factors— and their willingness to test their luck repeatedly.

And there's another smart way to exploit your Q.
Collaboration.
Harness your network to help you with your projects. If

nothing else, this prompts you to keep trying, to keep taking your Q-factor for a ride. Teamwork motivates us. For me, the students and postdocs—the many projects we do together—force me to continue to be productive.

Since success, too, is a collective phenomenon, our response to high-quality work or talented people is what shapes our fates. That may make success feel like a force well beyond our grasp. But if the Fifth Law tells us anything, it's that there's much we can control. Stubborn creativity, combined with a John Fenn–like tenacity, not only gives our lives their essential meaning, it also—as the data shows—provides the true secret to career-long success. That is what not only most effectively binds what we do with who we are but also explains why the people we most admire are those who recognize that while life may be finite, age is nothing more than a set of opportunities to celebrate with our friends.

•

The Japanese artist Katsushika Hokusai is one perfect, parting exemplar of all that. "All I have produced before the age of seventy is not worth taking into account. At seventy-three I have learned a little about the real structure of nature," he wrote at seventy-five. What followed made my day. "When I am eighty I shall have made still more progress. At ninety, I shall penetrate the mystery of things. At one hundred I shall have reached a marvelous stage, and when I am one-hundred-ten, everything I do, whether it be a dot or a line, will be alive."

Hokusai lived to be eighty-nine. He created his most memorable works in the final two decades of his life, including the iconic woodblock print *The Great Wave off Kanagawa*. The image is one I'm sure you know: an enormous white-capped wave slowly unfurls over a half-drowned skiff, dwarfing Mount Fuji in the background. It's an apt depiction of how success ebbs and flows over a lifetime, building sudden momentum and crashing over us, only to start all over again.

CONCLUSION

Before becoming a lovable genius with an unruly hairdo, Einstein was regarded by most of America as an arrogant elitist. He started making news only in 1919, fourteen years after his first paper on relativity, when researchers in England discovered that light does not travel straight but bends around the sun. This was a triumphant confirmation of his theory, and the British press was electrified by the discovery. Americans were a different story. The six editorials in the *New York Times* devoted to relativity mixed admiration with suspicion and even hostility. The source of this acrimony is somewhat puzzling, and may have been because Einstein was said to have asserted that "at most twelve people in the world" truly understood his work, a claim that was seen as off-putting and undemocratic. "The Declaration of Independence itself is outraged by the assertion that there is anything on earth or in interstellar space that can be understood by only a chosen few," exclaimed one of the editorialists. Not only was Einstein a European intellectual, out of touch with everyday people, he was — following Germany's disastrous role in World War I — German. To make matters more complicated, Einstein was Jewish and this drama was unfolding at a time of deep anti-Semitism and xenophobia in America. After a brief burst of attention in 1919, interest in relativity waned. Were it not for one twist of fate, Einstein's fame would likely have been of the fifteen-minute variety, and he'd be known today mostly in academic circles.

When, then, did Einstein become the embodiment of human genius? As it turns out, his fame has a precise birth date: April 3, 1921, the day he first set foot on American soil. The *New York Times* and the *Washington Post* dutifully sent reporters to the Battery in Lower Manhattan to interview the controversial physicist. To the journalists' bewilderment, however, they were not the only ones gathered on the East River to greet the arriving steamship. They found a crowd of nearly 20,000 people "cheering themselves hoarse." When Einstein disembarked, wearing a faded gray raincoat, smoking a "briar pipe," and gripping a violin case, he and his cohort were paraded in an open car around the Lower East Side. Their motorcade, followed by a police escort, "turned onto Second Avenue, where the sidewalks were lined nearly all the way Uptown with thousands who waved hands and handkerchiefs and shouted welcome to the visitors."

This outsized reception caught the press by surprise. Normally, a scientist's arrival would have been one of the many inconsequential news items that fill the back pages of every major newspaper. But the huge crowd, embracing Einstein with their hero's welcome, defied the journalists' expectations. This was big, they concluded. Einstein matters.

They were in for another surprise when they interviewed the physicist in person. Expecting a haughty intellectual or a frightening "Dr. Einstein"—after all, his theories had "destroyed space and time"—they instead encountered a man who wore shabby, unpretentious clothes, played the violin with a child's passion, and greeted the press "timidly," often answering questions with a bemused smile. After explaining relativity in the simplest terms he could muster, he added sheepishly, "Well, I hope I passed my examination." He was informal, funny, and humbly camera-shy. He was also full of quotable quotes, which made for good copy.

The next day Einstein made the front page of the *Washington Post*. "Professor Einstein Here, Explains Relativity," the *New York Times* also announced on its front page, adding, in a subtitle, "Thousands Wait for Hours to Welcome Theorist and His Party to America." There's a sudden change in tone in these articles, which describe him in language that is unequivocally warm. He's not the snobby scientist anymore. He's a dreamer, an artist, an "intuitive physicist," a witty and whimsical conversationalist. He's personable. But he's also popular. And, from that moment on, everywhere Einstein goes, he's treated like a movie star.

No one described the nature of Einstein's fame better than Charlie Chaplin, who hosted the scientist in Hollywood a decade later. Driving around town, the two men were greeted by people on the sidewalk with resounding enthusiasm. "They're cheering us both," said Chaplin. "You, because nobody understands you, and me, because everyone understands me."

Prior to his arrival in New York, Einstein was a physicist. Any news related to him was about relativity and his performance as a scientist. The day after the massive parade greeted his steamship, Einstein himself became the front-page headline.

But when I read those yellowed articles announcing Einstein's arrival in America, the real question I wonder about is why 20,000 ordinary New Yorkers caused a "near-riot" over a fairly obscure physicist. Why did they take a day off work to greet a controversial scientist?

The truth is, they *didn't*. Few of them, as they waved handkerchiefs in welcome, had any idea who the German physicist was. Einstein's monumental fame actually hinges on a huge misunderstanding: *The crowds were there to greet someone else.*

•

Twenty years ago, I had a revelation that changed the trajectory of my career. While driving to my first scientific conference as a newly minted faculty member, I was filled with fear. Not about the drive but about the conference.

I was twenty-seven back then, and a few months into my first real job, as an assistant professor at the University of Notre Dame. I was fast and determined as a graduate student, completing my Ph.D. in less than three years. Those were, I think, the only factors that could have landed me a faculty position, and I leaned hard on them. Not because they were my best assets, but because they were my *only* ones. Speed had its price. While a professor on paper, I was still a kid, a nervous and shy one at that. Sure, I'd managed to publish forty papers, but I didn't know how to ask a stranger for directions. I'd learned not to go to the administration building on campus to have a key made or to reserve a lecture hall, because I looked so hopeless people inevitably thought I was a graduate student who'd lost his way. Instead I'd call the office, asking questions in a tentative, heavily accented voice, and hanging up as quickly as possible.

As I neared St. Louis, that year's host of the American Physical Society's conference, I saw the city's famous arch from the highway. It was a welcome landmark, familiar from postcards, and it offered a tiny ray of hope that I could master the directions I'd written down. It was my first time in St. Louis, but even in the days before GPS, I wasn't overly worried about how I'd find the hotel. I was concerned about whom to talk to when I got there and where I would sit when lunch rolled around. At least from a distance, though, the city looked small—a grid of buildings and roads and sidewalks, some green, welcoming-looking parks—and it seemed suddenly navigable. I was finally a professor, I told myself. If I was going to teach my students about the world, I needed to act like a grown-up.

Sure enough, I did find my way to the hotel and figured out how to get to the conference. And by lunchtime, I'd decided to do something wildly uncharacteristic. If I had to eat a sandwich with some stranger—a nerve-racking proposition in and of itself—why not make it one of my personal heroes, a revered scientist who happened to be at the conference? Against the wishes of my violently beating heart, I introduced myself and asked if he had plans.

"I'm sorry, I do," he said, and I could have slapped myself for assuming this luminary of science would want to chitchat with a kid he'd never met before.

But then, casually and with a kind smile, he said that he was free for dinner.

The next five days were full of surprises. People were not just willing to talk; they were often eager to listen. They were open and curious. They were interested in the same things I was. And they doled out insight, suggestions, and phone numbers. The experience was my first practical lesson in networks, a topic that would become my life's work.

Some people are born with a talent for building meaningful links. I'm not one of them. In my case, networking was a skill I needed to acquire. I had to work hard at it, a conscious effort that began in St. Louis. Though I couldn't have known then, that trip was my first applied lesson in the mechanisms that drive success. Performance alone wasn't enough. If I wanted my work to have any impact, I couldn't avoid the people who needed to recognize my research. And if I wanted to encourage the success of others, I had to openly applaud their achievements. I was a participant in both sides of The Formula, as an individual and as part of the collective. That give-and-take is what underpins our success and ultimately determines our fates.

This is not a cynical endorsement of "networking" in the shallow and simplistic sense of the term. If my success is determined by the collective and not by individuals, then it's tempting to assume that my performance, talent, or passion doesn't matter. All I need to do is reach the right people and tell them exactly what they want to hear, and my success will snowball. But as the Third Law reminds us, that approach will only get you so far. If you want to win over the long term, performance is unavoidable. Your product needs to be highly fit and competitive.

You may outsmart your competitors with marketing, or be such a good networker that people fail to notice your questionable performance. But the real engine of success is the Third Law—fitness times preferential attachment. The two multiply, building on each other. Hoping for success with only one of those two factors is like multiplying any number by zero. It gets you exactly...nothing.

Before the St. Louis conference, I worked for a year as a postdoc at IBM. The guy in the neighboring office was an accomplished scientist, a full-time researcher at the prestigious lab. Seeing him as a kind of mentor, I asked him once about the most important project he'd ever worked on. He had several discoveries under his belt that he could have easily referred to. So I was taken aback, even disappointed, by his reply: the project he was currently working on, he told me. "My most important project? It's *always* the one I'm working on," he added.

At the time, I didn't understand his answer, to such a degree that I was convinced he was avoiding the question, that he was trying to brush me off. Still, the reply stuck with me over the years, in the way that profound ideas do. Now at fifty, I finally comprehend what he meant. *This* book is the most important thing I ever did. And the paper I'm writing *now* about the wiring of the brain will define my career. And our foodome project, an attempt to understand the patterns of personalized nutrition, which we're just getting going on, will be the one that will change the world. I honestly and sincerely believe all this about each of my current endeavors. If you're willing to listen (God help you), I'd be happy not only to talk for an hour or three about any of them but also to try to convince you that each will in fact be transformative. Ask me next year, and I'm sure I'll say the same thing...about some not-yet-conceived project.

With the Fifth Law in mind, I feel less delusional. Because there is no predictable pattern to the precise timing of our impact. It's completely random which of our projects will be our most important one. Luck, productivity, and our Q-factor together determine impact. So one of the few sureties I can lean on is that the more I try, the more opportunities I'll give my Q-factor to shine.

That's a reassuring reminder of the possibilities still ahead for me or any determined workaholic. I like to picture the late bloomer John Fenn accepting his Nobel in front of the king of Sweden. He's wearing a red bow tie and black tails, a bright smile gracing his aged face — finally getting his due at eighty-five after a lifetime of unwavering effort.

I also think about a paper Einstein wrote in 1935, at fifty-six, well beyond the age limit he himself had set as the twilight of creativity. The paper's message was clear: quantum mechanics, the prevailing theory of physics, was flawed. It predicted a strange phenomenon called "quantum entanglement," meaning faster-than-light "spooky action at a distance," an idea that violates Einstein's own theory of relativity. For decades, scientists wrote the 1935 paper off as the misguided ramblings of an aging genius. In the 1990s, though, that suddenly changed after physicists realized that entanglement is a key feature of quantum mechanics. The rediscovered Einstein paper became foundational to quantum computing. Today, its Einstein's most cited contribution to science, even surpassing his theory of relativity.

With that paper in mind, I hustle into the lab, grab a cappuccino, and get back to work.

Einstein's story also offers a telling example of the convoluted routes through which success emerges. After all, his is one of the most enduringly recognizable faces in the world, occupying such an exceptional position in our cultural awareness that *Time* magazine named him "Man of the Century." It's tempting to say that this attention is well deserved—that Einstein performed exceptionally well and reaped the benefits—but the reality is not so simple. True, no one questions Einstein's outstanding scientific performance, which then makes it logical to assume, just as those journalists greeting his steamship on the East River did, that the crowds assembled on the morning of April 3, 1921, to laud Einstein for his brilliance.

But the thing is, Einstein didn't arrive in New York as a scientist. He arrived as just another member of the delegation accompanying Chaim Weizmann, the president of the International Zionist Organization. Weizmann and his entourage were traveling to the States to promote the idea of a new Jewish state in what was then Palestine, a cause close to the hearts of a lot of New York Jews. Those 20,000 people celebrating the arriving ship? None of them cared much about relativity. They were, on the other hand, quite passionate about Zionism. Jewish community leaders encouraged attendance. Weizmann—who would later become Israel's first president—would be greeted by the mayor and given the key to the city. He was the first Jew to be bestowed that honor. It was a momentous occasion for a religious minority that had faced such frequent persecution. People came in droves to meet the hero of Zionism. The physicist accompanying him didn't even register.

We know this thanks to the Jewish press, which also covered the event on their front pages. The *Forward*'s headline proclaimed, "Great Parade for the Zionist Delegates in New York." The article describes the same parade that the *New*

York Times and the *Washington Post* also covered as headline news—except that the *Forward* and the rest of the Jewish press knew precisely why the crowd had gathered. Not only was Einstein absent from the headline, he was only mentioned in passing in the article itself, as a member of Weizmann's entourage.

Compare that with the opening line of the *Washington Post* article: "Several thousand persons gathered on the pier today to greet Prof. Albert Einstein, noted scientist and originator of the Einstein theory of relativity." While the article is quick to note that Einstein "landed here as a member of a party of distinguished Jews," it places about as much emphasis on the other arrivals as it does on Mrs. Einstein's response to the theory of relativity. Only after quoting her—"He has told me the theory a great many times, but it is all dim to me now"—does the write-up finally reveal, in a perfunctory nod, that Weizmann headed the Zionist delegation.

By erroneously handing Einstein the headlines, the gentile press did for Einstein what Arnout did for Kickstarter projects and Wikipedia editors—they gave him a huge kick, putting him on a path to success. From that day forward, Einstein was a celebrity, drawing crowds everywhere he went. Unparalleled by any scientist before or since, Einstein's fame was an accident utterly divorced from his scientific performance. He happened to be on the right steamship at the right time.

•

Einstein's narrative encapsulates the Laws of Success discussed in this book to an almost eerie degree. Our definition of success—that success isn't about you, it's about us? That's absolutely the case for Einstein, whose outsized recognition beyond the scientific community has a lot more to do with a left-field community's response than his performance.

The First Law—Performance drives success, but when performance is immeasurable, networks determine success? Einstein had already distinguished himself as a remarkable scientist, which was why the journalists were eager to interview him in the first place. But it was Einstein's network, his links to causes and key hubs *outside* the scientific community, that put him on that steamship to begin with. That network is largely invisible in the success story we commonly tell about Einstein.

The Second Law—Performance is bounded, but success is unbounded? As much as we lionize Einstein, several scientists—Newton, Bohr, Planck, Heisenberg—had just as deep an impact on physics as Einstein. His outsized presence in our collective memory is hard to justify based on performance alone. His unbounded success, however, goes without saying. Just show a picture of Einstein to anyone on the street.

The Third Law—Previous success × fitness = future success? Both of these factors played a role in Einstein's narrative. By handing him the headlines, the journalists provided the nudge that set his snowballing, widespread success in motion. But Einstein's excellence as a physicist was essential to the equation.

And while the first part of the Fourth Law, which says that team success requires diversity and balance, doesn't appear to apply to Einstein, since most of his papers were solo authored, the second half certainly does. Credit isn't about performance, it's about perception? Einstein's story hinges on a misattribution. Those crowds of Zionists were credited to Einstein not because he was the most important advocate of the cause. He was, at best, a bit player. But because he was the most widely recognizable person in the delegation to the gentile press, he got the headlines.

And finally, the Fifth Law, which says that success can come at any time as long as we're persistent? Remember Einstein's late-career paper about quantum entanglement? It was ultimately his most cited contribution to science, surpassing the impact of each of the five papers he wrote in 1905, a miracle year when he produced such blockbuster discoveries as the theory of relativity and quantum mechanics. And he never stopped trying, churning out idea after idea, paper after paper, until his death. That's a reminder of just how far persistence can take us when it's combined with a high Q-factor.

Stunningly, this simple list encompassed the success story of the most famous face in science. But he's not alone. The paths to success for anyone you can think of, from Paris Hilton to Mick Jagger to Nelson Mandela, hinge on these laws. That's because they're universal. And if we want to cultivate and encourage success in our own lives, they apply to us, too.

•

I opened this book with the statement that scientific laws are immutable—we can't rewrite them to serve our goals. Rather, we can use our awareness of them to inform our future choices and to benefit our world. The same is true for the Laws of Success. We can't alter them, but we can use them to evaluate when performance is sufficient for success and when it isn't. The lessons we can extract from these laws will help us find a balance, deciding how much effort we should devote to honing our skills vs. networking, assessing how credit will be allocated on projects we're involved in, and strategically choosing collaborators to boost creativity. When we break down and demystify success using the tools of science, we learn to see what we can control and what we can't. Most important, we can apply various laws in tandem to best enhance outcomes. And we can use this knowledge to dissect the success narratives around us, unraveling the mechanisms at work in the lives of the people we revere — an exercise that humanizes our heroes.

Like Einstein's, many success stories appear to hinge on one or a series of accidents. Hollywood celebrities are known to call up the tale of their big break — when a fortunate encounter or a powerful acquaintance placed them in the public eye. There is a luck element to this, for sure — and it usually has to do with that first nudge that kick-starts preferential attachment. But, as the Q-factor reminds us, luck is useless unless we repeatedly take advantage of opportunities when they do present themselves.

We now know that the Laws of Success underlie every success narrative, ordering what seems random in barely visible ways. That means, knowing what we now know, that we have the unique opportunity to situate ourselves for success. We can move beyond self-help tropes, which place far too much emphasis on enhancing performance, and instead approach our futures with strategies adapted to our goals and needs. We can use the Laws of Success to better our outcomes, just as we can exploit the laws of motion to engineer better airplanes.

We can also see how the inequalities around us are shaped by these laws and use our awareness of the mechanisms behind success to create a more equitable society. How? By kick-starting the success of the many deserving people around us. By helping the less visible nodes in our networks create vital links. By noticing children hindered by their circumstances and giving them a nudge. By recognizing that there's more to success than simple performance, we can assist hopeful up-and-comers with an arsenal of practical strategies.

Instead of praying for a lucky windfall, we now have a foundational science to work with in achieving both personal and societal goals. The science may be new, but the Laws of Success are not. Like all scientific laws, they're universal and eternal. They underpin millions of individual stories of failure and success, each of which can be examined and understood through this new lens. Everyone from Martin Luther King Jr. to the Beatles to Einstein were, for all their genius, ignorant of the laws that skyrocketed the exceptional accolades they received. We, now, are not. And that just might be the crucial advantage we can use in our quest to join their lofty heights.

Acknowledgments

I am regularly asked by my students, collaborators, and even my children to offer advice on how to succeed. Yet I often find my answers unsatisfactory—they are based on too few data points. In fact, my insights used to rely on one case study: my own. It wasn't until the emergence of the Science of Success that I was finally given the opportunity to expand these few data points to thousands, and sometimes to millions, learning from the successes and the failures of all of my colleagues. I decided to follow the data trail, turning the subject of success into a fascinating research topic that captivated many members of my lab. *The Formula* is the chronicle of that journey.

It wasn't a solitary journey. I am indebted to all who shared their passion and expertise, helping to unveil the Roots and the Laws of Success. It started many years ago at the Center for Network Science, first as a few isolated projects and later formalized through the Success Group, a cohort of researchers dedicated to exploring the topic. The contributions of some members of this group are discussed in the book; others are mentioned only in the notes. The members of the Success Group included Dashun Wang, Roberta Sinatra, Chaoming Song, Pierre Deville, Michael Szell, Gourab Ghoshal, Jim Bagrow, Burcu Yucesoy, Alexander Gates, Junming Huang,

Xindi Wang, Yasamin Khorramzadeh, Onur Varol, Maximilian Schich, Qing Jin, Wei Li, Yifang Ma, Nick Bloom, Luca Pappalardo, Paolo Cintia, Fosca Giannotti, Dino Pedreschi, and Hiroki Sayama. Our investigation into art also grew from our pursuit of success, thanks to the contributions of Sam Fraiberger, Roberta Sinatra, Christoph Riedl, and Magnus Resch. I benefited from discussions on art and success with Péter Küllői, Anne Thidemann, Attila Ledényi, and Attila Pőcze. I must also thank Orsolya Vásárhelyi and Milán Janosov, who helped me to teach my first Science of Success class at Central European University in Budapest. As I tried to narrate the story of success, I benefited from the help of several data artists and graphic designers, especially Mauro Martino, Kim Albrecht, Alice Grishchenko, and Gabriele Musella.

"We stand on the shoulders of giants," Newton once wrote, a statement that fully captures the research behind this book. Indeed, many brilliant colleagues have been indispensable, sharing great discoveries, offering help interpreting the research, and, in some cases, even allowing me access to unpublished material. I wish to thank all of them, including Arnout van de Rijt, Brian Uzzi, Balázs Vedres, Filippo Radicchi, Manuel Cebrian, Andres Abeliuk, Esteban Moro, Alan T. Sorensen, Sandy Pentland, Alex Petersen, Benjamin Jones, Bruce I. Sacerdote, Carlos Gershenson, Nicholas Christakis, Péter Csermely, David Galenson, Dean Keith Simonton, Dirk Brockmann, Duncan Watts, Erik Brynjolfsson, Fabio Pammolli, Frank Schweitzer, Gábor Kézdi, Gal Oestreicher-Singer, Gene Stanley, Keith Stanovich, Dirk Helbing, James A. Evans, Matthew J. Salganik, Matthew O.

Jackson, Pierre Azoulay, Csaba Pléh, Robert Oláh-Gál, Ronaldo Menezes, Santo Fortunato, and Sinan Aral. Additionally, many friends and colleagues, like György Dragomán, Viktor Segál, Gergely Böszörményi, Eszter Angyalosy, and Thea Singer, contributed ideas and advice that found their way into the book. Jay Zagorsky, József Baranyi, Ákos Erdős, Dániel Barabási, Janet K. Kelley, Ádám Halmos, and Arnout van de Rijt offered important feedback on the manuscript, and Péter Ruppert helped me to think about the business implications of our research. Special thanks to my Brookline neighbor Ákos Erdős, who, by gifting me his Lang Lang and Norah Jones concert tickets, offered me memorable experiences that found their way into the book. Also, thanks to my Budapest neighbors Tamás Hámori, who helped me understand the world of professional tennis, and László Heltay, who helped me navigate the world of classical music. Several early supporters, like Nassim Nicholas Taleb, Nicholas Christakis, Cesar Hidalgo, Alex Pentland, Santo Fortunato, James A. Evans, Gene Stanley, and Joseph Loscalzo, were willing to endorse the project in its infancy.

During the many years I've spent working on *The Formula*, James Stanfill, Jazz Robertson, Suzanne Aleva, and Brett Common have taken over many of the lab's administrative duties, allowing me to focus on writing this manuscript. Enikő Jankó and Sarah Morrison helped with editing during various stages of the writing process.

You can't have a successful book about success without a very professional publishing team. Special thanks go to my superstar agent, Doug Abrams, who would patiently remain on the phone for three hours at a time, helping me articulate my message.

This would be a very different book without his exceptional dedication to the project. His team at Idea Architects, including Jess Krager, Kelsey Sheronas, and Lara Love, were especially helpful in moving the project forward. Also thanks to the foreign agents, Camilla Ferrier, Chandler Crawford, and Jo Grossman, for making sure that *The Formula* is available everywhere. Ádám Halmos, my friend and my Hungarian publisher, has been my cheerleader throughout the project.

I cannot thank Carrie Braman enough for her dedicated editing and daily input over the past two years. She breathed life into the text, sourcing many key ideas, and helping bring the science out in a way that I did not think was possible. It was a pure joy working with her. Katherine Vaz joined the editing team at a critical juncture, and her skillful advice helped push the project past the finish line. James Stanfill sourced key ideas and was a vital force in shaping the initial chapters. John Parsley from Little, Brown saw the early potential of *The Formula*. Many thanks to him and to my editor, Phil Marino, who helped realize that vision. His pertinent input made the final book much more enjoyable.

Thanks to the many coffeehouses in Budapest and Boston—like Fixe, Mantra, Madal, and the sadly missed Alibi—and their fantastic baristas, who tolerated me for days at a time and fueled the momentum of the project with their great coffee.

And, finally, I would like to thank my wife, Janet, who understands that success as a family requires room to grow new ideas, and my children, Dániel, Izabella, and Lénárd, for the hours we missed while I worked on *The Formula*. I hope they will benefit from the many insights I gained by researching success.

Notes

Introduction: Success Isn't About You. It's About Us.

6 **The endeavor resulted in a truly fascinating paper:** Dashun Wang's first paper, about disasters, appeared as J. P. Bagrow, D. Wang, and A.-L. Barabási, "Collective Response of Human Populations to Large-Scale Emergencies," *PLOS ONE* 6, no. 3 (2011): 1–8. Our first success paper came out two years later: D. Wang, C. Song, A.-L. Barabási, "Quantifying Long-Term Scientific Impact," *Science* 342 (2013): 127–31.

11 **we also organized a symposium:** To learn more about the first scientific symposium on success, held at Harvard, see my Web page for the workshop at http://success.Barabásilab.com/2014/.

1: The Red Baron and the Forgotten Ace

19 **a young cavalryman named Manfred von Richthofen:** For more about von Richtofen's life, see https://en.wikipedia.org /wiki/Manfred_von_Richthofen. Other useful sources include "The 'Red Baron' Scores Two Victories," EyeWitness to History (2005), http://www.eyewitnesstohistory.com/richthofen .htm; "Mystery of Who Killed the Red Baron Manfred von Richthofen Finally Solved," *Daily Mail*, October 18, 2015; "Ace of Aces: How the Red Baron Became World War I's Most Legendary Fighter Pilot," *History Stories* (2016), https://www.history .com/news/ace-of-aces-how-the-red-baron-became-wwis-most -legendary-fighter-pilot. To get a more visual sense of the aerial combat he engaged in, see the History Channel documentary *The Red Baron: The Most Feared Fighter Pilot of World War I.*

261

20 **The Red Baron's story survives a century later:** For more on von Richtofen's entrenched presence in popular culture, see https:// en.wikipedia.org/wiki/The_Red_Baron_in_popular_culture.

21 **The paper explored the performance of German World War I aces:** See M. V. Simkin and V. P. Roychowdhury, "Theory of Aces: Fame by Chance or Merit," *Journal of Mathematical Sociology* 30, no. 1 (2003): 33–42, for more details on how the fame of the German aces grows exponentially with their achievement. In 2009, the same authors published a follow-up study to show how fame corresponds to merit in the case of Nobel Prize–winning physicists ("Estimating Achievement from Fame," https://arxiv.org/abs/0906.3558).

22 **Except then there's René Fonck:** To learn more about Fonck, see https://en.wikipedia.org/wiki/Ren%C3%A9_Fonck. See also "Rene Fonck—Top French Ace of WWI," by Stephen Sherman, http://acepilots.com/wwi/fr_fonck.html; "World War I: Colonel Rene Fonck," a 2017 biographical write-up on the website ThoughtCo.com by Kennedy Hickman, https://www .thoughtco.com/world-war-i-colonel-rene-fonck-2360477; and an article about his achievements and personality on Aerodrome .com: http://www.theaerodrome.com/aces/france/fonck.php.

23 **Claudette Colvin, an African-American teenager:** To learn more about Claudette Colvin's mostly unheralded contributions to the civil rights movement, listen to Amy Goodman's fascinating March 29, 2013, interview with her on *Democracy Now!*

24 **Edison gets credit for X-ray photography:** For details about misappropriated credit in the case of Thomas Edison and the Wright brothers, see Eric Goldschein and Robert Johnson's 2011 article in *Business Insider:* "The Wright Brothers Didn't Invent the Airplane...and Nine Other Inventors Who've Been Wrongly Credited."

33 **If you want to know who's more famous than Jesus:** The guidelines of the Pantheon Project, designed by Cesar Hidalgo from the MIT Media Lab, and its approach to defining and capturing "fame" are described in the "Methods" section of the project's website. See also A. Z. Yu et al., "Pantheon 1.0, a

Manually Verified Dataset of Globally Famous Biographies," *Scientific Data* 3, no. 2 (2016): 150075. A fun recap of some of the search categories and the famous figures who occupy them titled "Who's More Famous Than Jesus?" appeared in the March 14, 2014, *New York Times Magazine*. "The List of the 100 Most Famous People in History Only Has 8 Women on It," a 2014 opinion piece on Mic.com by Julianne Ross, highlights how a history of entrenched sexism is reflected in the Pantheon Project's list.

35 **"This [honor]":** There are different versions of the Aristotle quote that we paraphrase here. They are all rooted in Aristotle's *Nicomachean Ethics*, translated by Terence Irwin (Indianapolis: Hackett Publishing, 1999, NE I.5, 1095b23–30): "This [honor], however, appears to be too superficial to be what we are seeking, for it seems to depend more on those who honor than on the one honored, whereas we intuitively believe that the good is something of our own and hard to take from us. Further, it would seem, they seek to be honored by prudent people, among people who know them, and for virtue."

2: Grand Slams and College Diplomas

41 **exploring how success emerged in science:** How do we measure performance in science? My former lab member, James Bagrow, used *productivity* as a rough metric for gauging scientific performance in a 2008 paper. Bagrow and his colleagues collected data on the number of papers various physicists had published. They then compared that number to their visibility via their Google hits. They found a proportional relationship between productivity and visibility, a direct correlation between performance and scientific renown, one facet of success. See J. P. Bagrow et al., "How Famous Is a Scientist?—Famous to Those Who Know Us," *Europhysics Letters* 67, no. 4 (2004): 511–16.

41 **a rich trove of data gathered by the Association of Tennis Professionals:** For an example of what the ATP's point system looks like, in September 2015 Novak Djokovic's 12,785 points

made him the top player in men's tennis, and Federer was second-ranked with 6,725 points. In 2003, Justine Henin-Hardenne, the reigning women's champion at the time, had 6,628 points. For the sake of contrast, compare that with Anna Kournikova's 67 points during the same year, the paltry two-digit number that determined her 305 ranking. The points measure each tennis player's performance relative to the other players, and they provided Burcu and me with the key performance metric for our research linking performance to success.

43 **The tennis star Roger Federer:** According to *Forbes*, Federer was the fifth-highest-paid athlete in 2014, earning $67 million—$9 million from his tournament winnings and the rest from endorsements. That put him at the top of the list when it came to endorsement earnings. That year, no other athlete in any sport raked in as much money from endorsing brands.

43 **they reflect the *visibility* generated by his wins and losses:** Endorsement earnings are particularly sizeable and influential in sports like tennis and golf, which still reek, in the popular mind, of private clubs and prestige. And while tennis has a smaller worldwide audience than, let's say, soccer, its followers are undoubtedly wealthier: according to Ashlee Vance in a June 17, 2015, article in *Bloomberg News*, the average household income of a fan at the U.S. Open is $156,000. Luxury brands will pay crowd-pleasers a pretty penny in exchange for that fan's attention. Less visible players, those you might not recognize in the blur of competition, are far less richly rewarded. According to a 2015 article in *Victoria University News*, it costs roughly $160,000 to compete on the professional circuit, and few players make enough on the court to pay their bills. In fact, a study by the Australian Tennis Federation found that in 2013 only 150 professional tennis players were able to break even on prize money alone. Even top-ranked players have come to rely on endorsement dollars to pay for their coaching, their travel, and their time. So those who win tournaments are often rewarded twice over: sure, they earn coveted prize money, but they also earn visibility, and visibility is key to their endorsements and ultimately their wealth.

44 **She then invented a formula:** Our study, B. Yucesoy and A.-L. Barabási, "Untangling Performance from Success," *EPJ Data Science* 5, no. 17 (2016), can be accessed at the website developed by Kim Albrecht that is dedicated to the project, http:// untangling-tennis.net/. The website also provides a short video explaining the data and a visualization tool that allows users to search, sort, and compare the success and performance graphs of individual players.

44 **As Burcu crunched the numbers, a pattern emerged:** There were a few exceptions to the rule. Our data showed roughly a dozen rule-breakers whose popularity soared when it shouldn't have, causing an erratic spike in Wikipedia visits where one clearly shouldn't be. Interestingly, the outliers were young players, not seasoned veterans of the tennis world whose current on-court game no longer justified their renown. Take Ryan Sweeting, an unremarkable competitor whose ranking never surpassed sixty-fourth on the professional circuit. His fame barely registered on Burcu's graph until it increased tenfold practically overnight, as if he'd climbed fifty positions in the rankings. The reason for his sudden visibility prompted a chuckle from Burcu when she examined its source. People didn't flock to his Wikipedia page because of a stunning, drop-to-the-knees-and-kiss-the-racquet victory. Rather, it was his unexpected engagement to Kaley Cuoco, the actress who plays Penny on *The Big Bang Theory*. Cuoco and Sweeting had been dating for barely two months when their intent to marry reached the tabloids, so there was a certain degree of scandal surrounding the engagement, plenty of "what's the deal with the fiancé?" intrigue. That intrigue is captured in Burcu's graph: immediately following the engagement, Sweeting accumulated roughly 120,000 page views. The week of his marriage to Cuoco, his fame rose to an all-time high: 170,000 visits. And then there's Djokovic. No, not top-ranked Novak Djokovic, who has won twelve Grand Slam titles, but *Marko*, his tennis-playing kid brother, whose popularity was similar to a player ranked 30th but who never managed to climb higher than 581st on the

professional circuit. Marko's unearned fame has a simple origin: he's often confused with his wildly successful sibling. Of the millions searching for the hard-to-spell tennis-champion Djokovic, a small fraction land on Marko's page. That's enough to give him visibility that far exceeds his accomplishments, and enough to confuse Burcu's otherwise reliably accurate formula.

46 **graduates of elite colleges:** The statistics about Ivy League earnings come from the Department of Education. Christopher Ingraham's September 14, 2015, *Washington Post* blog article provides a chart that explains the data and details specifics about the finding.

48 **a trio of economists asked that very question:** To learn more about Boston-area exam schools and the authors' counterintuitive findings, see A. Abdulkadiroglu, J. Angrist, and P. Pathak, "The Elite Illusion: Achievement Effects at Boston and New York Exam Schools," *Econometrica* 82, no. 1 (2014): 137–96.

49 **Researchers found identical results from New York City to Romania to Hungary:** See a similar study by Cristian Pop-Eleches and Miguel Urquiola about the Romanian school system, "Going to a Better School: Effects and Behavioral Responses," *American Economic Review* 103, no. 4 (2013): 1289–324. While the authors did find that attending an elite school improves a student's final baccalaureate exam grade (the Romanian equivalent of the SAT), the gap is small. Because the improvement was so insignificant, the study reinforces the idea that individual achievement matters most. For a similar study from Hungary, see the blog post by Gábor Kézdi, on Defact.io, a site maintained by economists from Central European University: http://blog.defacto.io/post /157518958340/t%C3%A9nyleg-fontos-hogy-a-gyerek-a-legjobb.

50 **two Princeton economists:** Stacy Dale and Alan Krueger's brilliant 2011 paper, "Estimating the Return to College Selectivity over the Career Using Administrative Earnings Data," was published by the National Bureau of Economic Research (Working Paper No. 17159). It's a follow-up to their earlier paper "Estimating the Pay-off to Attending a More Selective College: An Application of Selection on Observables and Unobservables," *Quarterly Journal of Economics* 117, no. 4 (2002): 1491–1527. David

Leonhardt provides a good layperson's explanation of their findings in his February 21, 2011, *New York Times* blog post, "Revisiting the Value of Elite Colleges," which also explores the implications of the authors' findings.

51 **Nor am I suggesting that elite colleges:** Dale and Krueger acknowledge that there are enormous benefits to attending Ivy League colleges, which can and do provide network access to first-generation, low-income, and minority applicants. These students were exceptions to their overall findings.

52 **take a team sport like soccer:** Even with many individual sports like tennis and fencing, winning and losing are often dependent on factors beyond just a given athlete's performance. Her opponent's performance matters, too. If Anna Sharapova plays against Serena Williams, and Williams has an injury or a headache or just happens to miss a lot of the shots served at her, Sharapova benefits. If Sharapova is distracted by a personal issue or the sun's in her eyes or she's in a slump, Williams is more likely to emerge victorious.

52 **an Italian soccer league:** For our study on a judge's ability to properly evaluate soccer players, see "Human Perception of Performance," by Luca Pappalardo, Paolo Cintia, Dino Pedreschi, Fosca Giannotti, and A.-L. Barabási, available at https://arxiv.org/abs/1712.02224.

3: The $2 Million Urinal

54 **The better known of the two artists:** There are a number of great articles about Al Diaz and Jean-Michel Basquiat's early career. I especially like *Huck Magazine*'s October 2017 article, "The Strange Story of Jean Michel Basquiat's Original Partner in Crime," by Cian Traynor. *Dazed Digital* provides impressive details about the partnership and SAMO's origin story from Diaz's perspective in Ashleigh Kane's September 6, 2017, article, "The Story of SAMO, Basquiat's First Art Project."

55 **Diaz's partner created a large untitled painting:** Information about Basquiat's *Untitled* and its record-breaking sale at auction was sourced from the May 18, 2017, *New York Times*

article "Basquiat Sells for 'Mind-Blowing' $110 Million at Auction," by Robin Pogrebin and Scott Reyburn.

56 **That difference was part of a pattern:** Basquiat is often described as taking his career in his own hands, and Diaz among many others acknowledges Basquiat's willingness to engage in the commercial business of art. This is explored in Katherine Brooks's May 21, 2017, *Huffington Post* article, "How Jean-Michel Basquiat Became the Ultimate American Artist." Also see the detailed chronology of Basquiat's career at http://www.basquiat .com, where you can examine the network that pushed him to success. That's where the "Papa, I've made it!" quote came from.

58 **In 1917:** See Martin Gayford's excellent February 2008 *Telegraph* article "Duchamp's Fountain: The Practical Joke That Launched an Artistic Revolution," to get a better sense of *Fountain*'s origins.

59 **Dimitri Daskalopoulos, a Greek collector:** To see the Dimitri Daskalopoulos quote in context, check out "Marcel Duchamp: Money Is No Object: The Art of Defying the Art Market," by Frances Naumann, which appeared in the January 4, 2003, issue of *Toutfait*. This piece also illuminates Duchamp's significance in the art world.

60 **how, then, do we explain Basquiat's *Untitled*:** See Wikipedia's list of the most expensive paintings to get a sense of the increasing number of artworks that have sold for over $100 million: https:// en.wikipedia.org/wiki/List_of_most_expensive_paintings.

61 **few could remember what the fuss was about:** For more about how interest dwindled once credit for *The Man with the Golden Helmet* was reattributed, see "Credibility and Economic Value in the Visual Arts," H. Bonus and D. Ronte, *Journal of Cultural Economics* 21, no 2 (1997): 103–18. This paper also provides context for how difficult it is to assess value in art, a theme that is crucial to this chapter.

61 **Or the opposite happens:** Robin Pogrebin and Scott Reyburn's November 15, 2017, *New York Times* article, "Leonardo da Vinci Sells for $450.3 million, Shattering Auction Highs," provides further information on the painting's sale and history.

61 **Even the wildly famous *Mona Lisa*:** For more information about the *Mona Lisa* theft—it's a fascinating story—see Dorothy and Thomas Hoobler's long-form *Vanity Fair* article "Stealing *Mona Lisa*," which appeared in the magazine's May 2009 issue.

64 **I was curious about Mark Grotjahn:** Mark Grotjahn is a fascinating example of what it looks like when someone bypasses the art world's tacit protocols and practices, which place a lot of emphasis on prestige earned through gallery and dealer affiliations. For a more complete sense of how Grotjahn defies the expected routes to success in art, see Robin Pogrebin's July 30, 2017, *New York Times* article, "When an Artist Calls the Shots: Mark Grotjahn's Soaring Prices."

64 **Artists derive prestige from their affiliations:** See Wouter de Nooy's "The Dynamics of Artistic Prestige," *Poetics* 30, no. 3 (2002): 147–67, for more on the dependencies that govern the art world. De Nooy quotes Katherine Giuffre, who once compared the art world career ladder to a "sandpile, in which every actor's attempts to reach the top changes the shape of the climb." That's a useful metaphor for understanding success in art and it jibes with our findings. If a well-known artist suddenly exhibits at a left-field gallery, that gallery gains prestige. Prestigious artists go scurrying to it, beating a trail of footprints that morphs the topography of the network. Likewise, if a top-tier gallery exhibits an unknown artist, other gallerists will start seeing the artist with a new appreciation.

65 **The outcome of our effort was a map:** Our paper on art and networks, entitled "Reputation and Success in Art," by S. P. Fraiberger et al., will be published in *Science* in 2018.

67 **"To be successful as an artist":** I came across this Warhol quote in an excerpt of Phoebe Hoban's 2015 biography, *Basquiat: A Quick Killing in Art*, accessed via the *New York Times* website. Hoban describes Warhol's astute read on the art market and then quotes him: "Warhol, a wigged-out psychic, had presaged the whole thing. In *POPism*, he spelled it out to the next generation: 'To be successful as an artist, you have to have your work

shown by a good gallery for the same reason, say, that Dior never sold his originals from a counter in Woolworth's. It's a matter of marketing, among other things. If a guy has, say, a few thousand dollars to spend on a painting…he wants to buy something that's going to go up and up in value, and the only way that can happen is with a good gallery, one that looks out for the artist, promotes him, and sees to it that his work is shown in the right way to the right people. Because if the artist were to fade away, so would this guy's investment….No matter how good you are, if you are not promoted right, you won't be one of those remembered names.'"

69 **His fantastic illustrations:** To learn more about the Transylvanian artist Botond Részegh and his work, see http://reszegh botond.wordpress.com.

4: How Much Is a Bottle of Wine Worth?

77 **it's a job they approach with scientific seriousness:** To get a sense of a wine competition, like the one we open this chapter with, see the short film produced by the International Wine Challenge, which explains industry judging protocols. It's available at https://www.youtube.com/watch?v=-Nfnqhp5coA.

77 **He's a soft-spoken winemaker:** For details about Hodgson's story and research, see David Derbyshire's June 23, 2013, article, "Wine Tasting—It's Junk Science," in the *Guardian* (where the quote "Chance has a great deal to do with the awards that wines win" appeared); and W. Blake Gray's July 17, 2013, interview with Hodgson on the Winesearcher.com website. See also Will Storr's April 29, 2014, *Telegraph* article, "Is Everything We Know About Wine Wrong?," to get a better sense of Hodgson's background and the dilemmas that prompted his research.

79 **Usain Bolt, the fastest man on earth:** To see the minuscule difference between Bolt's and Blake's records in the hundred-meter dash, consult any site focused on running statistics. See also Robert Sutherland's August 14, 2016, article in the *Daily Telegraph*, "The Ten Fastest Men in 100m History," for more details.

80 **our performance follows something like a bell curve:** To learn more about the mathematical differences between bounded and unbounded distributions, see chapter 4 and section 4.9 in my book *Network Science* (Cambridge: Cambridge University Press, 2017), available at http://networksciencebook.com/.

80 **to forecast future outcomes in many sports:** Filippo Radicchi's predictions on Olympic records were published in "Universality, Limits, and Predictability of Gold Medal Performances at the Olympic Games," *PLOS ONE* 7, no. 7 (2012): e40335. He kindly shared with me his unpublished follow-up predictions for the 2016 Olympic Games.

83 **they sometimes get to taste 150 excellent wines:** For more information on how many wines a judge tastes a day and further details about the experience of wine judging see Wilford Wong's June 26, 2014, blog post "A Day in the Life of a Wine Judge," on Wine.com.

83 **Hodgson's data certainly suggests so:** See Hodgson's paper "An Examination of Judge Reliability at a Major U.S. Wine Competition," *Journal of Wine Economics* 3, no. 2. (2008): 105–13. It shows a lack of consistency between judges and a lack of consistency in judges over time. Equally fascinating is Hodgson's follow-up paper on the consistency in the awards that wines win, "An Analysis of the Concordance Among 13 Wine Competitions," *Journal of Wine Economics* 4, no. 1 (2009): 1–9.

85 **there's a purpose to his showmanship:** For details about Chia-Jung Tsay's findings, see "Sight over Sound in the Judgment of Music Performance," *PNAS* 110, no. 36 (2013): 14580–85. Also see Phillip Ball's August 2013 article in *Nature*, "Musicians' Appearances Matter More Than Their Sound," for a good explanation of the implications of her research.

87 **Take, for example, the Queen Elisabeth International Music Competition:** The patterns characterizing the Queen Elisabeth competition are described in detail in Renato Flores and Victor Ginsburgh's paper "The Queen Elisabeth Musical Competition: How Fair Is the Final Ranking?," *Journal of the Royal Statistical Society* 45, no. 1 (1996): 97–104. For a wider perspective, see also

V. Ginsburgh, "Awards, Success and Aesthetic Quality in the Arts," *Journal of Economic Perspectives* 17 (2003): 99–111.

90 **Wine and classical music share an aura of refinement:** Alex Mayyasi's September 11, 2013, article "The Science of Snobbery: How We're Duped into Thinking Fancy Things Are Better," which appeared in the *Atlantic*, is helpful for understanding how bias is further exacerbated in elite realms like classical music and wine judging. The quotes of wine terms come from Will Storr's *Telegraph* article (cited above), and were actual comments made by Jilly Goolden, a critic on the BBC's *Food and Drink* show.

91 **Europe's famous, long-standing pop song competition:** For specifics about the Eurovision Song Contest's immediacy bias, see Wandi Bruine de Bruin's paper "Save the Last Dance for Me: Unwanted Serial Position Effects in Jury Evaluations," *Acta Psychologica* 118, no. 3 (2005): 245–60. The paper explores how contest outcomes are shaped by the order of performances in four different arenas, including the Eurovision contest and professional figure skating. According to de Bruin, the immediacy bias is further exacerbated in the case of figure skating. That's because a skater's score from the first round determines her performance order in the second round. If she earns a low score in the first round and heads to the locker room crestfallen, she receives an earlier slot during the second round. If a skater in a later slot earns a high score, fist-pumping in excitement, she'll perform later once again. By using the first-round scores to determine the order of skaters in the second round, judges are doubling the problem. The initial random draw that determines a skater's performance slot in the first round ultimately affects her score in *both*. This bias could certainly be diminished by flipping the second-round slots. If first-round high scorers— those who have already benefited from serial position preferences—get early slots during the second round, they must once again prove their mettle, justifying their initial high scores. Those who earn low scores—presumably those who

appeared earliest on the roster during round one—could then overcome their initial disadvantage and even the playing field.

92 **Another example I find particularly startling:** Data about how immediacy affects outcomes in evaluating Spanish judge candidates came via Brian Uzzi from Northwestern University, and was collected by his former student, Guillermo Fernandez-Mazarambroz.

93 **the way the FDA approves new medical devices:** For details on FDA voting patterns and the biases that result from them, see D. Broniatowski and C. Magee, "Does Seating Location Impact Voting Behavior on Food and Drug Administration Advisory Committees?," *American Journal of Therapeutics* 20, no. 5 (2011): 502–6.

5: Superstars and Power Laws

98 **Tiger Woods was a mere nine months old:** For more on Tiger Woods's childhood story see *Tiger Woods: Prodigy* (Documentary Channel), available at https://www.youtube.com/watch?v=k-QS gd8bVI8. It's the source for the Earl Woods quote in the first paragraph of the chapter.

98 **At six, Woods placed eighth:** To get a sense of the breadth of Woods's early achievements on the green see his thorough time-line: http://tigerwoods.com/timeline. His achievements are also referenced in the documentary cited above. Also see "Timeline: A Troubled Champion," a *New York Times* interactive feature from 2009, which offers a good overview of Woods's impressive preprofessional golf career.

99 **A list of his records:** The list of Woods's professional achievements that I refer to is from Erik Matuszewski's December 30, 2016, article in *Forbes*, "41 Fantastic Facts and Figures for Tiger Woods' 41st Birthday."

99 **It's nearly impossible to find a more perfect bell curve in the real world:** You can see the bell curves the various performance criteria follow in golf in Charles Murray's 2003 book *Human Accomplishment*, published by HarperCollins.

99 **But he's not the best in all of them:** For stats on Woods's 2013 "strokes gained" and drive distance see the PGA's official website, pgatour.com, under "stats." That's also where I found information on Henrik Stenson's, Justin Rose's, and Lake List's performance in these same areas.

100 **his *success* is limitless:** To get a sense of Woods's wealth relative to other prominent African-Americans', see Matthew Miller's May 6, 2009, *Forbes* article, "The Wealthiest Black Americans." See the June 10, 2015, *Forbes* ("The World's Highest-Paid Athletes 2015") for Woods's number nine ranking at the time.

100 **An enormous amount of his wealth comes from endorsement deals:** For specifics on Woods's endorsements, see "Tiger Woods Sponsorship Deals and Endorsements," a *Telegraph* article from December 1, 2009. According to Wikipedia, the unique terms of Woods's Nike contract were discussed by Brian Berger on *Sports Business Radio* in 2006.

100 **Sherwin Rosen described superstars:** Sherwin Rosen's seminal paper, "The Economics of Superstars," *American Economic Review* 71, no. 5 (1981): 845–58, is referred to numerous times in this chapter. It was the first paper on the superstar phenomenon, taking an economist's look at the topic. An alternative take is offered in Moshe Adler's "Stardom and Talent," *American Economic Review* 75, no. 1 (1985): 208–12, which explores how success emerges when we can't distinguish between the performances of the various competitors. Adler's approach is more in line with the recent developments on the topic, as well as with our take in the chapter.

101 **how massive the rewards can be for those who reap them:** Data about Brown's and Sparks's October 2009 book sales from the *New York Times* Best Seller list was accessed via Nielsen Bookscan.

102 **the unbounded nature of success is based on a different mathematical relationship:** I discuss the difference between power laws and bell curves in great detail in *Linked: How Everything Is Connected to Everything Else and What It Means for Business, Science, and Everyday Life* (New York: Plume, 2003).

103 **the combined wealth of the top eight richest people:** See
Larry Elliot's January 15, 2017, article in the *Guardian*, "World's
Eight Richest People Have Same Wealth as Poorest 50%," for
more information on the widening global income disparity.

104 **Steven Weinberg is the best-paid physics professor:** For
more on Weinberg's story, see Selena Roberts's November 9,
2005, *New York Times* article, "Sports of the Times: An Awk-
ward Coexistence on Campus."

105 **Contrast that with today's business world:** Estimates on
CEO-to-worker pay ratios vary slightly depending on who is
included in the samples. The statistic included here is from Jena
McGregor's July 21, 2017, *Chicago Tribune* article, "Major Company CEOs Made 271 Times the Typical U.S. Worker in 2016."

105 **"A performer or author":** The Sherwin Rosen quote that
appears here is from "The Economics of Superstars," cited above.

106 **Think of the university's football coach:** Data on the Longhorns' income, and on college football profits more generally,
can be accessed at https://www.forbes.com/pictures/emdm45el
/1-university-of-texas-longhorns/#7398032730ed.

106 **his salary is derived from tuition dollars:** See the University
of Texas website for Weinberg's teaching schedule: https://
liberalarts.utexas.edu/plan2/curriculum/faculty/vineyard
#courses.

107 **it was cited 14,000 times:** For Weinberg's citation history, see
Google Scholar.

107 **each citation is worth a whopping $100,000:** The estimate on
the cost of a citation came from Esteban Moro. According to his
unpublished findings, the value of a citation in the United States
is slightly above $100,000—so a scientist like Weinberg who,
according to Google Scholar, has a paper with 14,000 citations
has an impact on science equivalent to roughly $1.4 billion.

109 **Timberlake is surely rewarded as if he is:** Justin Timberlake's
number nineteen ranking is from the June 29, 2015, *Forbes* "Celebrity 100" list.

109 **Rosen was right:** For more information about superstars'
swelling concert ticket revenue, see the December 25, 2010, *New*

York Times article "How Superstars' Pay Stifles Everyone Else," by Eduardo Porter. The article was adapted from Porter's book *The Price of Everything: Solving the Mystery of Why We Pay What We Do.*

110 **In the first decade of his professional career:** Tiger Woods's performance stats, and all subsequent discussion of the Tiger Woods effect, is sourced from Jennifer Brown's brilliant and thorough paper "Quitters Never Win: The (Adverse) Incentive Effects of Competing with Superstars," *Journal of Political Economy* 119, no. 5 (2011): 982–1013.

111 **Let's look at the data Brown collected:** It seems crazy to imagine that Brown's detailed analysis is possible, since any number of factors from mood to rain could potentially affect a player's score. But because year-by-year tournament data was available on Woods and his competitors, Brown could piece together just how powerful Woods's influence has been on the game. She was able to account for the variations in performance created by the unique challenges presented by particular courses. By studying the data gleaned from years of tournaments, she examined each golfer's performance on the same course over time. She could also account for a slew of other potential influencers: weather variations, crowd size, the intensity of media coverage, the prize money at stake, or the popularity of particular tournaments. She found, again and again, that Woods's effect on the competition was stronger than any other factor.

112 **Brown compared the scores of the tournament participants:** Woods's unexpected and prolonged break from professional play provided Brown with an opportunity to analyze other players' scores in his absence. Because the second surgery was unexpected, it allowed Brown to rule out a variety of other possible factors that might account for the noticeable superstar effect she'd found in the large data set. In this case, Woods wasn't selecting competitions that he knew he'd perform better at and sitting out others. His sudden nonattendance had nothing to do with the difficulty of particular courses or the relative strength of his competition. It was random.

113 **the degree to which it affected his performance:** Brown's research reminds me of a *This American Life* episode about a car dealership in New Jersey trying to make its monthly sales quota. The dealership had a large staff of mostly veteran salespeople, but there was one young guy with only four years of experience working on the team, and he consistently outperformed his coworkers. Not by a little, by *a lot.* At a dealership where many salespeople struggled to sell five cars a month, this guy was sometimes selling thirty or more. When he added up his commissions and bonuses, he was making almost twice the salary of his colleagues—six figures to their $60,000. If I hired this guy, I'd probably be patting myself on the back. But I also couldn't help but notice the resignation in the voices of his coworkers as they remarked on his ever-accumulating tallies. He was clearly intimidating other employees and, in all likelihood, decreasing the performance of the team. I wouldn't be surprised if the dealership as a whole ended up selling fewer cars. So if superstars scare the pants off the rest of us, lowering our performance, why hire them in the first place? For the full story about Jason Mascia, the car salesman I refer to here, listen to episode 129 of *This American Life*, "Cars," available at https://www.thisamericanlife.org/513/129-cars.

114 **research shows that when a university hires a scientific superstar:** To learn more about the benefits of superstardom on the productivity of colleagues, see the working paper "Why Stars Matter," by A. Agrawal, J. McHale, and A. Oettl, published in March 2014 by the National Bureau of Economic Research.

114 **a superstar's impact is just as profound when he or she departs:** For details on what happens to a scientist's collaborators after a superstar's death, see Pierre Azoulay, Joshua S. Graff-Zivin, and Jialan Wang, "Superstar Extinction," *Quarterly Journal of Economics* 125, no. 2 (2010).

116 **But his subsequent analysis is heartening:** Azoulay's follow-up study, P. Azoulay, C. Fons-Rosen, and J. S. Graff-Zivin, "Does Science Advance One Funeral at a Time?," National

Bureau of Economic Research Working Paper No. 21788 (2015), expands and hones his initial findings. He uses the term "Goliath's shadow," which I quote here.

117 **Scandal can overwhelm fame:** For more details on how we penalize superstars, see Azoulay's paper coauthored with Alessando Bonatti and Joshua L. Krieger, "The Career Effects of Scandal: Evidence from Scientific Retractions," National Bureau of Economic Research Working Paper No. 21146 (2015).

118 **"His entire identity and sense of self was taken away":** See Alan Shipnuck's February 13, 2015, article in *Golf*, "Tiger's Woes Aren't Just About His Game—Everything Goes Back to His Sex Scandal," to put this quote in further context and for more information on how public shaming has affected Woods's game and personal life.

6: Exploding Kittens and Sock Puppets

123 **For Elan Lee, it began with a stream of e-mail messages:** To learn more about the birth of the Exploding Kittens game, and the strange experience of watching firsthand while a Kickstarter campaign went viral, watch Elan Lee's speech on the JoCo cruise, given twelve days into the viral campaign: https://www .youtube.com/watch?v=tfB7IVTOkDk. The quote summarizing the highlight of the campaign came from this video. See also Jackie Bischof's February 2, 2015, *Newsweek* article, "A Card Game About Exploding Kittens Broke a Kickstarter Record."

125 **70 percent of Kickstarter projects fail:** Statistics about the success rates of Kickstarter projects are available at https:// www.kickstarter.com/help/stats. For more information about how Kickstarter fits into a bigger crowdsourced fundraising picture, see Catherine Clifford's January 18, 2016, article in *Entrepreneur*, "Less Than a Third of Crowdfunding Campaigns Reach Their Goal."

126 **Arnout randomly selected two hundred new Kickstarter projects:** For more details on Van de Rijt's Kickstarter experiment, see the paper he coauthored with S. Kang, M. Restivo, and A. Patil, "Field Experiments of Success-Breeds-Success

Dynamics," *PNAS* 111, no. 19 (2014): 6934–39. See also M. Restivo and A. van de Rijt, "Experimental Study of Informal Rewards in Peer Production," *PLOS ONE* 7, no. 3 (2012): e34358.

127 **This rich-get-richer phenomenon:** For more information on the Matthew effect and other examples of the rich-get-richer phenomenon see Robert K. Merton's brilliant paper "The Matthew Effect in Science," *Science* 159, no. 3810 (1968): 56–63. The biblical passage I quote comes from Merton's paper.

128 **Our map revealed something surprising:** Our analysis of the World Wide Web as a network was first published in R. Albert, H. Jeong, and A.-L. Barabási, "Diameter of the World Wide Web," *Nature* 401, no. 9 (1999): 130–31. For more about this work, and networks more generally, see my book *Linked: How Everything Is Connected to Everything Else and What It Means for Business, Science, and Everyday Life* (New York: Plume, 2003).

130 **That's a feedback loop with a dismal result:** For more information about how success breeds success in childhood literacy, see Keith Stanovich's thorough paper "Matthew Effects in Reading: Some Consequences of Individual Differences in the Acquisition of Literacy," *Reading Research Quarterly* 21, no. 4 (1986): 360–407. See also the interview with Stanovich at https://www.youtube.com /watchv=lF6VKmMVWEc, which illuminates his findings and their implications.

132 **These foundational questions prompted Arnout:** The Wikipedia experiment I describe here, along with the Change.org experiment I discuss elsewhere, are explored in Van de Rijt's paper "Field Experiments of Success-Breeds-Success Dynamics," cited above. The paper also describes another experiment on a fourth Internet platform which allowed Arnout to see if an initial positive rating led to more positive ratings by using the website Epinions.com. Each month, Epinions is used by roughly a million consumers, who can read evaluations of pretty much any product under the sun. Epinions pays reviewers to test the quality of these items—baby strollers, remote control cars, immersion blenders—and then write reviews of the products for the public to peruse. The website asks its readers, using a

simple system, to rate how helpful they found the reviews to be. If they found a particular review useful in evaluating the quality of a product, a reader can select "very helpful." A positive rating benefits the reviewers, who are paid more for product evaluations that are deemed more helpful. Arnout and his team read new, unrated reviews as they popped up on the site. Trying to account for quality in their endorsements, they chose 305 that they found helpful. They then gave a subset of these a "very helpful" rating, and left the others as their control group. And again, there was a marked difference in outcomes between the control group and those they endorsed. Presumably because Arnout accounted for quality when selecting reviews to include in his experiment, in the two weeks following the experiment's start, the majority—77 percent of the control group—earned at least one "very helpful" rating. But in the cases where Arnout intervened and offered the first positive rating, that percentage rose to 90 percent. In other words, when given an initial favorable endorsement, a full nine out of ten reviews received further positive feedback.

134 **The same team of researchers that discovered the competition's biases:** See Victor A. Ginsburgh and Jan C. van Ours's article "Expert Opinion and Compensation: Evidence from a Musical Competition," *American Economic Review* 93, no. 1 (2003): 289–98, for more information on how classical musicians benefit from winning the Queen Elisabeth competition. It's a follow-up study on Ginsburgh's 1996 paper about the competition discussed earlier.

137 **"I don't need to really say anything about the plot of this book":** See "R. J. Ellory's Secret Amazon Reviews Anger Rivals," Alison Flood's September 3, 2012, article in the *Guardian*, for details about the Ellory story. I use her quotes of both his positive and negative reviews. Her September 4, 2012, article, also in the *Guardian*, "Sock Puppetry and Fake Reviews: Published and Be Damned," provides a good discussion of the ethics and implications of sockpuppeting and an overview of how the practice benefits authors. A third *Guardian* article, also

by Flood, from July 23, 2010, "R. J. Ellory Wins Crime Novel of the Year Award," provides details about his career and his success as a crime novelist.

140 **by manipulating the "up-votes":** For more information on how up-and down-votes affect future ratings, see L. Muchnik, S. Aral, and S. J. Taylor, "Social Influence Bias: A Randomized Experiment," *Science* 341, no. 6146 (2013): 647–51.

141 **Arnout's next experiment:** See Van de Rijt's 2014 paper, cited above, for details about how further donations in the Kickstarter universe lead to "decreasing marginal returns." The same is true for ratings on Epinions.

144 **the artist who drew the goat wizards:** To learn more about Matthew Inman's runaway success as a comics creator, check out his own take from The Oatmeal at http://theoatmeal.com /misc/p/state. See also Krisztina Holly's July 28, 2016, article in *Forbes*, "Elan Lee's Secrets Behind the Largest Kickstarter Campaign in History," which acknowledges the role Inman played in the success of the card game.

7: The Ear of the Beholder

147 **Kate Mills, publishing director at Orion Books:** Kate Mills's quote, and more details about the Robert Galbraith story, come from Sam Marsden's July 14, 2013, article in the *Telegraph*, "The Cuckoo's Calling: Publishers' Embarrassment at Turning Down a J. K. Rowling Detective Novel."

147 **Wansell praised *The Cuckoo's Calling*:** For more information on the initial positive reviews the book received, including Geoffrey Wansell's glowing response, see Joe Collins's July 15, 2013, article in *New Statesman*, "What Did Critics Really Think of *Cuckoo's Calling* (Before They Knew It Was by J. K. Rowling)?"

148 **Stephen King conducted a similar experiment:** For more details on King's fascinating multibook experiment with writing under a pseudonym, see https://en.wikipedia.org/wiki /Richard_Bachman. See also Jake Rossen's July 10, 2017, article in *Mental Floss*, "Known Alias: How Stephen King Was Outed as Richard Bachman."

149 **she'd been a single mother collecting welfare:** See Rowling's 2008 Harvard commencement speech for more about her circumstances while writing *Harry Potter and the Sorcerer's Stone* and to read the quote in context: https://news.harvard.edu /gazette/story/2008/06/text-of-j-k-rowling-speech/.

151 **Seeking to understand how popularity influences success:** To learn more about the MusicLab study, see M. J. Salganik, P. Sheridan Dodds, and D. J. Watts, "Experimental Study of Inequality and Unpredictability in an Artificial Cultural Market," *Science* 311, no. 5762 (2006): 854–56. The paper's supporting online material provides impressive details on the experiment and its findings. For a good layperson's overview of the paper, see Jesse Marczyk's September 3, 2013, blog post, "The Popularity of Popularity," in *Psychology Today*.

153 **a song floated to the top and stayed there:** The flocking effect discussed here led to pronounced unevenness in the number of downloads particular songs received. In the control group, which lacked social influence, all songs had the same chance of being listened to. A participant would click on one and decide if he liked it, basing his opinion exclusively on his own experience of the song. That was gone once the participants were privy to their group's download counts. Only about two hundred participants downloaded the songs deemed less popular, while those deemed excellent were downloaded by more than three thousand listeners, nearly half of the participants in each group. That means that a "winner-take-all" dynamic—a consequence of preferential attachment—emerged once social influence was turned on.

153 **a term Robert Merton coined in 1948:** For further details on the concept of the self-fulfilling prophecy, see Robert Merton's seminal paper, "The Self-Fulfilling Prophecy," *Antioch Review* 8, no. 2 (1948): 193–210.

153 **to describe gaps in educational achievement:** Merton recognized that there were plenty of other applications for the term "self-fulfilling prophecy." Another example is a financial panic— we're told the market is failing, and so we sell, hence it fails. And then there's the placebo effect: We think that something is good

for us, so it is. It's worth noting that the placebo effect isn't insignificant. It's actually built into our genes, into neural processes of perception, and it's so strong that doctors often can't distinguish between it and the biological effect they're attempting to study. See, for example, K. T. Hall, J. Loscalzo, and T. J. Kaptchuk, "Genetics and the Placebo affect: The Placebome," *Trends in Molecular Medicine* 21, no. 5 (2015): 285–94.

154 **The experiment took place at the Oak School:** To learn more about the Oak School study, see Robert Rosenthal and Lenore Jacobson's *Pygmalion in the Classroom: Teacher Expectation and Pupils' Intellectual Development* (New York: Holt and Winston, 1968).

155 **the researchers deliberately deceived the new participants:** For further details on the second MusicLab study discussed here, see Matthew Salganik and Duncan Watts, "Leading the Herd Astray: An Experimental Study of Self-Fulfilling Prophecies in an Artificial Cultural Marketplace," *Social Psychology Quarterly* 71, no. 4 (2008): 338–55.

156 **And it happens in science:** For more information on how reputation signaling affects a famous scientist's coauthors, see T. S. Simcoe and D. M. Waguespack, "Status, Quality, and Attention: What's in a (Missing) Name?," *Management Science* 57, no. 2 (2011): 274–90.

159 **to understand how these latecomers became the hubs:** For the role of fitness in competition for success, see A.-L. Barabási, R. Albert, H. Jeong, and G. Bianconi, "Power Law Distribution of the World Wide Web," *Science* 287, no. 5461 (2000): 2115; and G. Bianconi and A.-L. Barabási, "Competition and Multiscaling in Evolving Networks," *Europhysics Letters* 54, no. 4 (2001): 436–42.

162 **Manuel and his team had developed an algorithm:** See A. Abeliuk et al., "The Benefits of Social Influence in Optimized Cultural Markets," *PLOS ONE* 10, no. 4 (2015): 1–20, the brilliant paper coauthored by Manuel Cebrian, for more information about how the Australian team developed and honed the algorithm to detect the fitness of songs.

164 **After getting his Ph.D., Dashun joined IBM:** For more specifics on the ranking algorithm described here, see Ting Wang and Dashun Wang's paper "Why Amazon's Rankings Might Mislead You: The Story of Herding Effects," *Big Data Journal* 2, no. 4 (2014): 196–204.

166 **"Had things turned out only slightly different":** To read Duncan Watts's editorial on J. K. Rowling and success, see "J. K. Rowling and the Chamber of Literary Fame," *Bloomberg*, July 19, 2013.

168 **the success of *Harry Potter* wasn't a fluke:** For *Harry Potter*'s publishing history and the book's slow initial rise in popularity, see https://en.wikipedia.org/wiki/Harry_Potter.

169 **when Ben Cohen and Jerry Greenfield opened an ice-cream shop:** For more information on Ben & Jerry's success story, see *Entrepreneur*'s October 10, 2008, profile of the duo at https://www.entrepreneur.com/article/197626. Also see *Peace, Love, and Branding*, a 2014 short film by Fast Company that provides details on the company's origins and marketing tactics (https://www.youtube.com/watch?v=JNuDGsSdEoU).

8: Kind of Conventional, Kind of Innovative, *Kind of Blue*

175 **five musicians handpicked by Miles Davis:** More information about the *Kind of Blue* recording sessions and the record's rampant success can be found on Wikipedia at https://en.wikipedia.org/wiki/Kind_of_Blue. See also "Between Takes: The *Kind of Blue* Sessions," an excerpt of Ashley Kahn's liner notes for the record's fiftieth-anniversary reissue on NPR's *Morning Edition*, January 29, 2009, which provides good context on the experience of recording the album.

176 **the secret was the simplicity of the charts:** For an inside take on the *Kind of Blue* recordings, see Bill Evans's liner notes, published March 2, 2018, in *SFJazz* as "Improvisation in Jazz."

177 **Brian examined the public's response to musicals:** To learn more about Brian Uzzi's brilliant research on the success of Broadway musicals, see B. Uzzi and J. Spiro, "Collaboration and Creativity: The Small World Problem," *American Journal of*

Sociology 111, no. 2 (2005): 447–504. The *Chorus Line*, *Producers*, and *Carousel* examples I discuss here, and the important relationship between Rodgers and Hammerstein, are highlighted by the authors in the paper.

180 **In examining the entire history of jazz:** For more details on the fascinating and comprehensive study of success in jazz, which I discuss here and at the end of the chapter, see the work of Balázs Vedres, my colleague in Budapest, specifically his article "Forbidden Triads and Creative Success in Jazz: The Miles Davis Factor," *Applied Network Science* 2, no. 3 (2017). For a summary of the author's main findings see http://blogs.springer open.com/springeropen/2017/10/05/jazz-bands-succeed-by -missing-links-among-musicians/.

180 **Balázs identified comparable dynamics in video game development:** For specifics about the study on teams in video game development, see Mathijs de Vaan, David Stark, and Balázs Vedres, "Game Changer: Structural Folds with Cognitive Distance in Video Game Development," *American Journal of Sociology* 120, no. 4 (2015): 1144–94.

181 **the highest-impact papers in science are produced not by solo geniuses:** The research about solo vs. team work was done by my former postdoc Stefan Wuchty, working in Brian Uzzi's lab, and was published in S. Wuchty, B. F. Jones, and B. Uzzi, "The Increasing Dominance of Teams in the Production of Knowledge," *Science* 316, no. 5827 (2007): 1036–39.

182 **Jim explored an enormous data set from the computer-programming site GitHub:** To learn more about the work of James Bagrow on leadership in GitHub, see Michael Klug and James P. Bagrow, "Understanding the Group Dynamics and Success of Teams," *Royal Society Open Science* 3, no. 160007 (2016).

184 **lopsided contributions are not unique to GitHub:** For more information about how work is distributed on Wikipedia editing teams, see Anniket Kittur and Robert E. Kraut, *Beyond Wikipedia: Coordination and Conflict in Online Production Groups* (New York: ACM Press, 2010).

184 **how teams consisting of high school students conduct research in synthetic biology:** The results on the team dynamics of iGEM, capturing the collaboration patterns of high school synthetic biology teams, came from an ongoing study in my lab led by Marc Santolini.

184 **"No grand idea was ever born in a conference":** The full F. Scott Fitzgerald quip, "No grand idea was ever born in a conference, but a lot of foolish ideas have died there," appeared in "Notebook E" in *The Crack-Up* (1945), a posthumous collection of letters, essays, and notes edited by Edmund Wilson.

185 **William Muir studies animal breeding:** To learn more about Muir's study, see W. M. Muir, "Group Selection for Adaptation to Multiple-Hen Cages: Selection Program and Direct Responses," *Poultry Science* 75, no. 4 (1996): 447–58. Also see "When the Strong Outbreed the Weak," David Sloan Wilson's July 11, 2016, in-depth interview with Muir for the Evolution Institute, https://evolution-institute.org/when-the-strong-outbreed-the-weak-an-interview-with-william-muir/.

187 **the infamous example of Duke University:** See "Discord Turns Academe's Hot Team Cold," Janny Scott's November 21, 1998, *New York Times* article, for more discussion of the too-much-talent effect on Duke University's English department.

187 **the "too-much-talent" effect in professional sports:** For more information about the issues that occur on superstar teams, see Roderick I. Swaab et al., "The Too-Much-Talent Effect: Team Interdependence Determines When More Talent Is Too Much or Not Enough," *Psychological Science* 25, no. 1581 (2014).

188 **Could they measure the intelligence of a group:** To learn more about collective intelligence, see Anita Williams Woolley et al., "Evidence for a Collective Intelligence Factor in the Performance of Human Groups," *Science* 330, no. 6004 (2010): 686–88.

189 **groupthink emerges when teams become too cohesive:** For more examples of groupthink and its consequences, and to learn

more about the Bay of Pigs crisis teamwork failure, see
J. Richard Hackman and Nancy Katz's "Group Behavior and
Performance," in S. T. Fiske, D. T. Gilbert, and G. Lindzey, eds.,
Handbook of Social Psychology, 5th ed. (New York: Wiley, 2010).

191 **he turned a bank's call center into his laboratory:** To learn
more about Sandy Pentland's badge-data research, see two
excellent articles in the April 2012 *Harvard Business Review:*
"The New Science of Building Great Teams: Analytics for Success," featuring Pentland and moderated by Angelia Herrin;
and Pentland's "The New Science of Building Great Teams:
The Chemistry of High-Performing Groups Is No Longer a
Mystery."

194 **Orchestrating success is a delicate balancing act:** For specifics on the team dynamics that contributed to *Kind of Blue*, see
John Szwed, *So What: The Life of Miles Davis* (New York: Simon
& Schuster, 2002), especially pages 174–77, on Davis's preparation and approach to the seminal album. The Wynton Kelly
example is discussed there.

194 **He brought together "forbidden triads":** Balázs Vedres's key
finding was that the type of relationship Kelly brought along
was essential to success in jazz. Indeed, across all jazz albums,
the densities of such forbidden triads have an inverted, U-shaped
relationship to success, suggesting that too little or too much of
any kind of triad is poisonous to success. If you compare two
jazz recordings with the same number of collaborators, the one
that features more forbidden triads will experience significantly
more long-term success than the one with only open and closed
triads. This approach to leadership was arguably the most
important aspect of Davis's success. Though he was, of course, a
gifted trumpeter, his musical genius rested at least in part on his
casting decisions. Balázs found, in fact, that the exceptional success *Kind of Blue* experienced, even compared to the many other
albums Davis put together, is rooted in the many forbidden triads employed there. The more forbidden triads assembled by
Davis in one of his sessions, the more successful it became.

9: The Algorithm That Found the Overlooked Scientist

196 **I first learned about Douglas Prasher three years ago:** For more information about Prasher's story, see Yudhijit Bhattacharjee's excellent July 18, 2011, *Discover Magazine* article, "How Bad Luck and Bad Networking Cost Douglas Prasher a Nobel Prize." Also see "What Ever Happened to Douglas Prasher?," Bob Grant's February 26, 2013, op-ed in *The Scientist*.

196 **We often view science as the quest of the lonely genius:** To get a sense of the increasing dominance of teams in science, see Brian Uzzi's article "The Increasing Dominance of Teams in the Production of Knowledge," discussed in the previous chapter and cited there.

198 **Hua-Wei jumped on the problem:** For details on our credit allocation algorithm, developed by Hua-Wei while he visited my lab, see Hua-Wei Shen and Albert-László Barabási, "Collective Credit Allocation in Science," *PNAS* 111, no. 34 (2014): 12325–30.

199 **There were only a few cases where our algorithm and the Nobel Committee disagreed:** Credit misallocation is essentially written into the history of science. It's a throwback to an era when aristocratic white men, hobby scientists supervising underlings and assistants, received not just some but *all* the credit for discoveries and insights often produced by vast teams. For example, according to S. Shapin ("The Invisible Technician," *American Scientist* 77, no. 6 [1989]: 554–63), the anonymous technicians who helped Robert Boyle, a well-known seventeenth-century chemist—the people who actually performed his experiments and whose living hands scrawled key observations in laboratory notebooks—are lost to history. Etchings from seventeenth-century London depict single scientists in elaborate feathered hats who stand heroically in the foreground of labs peopled not by collaborators but by nameless putti. The putti—cherubs thought to be visible only through physical illusion—are stand-ins for the lab assistants who actually operated the scientific instruments. Such technicians were unnamed, "ghost authors" even in their own time. But, tellingly,

the etchings ensure their anonymity further by rendering them literally invisible. Thus, our tendency to focus on individual accomplishment over team achievement is now deeply ingrained in the scientific nomenclature. We refer to major work as belonging to a single thinker: Euclidian geometry, Mendelian inheritance, Newton's laws of motion, Einstein's relativity. We also hire, promote, and make tenure decisions based on an individual's body of work, despite how rare solo authorship is in this day and age.

202 **And yet, there was something unique about Battier:** See Michael Lewis's wonderful profile of Battier, "The No-Stats All-Star," in the February 13, 2009, *New York Times Magazine*, for details on Battier's tactics. This was the source for the quote about Kobe Bryant.

202 **Harry Truman once said:** I came across the Harry Truman quote in an editorial in *Nature* 535, no. 7612 (2016): 323. Its attribution to John Wooden and the English journalist Charles Edward Montague is discussed here: http://forum.quoteland .com/eve/forums/a/tpc/f/99191541/m/7123950067.

205 **I'll never forget the devastating photo of the Syrian toddler:** For details about the surge in fundraising for refugee causes prompted by Aylan Kurdi's photo, see Luke Mintz's July 12, 2017, article, "Photo of Syrian Toddler Boosted Fundraising for Refugees 100-Fold," in *Business Insider*.

208 **As a tried-and-true method, recommended by grandparents everywhere, there are clear benefits to apprenticeship:** For details about Eliasson's *New York City Waterfalls* artwork, see https://en.wikipedia.org/wiki/New_York_City_Waterfalls.

208 **I tell my students that working with a recognized name is the best way to build a reputation:** The changes in credit allocation for the 1997 Nobel Prize in Physics is discussed in detail in the *PNAS* paper by Hua-Wei Shen and myself, cited above.

210 **Darlene Love was on her hands and knees in a bathroom:** Darlene Love's story (and the equally compelling stories of many other African-American women backup singers) is beautifully told in *Twenty Feet from Stardom* (2013), directed by

Morgan Neville. You can see Love's Rock & Roll Hall of Fame induction speech by Bette Midler here: https://www.youtube.com/watch?v=Oo4gHVT82Uk.

213 **Gendered pay, of course, isn't the only manifestation of credit misallocation:** The gender pay gap and the tenure gap in academia are widely acknowledged and numerous articles have been written on the topic. It is something we are also exploring in my lab in a joint project with Junming Huang, Roberta Sinatra, and Alex Gates.

213 **The data shows that women economists:** For more details on the troubling differences in the tenure rates of male and female economists, see Heather Sarsons's brilliant "Recognition for Group Work: Gender Differences in Academia," *American Economic Review* 107, no. 5 (2017): 141–45.

215 **Sixteen years later, the recipients of Prasher's envelopes:** Both Chalfie and Tsien named Prasher as a coauthor when they published their first article on GFP, so he contributed to both Nobel Prize–winning discoveries. And he had a solo article, the one he'd written before he quit, announcing the cloning of GFP. That's why our algorithm selected him for the Nobel Prize. He was the only scientist whose work was most consistently linked to the success of the glowing molecule. Chalfie was not shy about confessing this: "They could've easily given the prize to Douglas and the other two [Osamu Shimomura and Roger Y. Tsien] and left me out," he said after his win.

216 **Seventeen years after leaving academia:** One day the Science of Success may help correct some of these egregious credit misallocations. After all, I learned about Prasher from our predictive algorithm, which quickly zoomed in on his monumental contribution to GFP. It did a better job than the Nobel Committee, mainly because Prasher's crucial role was not evident in any single paper. It was a secret distributed across thousands of research papers by scientists who co-cited Prasher's seminal work along with the work of those who eventually walked away with the prize. And because the Nobel Committee didn't have an algorithm that could reveal the true credit share, its members

made a decision based on the recommendations they received. And why would someone recommend a scientist for a Nobel Prize whom they'd never met, who hadn't written a paper for fifteen years, and who hadn't attended a single conference? As far as the anonymous recommenders and the committee were concerned, Prasher was one of dozens of names on the prizewinning papers. For all intents and purposes, he hardly existed.

10: Einstein's Error

222 **Age is, of course, a fever chill:** See page 186 in *Greatness: Who Makes History and Why*, by Dean Keith Simonton (New York: Guilford Press, 1994), for the Einstein quote and Dirac poem.

222 **While Dirac failed to follow his own dictate:** See Dean Keith Simonton, "Creative Productivity: A Predictive and Explanatory Model of Career Trajectories and Landmarks," *Psychological Review* 104 (1997): 66–89, for details on Simonton's research. See also Dean Keith Simonton, "Age and Outstanding Achievement: What Do We Know After a Century of Research?," *Psychological Bulletin* 104, no. 2 (1988): 251–67.

222 **Must we inevitably lose our mojo as we age?:** Benjamin Jones, an economist whose interests parallel Simonton's, surveyed Nobel Prize winners between 1900 and 2008 and came to a similar conclusion. See his "Age and Great Invention," National Bureau of Economic Research Working Paper No. 11359 (2005); and Benjamin F. Jones and Bruce A. Weinberg, "Age Dynamics in Scientific Creativity," *PNAS* 108, no. 47 (2011): 18910–14. He did, however, see systematic changes over the past decades. Both in physics and in medicine, a scientist's chance of receiving a Nobel for work they completed before turning thirty was the highest in 1920 and has been decreasing ever since. In other words, scientists now are slightly older when they break through. Overall, he saw a six-year average increase in the age of major innovators over the course of the twentieth century, a shift he attributes to the increased years it takes to complete advanced degrees in the modern era. But even accounting for this shift, the winners' landmark work typically

emerged in their third or fourth decade, shortly after they'd completed their training and taken a few years to get their sea legs, so to speak, in the scientific world. Because there was such an obvious relationship between when landmark work was produced and the prizewinners' age when they completed it, Jones could develop a predictive formula, foreseeing precisely when a researcher would break through. When there's a predictive formula on hand that's even remotely relevant to my fate, I have to, of course, try it on for size. And since Jones's formula is not really about Nobel Prize winners but about peak creativity, it applies to me as well. According to Jones's formula, my highest-impact work should have come at thirty-six. It's pretty close: I was thirty-one when I completed my work about preferential attachment in networks, which is my most cited work to date.

227 **Roberta's late-night "aha" moment:** Our discovery of the Fifth Law and the Q-factor was published in Roberta Sinatra, Dashun Wang, Pierre Deville, Chaoming Song, and Albert-László Barabási, "Quantifying the Evolution of Individual Scientific Impact," *Science* 354, no. 6312 (2016): 5239. Note that in some areas, creativity does have an age. In the 1990s, David Galenson, an economist at the University of Chicago, examined the ages when artists made their highest-selling pieces. He saw, essentially, two schools of American painters, with wildly different ages of major achievement. Some, like Andy Warhol, Frank Stella, and Jasper Johns, tended to produce high-value pieces very early on in their artistic lives. Others, like Willem de Kooning, Jackson Pollock, and Mark Rothko, made their best-selling works late in their careers. Galenson discovered a pattern here beyond the Fifth Law. The late bloomers all had something in common: they approached their canvases via a process of trial and error, repeatedly wrestling with the same subject and doggedly honing their technique. Galenson called this wise crew "experimental artists." On the other hand, the young upstarts like Andy Warhol, Jasper Johns, Picasso, and Van Gogh, were "conceptual artists" interested in

expressing revolutionary ideas, often in lieu of technique. By classifying each artist as belonging to the conceptual or experimental camp, Galenson could make a reasonable guess as to the value of a work that came up for auction. An early-career work by Warhol, for example, was worth millions of dollars more than a late-career one. The opposite was true for Pollock. To learn more about Galenson's work, see *Old Masters and Young Geniuses: The Two Life Cycles of Artistic Creativity* (Princeton, NJ: Princeton University Press, 2006). Galenson's findings parallel Dean Keith Simonton's, who looked at famous writers and found general, discipline-based trends. In poetry, Simonton discovered, creative landmarks were reached relatively early on average. Interestingly, novelists typically take longer to blossom, often not publishing their landmark work until their late forties or early fifties. This yawning age difference between successful poets and prose writers is seen throughout history and across cultures, a remarkably consistent trend.

231 **Fenn's story is a happy one:** For more about John Fenn's fascinating life, see Carol Robinson's eulogy in *Nature* 469, no. 300 (2011). Despite the happy ending I describe here, it's worth noting that there's a tragic epilogue to Fenn's tale of late success. While Yale didn't think that the elderly scientist belonged on its faculty, it was eager to claim his late-career discovery. Yale sued Fenn for roughly a million dollars in 1993, arguing that his patent was their intellectual property, since the idea was born under their roof. Never mind that it was *their* mandatory retirement policy that forced him out of his ivied laboratory, hat in hand. And Yale won, collecting $500,000 in legal fees and $545,000 in damages. For details on this, see "Nobelist Loses to Yale in Lawsuit," Kate Moran's article in the May–June 2005 issue of the *Yale Alumni Magazine*.

231 **Fenn embodies the Fifth Law's simple message:** For a list of people of all ages who found success—including those I mention here—see http://brainprick.com/you-can-succeed-at-any-age -never-too-young-never-too-old/.

233 **So, if an individual with a low *Q*-factor:** See "Seven Steve Jobs Products That Failed," Chandra Steele's August 26, 2011, article in *PC Magazine*, which lists some of the numerous failures in Jobs's rampantly successful career.

234 **This career model defied many of my expectations:** I was also convinced that we get better and better at sniffing out new ideas to explore, honing a kind of sixth investigative sense with each passing year. I certainly believed that some of us are better than others at generating these starting ideas, as if we are all pulling our ideas from different distributions. Once again, our findings showed that neither was the case—the pool from which we picked our random numbers was the same for all of us and didn't change over time. We all grab our ideas from the same distribution, which means that no one is better than their peers at systematically reaching for higher r. The model that most accurately described innovation, then, was deceptively, stunningly straightforward: we just pick random ideas, enhancing them with a Q-factor that remains unchanged during our career. That means that the more we try, the more likely it is that we will stumble across that magic high-r idea. A rich vein of inquiry will work in tandem with our inherent Q, amplifying our success.

235 **Does this finding apply to those outside the sciences?:** The Twitter study I mention here is an ongoing project in my lab, done in collaboration with Onur Varol and Alexander Gates.

240 **The Japanese artist Katsushika Hokusai:** To learn more about Hokusai, see https://en.wikipedia.org/wiki/Hokusai.

Conclusion

243 **This outsized reception caught the press by surprise:** For more details on the confusion surrounding Einstein's visit—and his enduring fame since—see Marshall Missner's brilliant, thorough, and largely unheralded discussion of the topic, "Why Einstein Became Famous in America," *Social Studies of Science* 15, no. 2 (1985): 267–91. We also traced the story as it unfolded

in the press of the day by reading the following primary source articles, some of which are quoted in this conclusion:

"Einstein's Discoveries: A Revolution in Physics, but Not Philosophy," by Eugene L. Fisk, *New York Times*, January 5, 1919.

"Eclipse Showed Gravity Variation," *New York Times*, November 9, 1919.

"Lights All Askew in the Heavens: Men of Science More or Less Agog over Eclipse Observations," *New York Times*, November 10, 1919.

"Don't Worry About New Light Theory: Physicists Agree It Can Be Disregarded for All Practical Purposes," *New York Times*, November 16, 1919.

"Einstein Expounds His New Theory," *New York Times*, December 3, 1919.

"How Tall Are You, Einstein Measure?," *New York Times*, December 4, 1919.

"Assaulting the Absolute," *New York Times*, December 7, 1919.

"Einstein's Thirteenth Man," by O. W. Tefft, *New York Times*, December 10, 1919.

"A New Physics Based on Einstein: Sir Oliver Lodge Says It Will Prevail, and Mathematicians Will Have a Terrible Time," *New York Times*, September 6, 1920.

"Disturber of Minds Unpopular," *New York Times*, September 6, 1920.

"Measurer of the Universe," *New York Times*, January 31, 1921.

"Poor Says Einstein Fails in Evidence," *New York Times*, February 8, 1921.

"Professor Einstein Here, Explains Relativity," *New York Times*, April 3, 1921.

"Thousands Greet Einstein at Pier: Mayor Hylan's Committee Welcomes Scientist and Party Down Bay," *Washington Post*, April 3, 1921.

"Einstein Sees End of Space and Time," *New York Times*, April 4, 1921.

"Psychopathic Relativity," *New York Times*, April 5, 1921.

"Holds Up Freedom of City to Einstein," *New York Times*, April 6, 1921.

"Relativity at the City Hall," *New York Times*, April 7, 1921.

"Einstein to Have Freedom of the State," *New York Times*, April 7, 1921.

"Falconer Is Denounced," *New York Times*, April 7, 1921.

"Freedom of City Given to Einstein," *New York Times*, April 9, 1921.

"The Skyscraper Built by Einstein," a review by Benjamin Harrow, *New York Times*, April 17, 1921.

"The Universe in a Nutshell: World Dimensions and World Distances and the Einstein Relativity Theory," by Leo Gilbert, *New York Times*, April 17, 1921.

"Kindred Studies Up on Einstein Theory: Tells House It May Bear on Legislation as to Relations with the Cosmos," *New York Times*, May 17, 1921.

"Einstein Honored at Boston," *New York Times*, May 19, 1921.

"Rush to Greet Einstein: War Veterans Fight Off Great Crowd of Welcomers in Cleveland," *New York Times*, May 26, 1921.

Index

Adler, Moshe, 274n

Altavista, 158

Amazon, 128, 137–39, 140, 164–65, 166

ambition, 47, 50–51, 52, 71

American Physical Society conference, 245–48

animal breeding, 185–87, 195

Aral, Sinan, 140

Aristotle, 34–35, 263n

arts: measurement of success in, 10–11, 13, 25, 57, 59–60, 68, 73, 109; and networks, 57, 62, 63, 64–68, 69, 70, 71, 269–70n; relationship between artists and institutions, 64–71, 269–70n; and superstar effect, 113; and timing of success, 229, 292–93n; value in, 60–64, 68, 69, 83, 109

Ashkin, Arthur, 209

Association of Tennis Professionals, 41–42, 263–64n

audience: relationship to success, 13, 14, 95, 104–6, 109–10; and team success, 190

Australian Tennis Federation, 264n

Azoulay, Pierre, 114, 116–17

Bagrow, James, 182–84, 188, 263n

Barabási, Dániel, 39–40, 45–47, 49, 51–52, 145–46, 235

Barabási, Izabella, 130

Barabási, Leó, 143, 145

Bashō, 34

Basquiat, Jean-Michel, 54–57, 60, 68, 267n, 268n

Báthory, Elizabeth, 34

Battier, Shane, 202–3

bell curve, 80–81, 99, 102–3

Ben & Jerry's, 169–71

Berlin, Irving, 178

Beyoncé, 108

Bezos, Jeff, 190

Blake, Yohan, 79, 80

Bohr, Niels, 252

Bolt, Usain, 79–81

Boston Latin Academy, 47–49

Boston Latin School, 47–49

Boyle, Robert, 288–89n

301

About the Author

Albert-László Barabási is the Robert Gray Dodge Professor of Network Science and a Distinguished University Professor at Northeastern University, where he directs the Center for Complex Network Research and holds appointments in the Department of Medicine at Harvard Medical School and the Department of Network and Data Sciences at Central European University in Budapest. A native of Transylvania, Romania, he received his master's in theoretical physics at Eötvös University in Budapest, Hungary, and his Ph.D. at Boston University. His book *Linked: The New Science of Networks* (Perseus, 2002) is currently available in fifteen languages. *Bursts: The Hidden Pattern Behind Everything We Do* (Dutton, 2010) is available in five languages. He is the author of *Network Science* (Cambridge, 2016) and the coeditor of *The Structure and Dynamics of Networks* (Princeton, 2005) and *Network Medicine* (Harvard University Press, 2017). His work has led to many breakthroughs, including the discovery of scale-free networks, which continues to make him one of the most cited scientists today.

Barabási is a Fellow of the American Physical Society and of the American Association for the Advancement of Science. He was awarded the FEBS Anniversary Prize for Systems Biology in 2005 and the John von Neumann Medal for outstanding achievements in computer science and technology in 2006, the C&C Prize from the NEC Foundation in 2008, the U.S. National Academies of Sciences Cozzarelli Prize in 2009, the Lagrange Prize for his contributions to complex systems in 2011, the Prima Primissima Award for his contributions to science in 2014, and the Senior Scientific Award of the Complex Systems Society in 2017. He was elected a member of the Hungarian Academy of Sciences, the Romanian Academy, Academia Europaea, the European Academy of Sciences and Arts, and the Massachusetts Academy of Sciences, and he received Doctor Honoris Causa degrees from Universidad Politécnica de Madrid, the University of West Timişoara, and Utrecht University.